Managing Research Data

Managing Research Data

Edited by
Graham Pryor

facet publishing

Published by Facet Publishing,
7 Ridgmount Street, London WC1E 7AE
www.facetpublishing.co.uk

Facet Publishing is wholly owned by CILIP: the Chartered Institute of
Library and Information Professionals.

British Library Cataloguing in Publication Data
A catalogue record for this book is available from the British Library.

ISBN 978-1-85604-756-2

First published 2012

Text printed on FSC accredited material.

Mixed Sources
Product group from well-managed
forests and other controlled sources
www.fsc.org Cert no. SA-COC-1565
© 1996 Forest Stewardship Council

Typeset from editors' files by Facet Publishing in 10/13pt Garamond
and Frutiger.
Printed and made in Great Britain by MPG Books Group, UK.

Contents

Preface

Data management is an active process by which digital resources remain discoverable, accessible and intelligible over the longer term, a process that invests data and datasets with the potential to accrue value as assets enjoying far wider use than their creators may have anticipated. In the world of research, such a value-adding process is a significant contributor to the much desired achievement of impact.

Initially, the aim of this book was to introduce and familiarize the library and information professional with the principal elements of research data management. Traditionally, librarians have acted as the trusted and expert stewards of the nation's intellectual output but in the digital age they have lost ground in their engagement with the needs of the academic research community, which has found itself made increasingly self-sufficient by developments in information technology.

But it soon became apparent when assembling a representative selection of chapters, with the intention of providing an adequate picture of the prevailing research data landscape, that by explaining the reasons for pursuing effective data management and by describing the measures that should and are being taken, this volume would serve as both an introduction and a summary for a much broader community of stakeholders.

Hence, within these pages you will discover a wealth of information and instruction covering such core issues as the terms of compliance with funder expectations for data management and sharing, an explanation of the context and recommended approaches to individual and institutional data management planning, a discussion of the roles and responsibilities of key players in the research data lifecycle, as well as detailed reports of initiatives, strategies and organizations being deployed nationally and on a global scale.

That initial aim remains, but in truth we all of us today 'do data', as information professionals, practising researchers or policy makers. I do hope this book will help you do it better.

Graham Pryor

Contributors

G. Sayeed Choudhury

G. Sayeed Choudhury is the Associate Dean for Library Digital Programs and Hodson Director of the Digital Research and Curation Center at the Sheridan Libraries of Johns Hopkins University, Baltimore. He is also the Director of Operations for the Institute of Data Intensive Engineering and Science (IDIES) based at Johns Hopkins.

Ellen Collins

Ellen Collins is a social researcher with a background in culture, libraries and information. As Research Officer at the Research Information Network, London, she has managed research projects investigating data centre usage, information practices in the humanities and physical sciences and information handling in collaborative research.

Sheila Corrall

Sheila Corrall is Professor of Librarianship and Information Management and Graduate Research Tutor in the University of Sheffield Information School, where her research and teaching focus on strategic management, collection development, information literacy and professional competencies. She has worked in public, special, national and academic libraries, including positions as director of library and information services at three universities.

Martin Donnelly

As Senior Institutional Support Officer with the Digital Curation Centre in Edinburgh, Martin has steered the development of the data management planning tool, DMP Online. Before joining the DCC he was Technology Assessor at the Humanities Advanced Technology and Information Institute at the University of Glasgow.

Peter Halfpenny

Peter Halfpenny is Emeritus Professor of Sociology at the University of Manchester. He was Deputy Director of Manchester Informatics for four years and Executive Director of the ESRC National Centre for e-Social Science for five years. His interests are advanced computer applications in the social sciences.

Sarah Higgins

Sarah Higgins lectures in Archives Administration and Records Management at Aberystwyth University, where her research focuses on the lifecycle management of digital materials by archives services, libraries and other information professionals. She was formerly an adviser with the Digital Curation Centre where she led the DCC Curation Lifecycle Model Project and the standards advisory function.

Sarah Jones

Sarah Jones trained as an archivist and has been working as a researcher in the Humanities Advanced Technology and Information Institute (HATII), in Glasgow, since 2006, initially for the Arts and Humanities Data Service and then for the Digital Curation Centre (DCC). She led the national Data Audit Framework (DAF) project and has developed a body of policy and data management resources for the DCC.

Brian F. Lavoie

Brian Lavoie joined OCLC Research in 1996, since when he has worked on a range of projects – from the development of OCLC's Four-Figure Cutter Tables and automated cuttering tools, to analysing the structure and content of the world wide web. Brian's academic background is in economics (he has a PhD in agricultural economics) and his research interests include the analysis of aggregate collections, economic issues associated with information and the provision of information services, system-wide organization of library resources and digital preservation. Brian served as co-chair of the Blue Ribbon Task Force on Sustainable Digital Preservation and Access and is a member of the PREMIS Data Dictionary Editorial Committee.

William Michener

William Michener is Professor and Director of e-Science Initiatives in the University Libraries System at the University of New Mexico. He has been involved in numerous environmental informatics research and technology development projects and currently serves as Director for DataONE. He also serves as editor of *Ecological Archives* and associate editor of the *Journal of Ecological Informatics*.

Rob Procter

Rob Procter is Professor and Director of the Manchester e-Research Centre, where he is responsible for developing the Centre's research strategy, co-ordinating developments in the application of e-infrastructure tools and services in social science research, and leading studies of socio-technical issues influencing the wider take up of e-infrastructure-based solutions. He was Research Director of the ESRC-funded National Centre for e-Social Science from 2004 to 2009 and is now part of the Digital Social Research Directorate.

Graham Pryor

Prior to joining the Digital Curation Centre in Edinburgh, where he is Associate Director, Graham Pryor spent nine years as Director of Information Systems and Services at the University of Aberdeen; this followed a number of senior information management posts within the defence and energy sectors.

Andrew Treloar

Andrew Treloar is the Director of Technology for the Australian National Data Service. His research interests include data management, institutional repositories and scholarly communication.

Alex Voss

Alex Voss is a Lecturer in Software Engineering in the School of Computer Science at the University of St Andrews. His research interests are the development, operation and use of distributed systems, especially the ways in which such systems are integrated in and supported by socio-technical arrangements. His current focus is the use of cloud computing in research applications.

Angus Whyte

Angus Whyte has a background in social informatics. After gaining his PhD in information science from the University of Strathclyde in 2008 his research focused on developing and evaluating systems for collaboration and participation. He joined the DCC in 2007 to study and support researchers' curation practices and has been responsible for a number of publications in the field of data sharing and curation.

CHAPTER 1

Why manage research data?

Graham Pryor

Consider this: every year around £3.5 billion of taxpayers' money is spent on research undertaken by UK universities. That is a considerable level of investment and members of the public might reasonably assume that all due care will be taken to ensure this national endowment is applied wisely. Justifiably, they might also expect that the fruits from such rich endeavours will be afforded the attention necessary to ensure an optimum return on investment. So what are these 'fruits' and how indeed in practice is their value observed?

A challenge for the information professional

Way back in 1979, Dennis Lewis, then head of ASLIB, the UK's Association for Information Management, wrote what came to be known as the Doomsday Scenario for librarians. His main claim was that information professionals wouldn't be around by the year 2000, meaning that the *types* of information professionals he saw working in 1979 (mainly librarians and information scientists) would be long gone, swept away by a new information age that would by implication belong to computing scientists. In the event, it didn't happen quite like that and the traditional custodians of documented knowledge, with their armoury of skills in appraising, classifying, preserving, storing and retrieving information somehow managed to reinvent themselves as the purveyors and stewards of digitally encoded knowledge, albeit they have confined themselves in the main to handling published materials. But the challenge has not gone away. Inexorably it has continued to increase in scale and complexity, re-presenting itself in a multiplicity of dimensions until, most significantly today, the accessible output from scholarly research is no longer to be considered exclusively through its documented or published form. We are talking here about digital data, a component of the knowledge enterprise that is as urgently in need of effective stewardship as any of the more traditional products of scholarly research.

This book is an attempt to explain to the library and information community what has to be done at a local, national or international level to engage with this fresh challenge, and why it is important that the traditional role of the information professional should undergo some urgent re-tooling, not only to sustain the profession but also to ensure that the research community can benefit more completely from its centuries-old reserve of knowledge management acumen.

This introductory chapter will survey the key changes that have taken place in the information landscape during the past decade, within the research community and at the level of national and international policy. Each of the themes it introduces will be explored in greater detail in the succeeding chapters. For the information professional it is anticipated that such an approach will offer the prospect for familiarization with a new arena of activity, to enable gaps in understanding to be filled and for fresh workplace or career opportunities to be revealed. These are the fruits on offer within this volume. To resume that initial metaphor more appositely, our key questions must be: what should we recognize today as the fruits from scholarly research and what needs to be done to preserve and enjoy them?

The data deluge

Overwhelmingly, the output from research in the 21st century is data, produced chiefly in electronic form and having a scale of generation that is rapid, vast and particularly remarkable for its exponential rate of increase. Although this condition is to be found in all disciplines it is at its most dramatic in the sciences, where the annual rate of increase is in the region of 30%. Consider the biosciences, where the raw image files for a single human genome have been estimated at 28.8 terabytes, which is approaching 30,000 gigabytes (MacArthur, 2008). Or the high energy physics community, where the Large Hadron Collider (LHC) experiment at the European Organization for Nuclear Research (CERN), in Geneva, to which 19 UK universities have contributed, is expected to produce around 15 petabytes (15 million gigabytes) of data annually. A private individual attempting to store that quantity of data would require in excess of 1.7 million dual-layer DVDs! Yet the LHC is not unique among the global research community in generating massive data volumes.

Research programmes are funded and undertaken nationally and internationally. Expenditure on research can attain colossal proportions. In the USA, research spending on science and engineering alone reached almost $55 billion in 2009 (Britt, 2010), while between 2007 and 2013 the European Commission is spending €50 billion (£42.4/$61.5 billion) on its framework programme for research. Weighing the anticipated output from all of these programmes in a global context, it is easy to comprehend the source of the now-familiar *digital deluge*, a term that describes not only the data directly generated by these programmes but includes the further proliferation that occurs when they are shared or accessed by interested communities around the world.

At this point it is pertinent to be reminded of observations by research colleagues in the humanities that they don't actually work with data, an assertion based on the mistaken belief that data is exclusively the stuff of science, whereas as humanists they might claim instead to work with information and knowledge. Yet data is the primary building block of all information, comprising the lowest level of abstraction in any field of knowledge, where it is identifiable as collections of numbers, characters, images or other symbols that when contextualized in a certain way represent facts, figures or ideas as communicable information. Moreover, in the digital age, the information and knowledge to which humanists will steadfastly lay claim can only be communicated to another person, whether across campus networks or via the internet, after they have been encoded as transmittable data.

In the specific arena of academic research, data is the output from any systematic investigation involving a process of observation, experiment or the testing of a hypothesis, which when assembled in context and interpreted expertly will produce new knowledge. So we all 'do data', whether we are humanists, scientists or social scientists. That data is a serious business for humanists too was underlined by the outcry in 2008 when funding was withdrawn from the UK's Arts and Humanities Data Service (AHDS), a national service established to enable the discovery, creation and preservation of digital resources across the arts and humanities research, teaching and learning community.

But while data may be the principal output from scholarly research, whatever the discipline, like the tip of an iceberg only a small proportion will be made visible. As the most conspicuous and probably the most familiar intellectual product of research that is conducted in a university, the scholarly article or paper has long been established as the means to deliver the results of experiments or the proof to a new hypothesis. For acceptance by a reputable journal, the organ through which the research paper will normally be assessed, published and delivered, the output from an often lengthy and laborious research process will have to be massively and selectively compressed. To be peer reviewed, to be selected from among and inserted alongside a host of competing articles, as well as to function both informatively and accessibly, published research can only represent those particular aspects of the experimental or investigative process that are essential to making the case and providing the necessary evidence to prove a hypothesis. Hence, a severe routine of selection, reduction and distillation from the greater expanse of experimental and evidential data generated and collected within a research programme will eventually reduce down to a publishable document, finely tuned to deliver a measured and measurable argument, with the greater volume of data from which the paper has been produced remaining hidden and largely inaccessible.

When there is such a focus on pruning research output to meet the strictures of the publishing process, should we expect that all possible value has been wrung from the broader wealth of data that was gathered or produced during the lifetime of a project? It is unlikely. And can we reasonably anticipate that it will have been left in a condition that will facilitate further use by the original researcher, or by others? Probably not.

The wealth of data and the merits of planning

From these initial observations it is evident that the data deluge of the 21st century is a phenomenon that, if left unchallenged and unmanaged, is likely to result in considerable financial waste as well as opportunity loss. When considering the massive investment of time, intellectual effort and hard cash that goes into a research programme, should we not be expecting to draw more from the data generated than can be extracted from a well honed paper or series of papers? Surely data produced so expensively should not be treated as spoil, put aside like the waste materials from an intellectual mine? Neither is this a simple monetary argument, for without due attention, without the systematic shaping of datasets for subsequent reuse or re-purposing, such careless disdain for source data is likely to spawn a host of missed opportunities in economic, social and scientific advancement. The value of research data is not to be measured simply by the accountant's abacus.

That the research output from our universities has a direct impact on our lives and our state of physical and mental well-being is no mere accident but the consequence of strategic decisions taken at a national level. Take, for example, the UK's Engineering and Physical Sciences Research Council (EPSRC), which funds research across a broad range of disciplines including information technology, structural engineering and materials science and which seeks to align research with outcomes having relevance to society and business. In its 2008–2011 plan the EPSRC has identified £1.9 billion of research themes that will sustain advances in energy, the digital economy and next generation healthcare (EPSRC, 2009). It is public investment on this scale, coupled with a determination to produce results of benefit to the common good, which provides a meaningful indicator of the potential and critical value inherent in the data generated from research.

The expectation by the major funders that research data as a recognized asset will be afforded due care and attention has become more overt in recent years, confirmed by an emerging requirement for the inclusion of data management plans within research grant proposals. Their message is clear: data should no longer be abandoned on the workbench like wood shavings in a carpenter's shop; increasingly it is expected to join the finished assembly of scholarly output as a valued and managed component with an extended life and sustained usability.

To emphasize their collective solidarity behind that message, Research Councils UK (RCUK) have published seven *Common Principles on Data Policy* (RCUK, 2011), with the intention of providing an overarching framework for individual research council data policies. While recognizing 'that there are legal, ethical and commercial constraints on release of research data', the Principles also state emphatically that 'publicly funded research data are a public good, produced in the public interest, which should be made openly available with as few restrictions as possible in a timely and responsible manner that does not harm intellectual property'. The Principles take care to support caution against the inappropriate or premature release of data, as well as to urge the proper acknowledgement of sources. They also point out that 'it is appropriate to use public funds to support the management and sharing of publicly-funded research data', which neatly makes the connection with the councils' role as funders of research.

In the UK today, most domain-based research funders expect grant applicants to submit a statement describing their plans for access, management and the long-term curation of research outputs, although the approach varies according to individual funder, as described in a critical analysis of individual funder requirements available from the Digital Curation Centre (DCC) website (www.dcc.ac.uk/webfm_send/339). Although the Arts and Humanities Research Council (AHRC), Economic and Social Research Council (ESRC) and Natural Environment Research Council (NERC) each focus on the long-term sustainability of digital resources, the biomedical funders – Biotechnology and Biological Sciences Research Council (BBSRC), Medical Research Council (MRC) and the Wellcome Trust – are more concerned with the data-sharing potential of research resources (DCC, 2011). Such heterogeneity of approach perhaps reveals differences in individual research cultures and goals; in practical terms it may also produce additional challenges for the authors of cross-disciplinary research proposals, who will need to satisfy the content and formatting requirements of very different data management plans as defined by different funding agencies. Measures to address this diversity of demands are discussed in some detail in Chapter 5.

When the funding bodies also provide infrastructure services in the shape of national data centres (whose features are described more fully in Chapter 8), to which data can be offered for deposit and through which researchers will enjoy the support of a structured curation management programme, data management plans serve as an effective instrument for the eventual delivery of data to those centres. But elsewhere there exist neither carrots nor sticks to ensure that, once funds are released, there will be any rigorous adherence to the agreed plan. This lack of any monitoring function is not peculiar to UK funders; in the USA the National Science Foundation (NSF) announced that from 18 January 2011 all research proposals submitted to the NSF must include a supplementary two page data management plan, which will describe 'how the proposal will conform to NSF policy on the dissemination and sharing of research results' (NSF, 2010). That may convince scrutineers in the NSF that a proposal is on-message but it is a long way from ensuring that the data produced will be properly prepared, managed and preserved for long-term access and reuse. It certainly carries no sanctions to ensure compliance with any front-loaded statement of conformance. So if there is no rigour being applied by the funding agencies and with the majority of disciplines lacking the services of a national data centre, who is providing due care and attention to our research data output – the academic research community itself?

The research lifecycle

The research lifecycle has been described variously as a linear or cyclical model but in practice it consists of multiple investigative sub-cycles including tools, methodologies and a series of reiterative steps that serve to reinforce surges of forward progress in the overall sequence of activity. This process may be described more simply as following the pattern illustrated in Figure 1.1. It has six sequential phases, commencing usually with an idea or hypothesis and concluding with the delivery of a product, most often in the shape of a published report or other scholarly text. To an ever-growing extent the published report is accompanied by supplementary data, in the shape of files containing datasets produced during the research programme, or links to databases with supporting information or protocols, which themselves may provide the spark to animate further investigation.

In each and every phase of the lifecycle the researcher will gather and use data and/or generate new data. In the initial phase, typically, when structuring a hypothesis and planning the research programme, existing published data will be gathered and reviewed; some will be used to set the scene, other data will be selected as the raw material for new research. Later, the research process itself will necessitate pulling in further data from published sources or from collaborators in the field, either for speculative reanalysis within new contexts revealed by the research programme or to provide authoritative benchmarks for comparing or measuring the output from new research. This phase will also be the principal source of new data arising from investigation or experimentation. As depicted by Figure 1.1, all of the six phases will be datacentric to some degree in that they will each depend on the use or generation of data, not least at the point of reuse, where data produced, filtered and synthesized may present opportunities for new research. This last function is perhaps the most crucial to developing the body of knowledge and deserves further explanation.

For certain groups of researchers, such as systems biologists, the availability of others' research data is no less than fundamental to their own work process. Systems biologists, who will often have an interdisciplinary background, work in complex teams

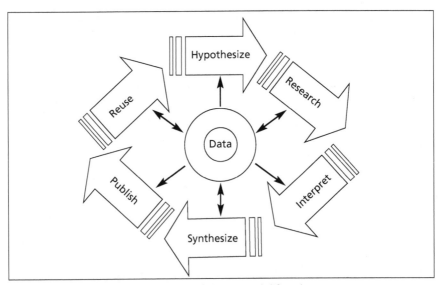

Figure 1.1 *The six datacentric phases of the research lifecycle*

that include an array of complementary experts, for example bioinformaticians, biophysicists and mathematicians. Their modus operandi is to produce new knowledge by modelling existing knowledge taken from large datasets generated within the global experimental and theoretical research community. At the risk of stretching a point, it is worth also referring here to a more popularly cited instance of effective data reuse, where new research has been enabled by the digitization of weather records extracted from a previous century of ships' logs, with data not originally gathered for that purpose now being used in research into climate change.

Despite its obvious 'datacentricity' the diagram at Figure 1.1 presents the researcher as a user or producer of data rather than as a data manager or custodian. And why should we expect anything more? As observed in the 2009 Research Information Network (RIN) study of researchers in the life sciences, 'data curation is only one element in the research lifecycle [and there is] little evidence that planned data management has yet been adopted as standard practice' (RIN, 2009, 49). Data can be difficult and costly to acquire or produce; it may take years to gather, often depending on the careful establishment of intricate relationships with collaborators or target study groups. Furthermore, in highly innovative fields of research it is likely that new techniques of data production and manipulation may first need to be developed. These are the issues that will absorb researchers and in which they will exercise skill: the getting of data in order to conduct research, often within a limited timescale, not the management or curation of data over the long term.

For researchers, career rewards are secured from the quality of their research output rather than from any efficacy in data curation, and while there may be a guarded acknowledgement of the value that may be achieved from sharing data, the effort necessary to preparing data for sharing is generally regarded as an unwelcome burden, requiring skills that are not necessarily present in a researcher's basic toolkit for conducting research.

A data curation lifecycle

But the needs of a full and effective data management programme are not so different from those depicted in the research lifecycle. The DCC's curation lifecycle model (Figure 1.2; DCC, 2009), which like the research lifecycle has its critical starting point at the research conceptualization stage, is designed to ensure that all necessary phases of curation are planned and undertaken in the correct sequence.

Data, meaning any digital information recorded in a binary as opposed to decimal form, where binary is the numerical format that computing devices employ to store and manage information, is shown at the centre of the curation lifecycle. It includes both digital objects (e.g. text files, image files or sound files) and databases (structured collections of records or data stored in a computer system). Notes provided to support the model describe the full lifecycle actions necessary for the preservation and curation of data, such as the assignment of metadata. These actions, together with an

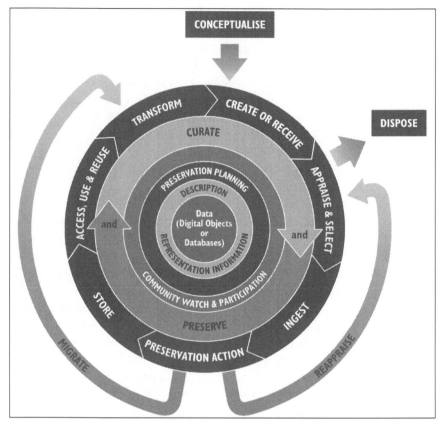

Figure 1.2 *The DCC curation lifecycle model [reproduced by permission of the DCC]*

explanation of other sequential and occasional actions, are described in more detail in Chapter 2. In the outermost ring, in an implicit reflection of the research lifecycle, the series of sequential actions starts with planning for the creation, capture and storage of data, eventually concluding with some predicted transformation of the curated data – although transformation is itself but a new beginning! Additionally, three occasional actions are also shown as pivotal to the concept of data curation, since disposal, reappraisal and migration are key to decisions informing a process that will enable a view over the longer term.

A routine of decisions about data disposal is needed to take account of not only changes in the potential long-term value of datasets but also any legislation governing the length of time that certain types of data must be preserved. The nature of some data, where for instance confidentiality is an issue, may even dictate the use of secure destruction methods. In all cases, the cost of curating data over the long term will require serious consideration and periodic review presents one means of achieving cost containment. Reappraisal is also necessary where data has failed to meet formal validation procedures, since there is little point in retaining data that is neither reliable nor robust. Finally, migration of data may be undertaken following reappraisal or decisions about disposal and usually involves transformation to a different format, an undertaking that is essential if data is to continue to function within a changed storage environment or where it is necessary to ensure the data's immunity from hardware or software obsolescence.

The intention of the lifecycle model is unambiguous: to explain how maintaining, preserving and, most crucially, adding value to or extracting value from research data should be achieved throughout an optimized lifecycle. It does this by prompting us to ask what are the essential ingredients of an effective digital curation architecture. Notice too how the language used in the model is all about data handling and the needs of the data itself. It is a step beyond the view provided in Figure 1.1, where data is shown as an anonymous factor of production, feeding and enabling the research process. Here in the DCC model, the emphasis is on the changing aspects of the data rather than the research. In the DCC model data is to be captured and matured according to a plan, with a structure that is independent of the individual idiosyncrasies of research programmes. In this model the tone is redolent of care, where data is nurtured, massaged and preserved according to a dynamic and continuous process. There is one inherent omission: the sequences and activities are explained in careful detail yet who should be responsible for enabling or pursuing these preservation actions is less clear.

The sustaining professional: a longer view

Digital curation involves the active management of research datasets in order to preserve their long-term research value, yet this is a concept with limited appeal to the majority of a research community that receives short-term funding and is composed of a highly mobile workforce. Typically, within or across disciplines, members of that workforce will over time combine, disperse and recombine with seeming fluidity; the research they undertake will rarely follow an exclusive and linear path and as a community they will exhibit changing patterns of allegiance and interests. The dedication and opportunity to plan and work with data over the longer term must therefore belong with a different kind of community, one that is organizationally stable, sustainable and with the freedom and capacity to make plans and projections that will exceed the kind of short-term goals and funding allocations common to research themes and projects. The terminology used in the DCC curation lifecycle model also suggests a different kind of skill set to that traditionally associated with researchers, one that instead implies the stewardship and husbandry of data rather than its active use. It was not necessarily the intention of its author, the DCC's Sarah Higgins, who gives further insight into the curation lifecycle in the next chapter, yet the greatest resonance of this model is with the information practitioner, the archivist perhaps, or the librarian.

Those researchers who have recognized the need better to manage their data are faced by a dilemma. While they may eschew responsibility for acquiring and applying skills in data management (or curation) beyond the basics necessary to enable their research, in surveys sponsored by the Joint Information Systems Committee (JISC) and RIN, researchers have consistently remarked that in order properly to discharge their function information professionals employed to provide support to any research group will require a substantial level of discipline knowledge. If interpreted unsympathetically, the inference here is that a level of discipline expertise would be expected that would put data curators almost on a par with the researchers themselves, thereby ruling out most professionally trained information practitioners from providing data management support to a university research team. It should not be the case, although such pejorative attitudes are heavily reinforced by a culture of self-sufficiency among the research community, in which the tendency to rely on oneself or one's trusted colleagues rather than central services is endemic.

Cultural barriers

Project StORe, an initiative from the JISC repositories programme, confirmed this culture as a significant barrier to change. One of the earliest of recent studies of research information behaviours, the 2006 StORe survey of seven scientific disciplines found researchers claiming undisputed rights to the management of their data with uncompromising declarations such as 'it's my responsibility' and, more dismissively, 'the university has assigned a librarian to our department . . . but I have not used her services' (Pryor, 2006). Such ingrained attitudes do pose a serious challenge to enthusiastic information professionals with a mission to engage with the research data agenda and it would appear that, before they can make headway, information professionals have a two-pronged challenge to overcome. The first involves regaining a greater parity of esteem with the research community, without which they will lack credibility; the second requires them to persuade and demonstrate that they have a material contribution to make, one that is likely to be of tangible benefit to researchers and the research programme. The former should follow the latter, but information professionals must be active in taking the lead; they can't wait for the researchers to come knocking. True, researchers may admit they are concerned about such issues as accessibility and barriers to acquiring information, but such is the pace of research that they will not set aside the time to seek assistance from beyond their own research group or to indulge in much more than a quick session with Google. It is, therefore, up to the information professional to learn about these concerns and to use them as a pretext for offering genuine advice and assistance, which has to be the first step in proactively reconnecting with the research community.

The re-purposed librarian

In recent years the traditional role of professional information intermediaries has been largely replaced by services that give direct access to ubiquitous online resources. Not by design but from reliance on the availability of search engines, many researchers have effectively removed themselves from the mainstream library user population. Of course there is potential risk to them from this behaviour, given the limitations of generic search engines such as Google, and if steps could be taken to reconnect researchers with information professionals the resulting benefits to information discovery would, in turn, enhance the research process. Nonetheless, as a consequence of this change in dependency, libraries and librarians have become associated primarily with serving the needs of the undergraduate population, whereas for centuries they occupied a more august role as the recognized exponents of skill in classifying and organizing information and knowledge, including its appraisal, selection and annotation. In that role they have long been the natural source of expertise in storing and preserving information and, until the recent growth in online tools for the discovery and download of information, they had been unrivalled in their ability to retrieve information, to distribute and to share it, as well as manage access to it. This veritable catalogue of qualifications will become a repeated motif throughout this chapter, since it remains highly appropriate to the management of research data and obligingly describes a toolkit waiting to be opened and deployed!

The situation in the USA is somewhat more encouraging than in the UK. In spring 2010, for example, the library at the University of Virginia opted to pursue a new strategic direction and focus more on providing structured support to data management, with the primary aims of building data literacy among library staff, developing knowledge of how researchers at the university actually manage their data and creating opportunities for active consultation and collaboration. In the face of universally shrinking budgets, this strategy required the identification of services most likely to produce the greatest value to the institution, as well as hard and radical decisions over which existing services to drop or change in favour of the new regime. What emerged was a new Scientific Data Consulting Group (University of Virginia, 2011) consisting mainly of existing library staff who had been 're-purposed'. One must assume that Virginia's research community, like that also at the University of Minnesota, is proving receptive to this initiative.

At Minnesota a programme of assistance in the creation of data management plans was launched proactively in advance of the NSF declaration, building on the results from studies of researcher needs conducted at the university in 2006 and 2007 (University of Minnesota, 2007). The response to those studies was generally positive, attracting such statements from faculty staff as 'If there were a workshop on organization and file management, I would go. The Libraries do this so well.' The University of Virginia initiative too appears to be flourishing. Guidance to help Virginia's researchers comply with the National Science Foundation's requirements for data management plans has been produced and the university has joined a group of major research institutions working to develop a flexible online tool that will help researchers generate data management plans. This group includes the UK's DCC, which developed the first such online tool (downloadable from www.dcc.ac.uk/dmponline).

Risky business

In the UK the needs of the research community are no less pressing, where of particular concern is how bare and basic are some of these unsatisfied needs. Witness the practices recorded by a scoping study undertaken by the project Incremental, a collaboration between Cambridge University Library and the Humanities Advanced Technology and Information Institute (HATII) at the University of Glasgow. From a series of in-depth interviews Incremental documented the extent to which some research datasets exist in a state of relentless jeopardy, perhaps the most serious revelation being that researchers at both institutions were having difficulty in finding even their own data. This was principally because of their use of inconsistent file structures and naming conventions, the extensive and risky practice of storing critical research data on cheap and flimsy media such as flash drives, and the scant deployment of networked storage facilities in some areas (Incremental, 2010). An already difficult situation was found to have been compounded by the creation of only minimal documentation to describe the nature and condition of the data that had been stored and, most surprisingly, a severely limited awareness of the opportunities and routines for data back-up. Incremental's response has been immediate and pragmatic: to meet researchers' demands for simple, clear, engaging and available help and support by producing accessible visual guidance on the creation, storage and management of data, supported by discipline-specific training in data curation principles and techniques. But no explanation for the prevalent dearth of basic data management practice was given in the study report other than an acknowledgement that the technological and human infrastructures currently provided by institutions are often insufficient to meet researchers' data management needs, as a consequence of which they are forced to do the best they can with the limited time, skills and resources available.

National centres, services and strategies

As an exemplar for building bridges between the information and research communities Incremental has proved to be a success. But it is nevertheless a pilot project with limited scope and a very specific locus. In the UK generally there remains an uphill struggle to identify resources sufficient to bridge an apparent gulf between the actual capabilities of information professionals and their perceived inadequacies in the mind's eye of researchers. Under such circumstances is there perhaps an alternative body better positioned for the challenge? Incremental is one of eight projects funded under the JISC's research data management infrastructure programme (JISC, 2010), with whom its findings resonate. This is a generously resourced programme with a strategic ambition to provide the UK higher education sector with examples of good practice in research data management. But beyond this developmental community there are several national organizations already well established in the data curation field, not least the data centres previously mentioned. One, the UK Data Archive (UKDA), has been operational for over 40 years, curating the largest collection of digital data in the social sciences and humanities in the UK.

As respected centres of expertise, these data centres provide not only guidance on data management practice but also the costly infrastructure necessary for the storage, preservation and access management of data deposited with them. They also reflect and influence the development of data management policy by the research councils that, typically, are their principal source of funding. In the case of the UKDA, for example, involvement in drafting the ESRC's Research Data Policy (ESRC, 2010) allowed UKDA staff to draw on their skills and enduring practical experience as well as to consult with other expert bodies such as the DCC, leading to the publication of a well informed and practical document that identifies the responsibilities of research grant holders, the ESRC and the data service providers. This was an exercise in the construction of policy as a tool for support and assistance rather than the composition of a political decree, an object rarely afforded much regard within academia! Similarly, the Natural Environment Research Centre's (NERC) network of data centres supports an integrated Data Discovery Service, covering the several strands of environmental research funded by the NERC, and providing an authoritative interface between the broader body of data users and the NERC research community.

Other centres hosted in the UK include the Archaeology Data Service and the European Bioinformatics Institute, with further domain-specific services under development, such as those being designed to support projects funded by the Medical Research Council. But notwithstanding the value and success of these organizations as assured custodians of the knowledge produced in their individual subject domains, they do not represent or serve all the fields of active research; nor are their services necessarily inclusive across their own domains, where they may adopt a selective approach to the preferred coverage and range of data that they will accept. Neither should we be complacent in regarding their custodianship as assured and sustainable: witness the demise of the much-appreciated AHDS in 2008, which has been reported as a direct consequence of unsympathetic financial pruning by the AHRC.

A case for the proper management of research data can be advanced on financial or ethical grounds but agreeing the roles and responsibilities for managing the research data deluge, as well as enabling a coherence and consistency of approach, remains a complex question requiring active participation and commitment from a range of stakeholders. In the UK the initiative to inject coherence to the research data community has been taken by the JISC, through the DCC, which it funds and which was launched in 2004 as a key component of the JISC's Continuing Access and Digital Preservation Strategy (www.dcc.ac.uk/about-us/history-dcc). In late 2010 the DCC's role was extended to accommodate aspects of a further initiative to create a UK Research Data Service, with funding from the Higher Education Funding Council for England (HEFCE), whereby it will from 2011 provide data management services in support of a new national cloud computing and storage infrastructure for research.

At the other end of the digitally connected world the Australian National Data

Service (ANDS) has embarked on a ten year programme to transform collections of Australian research data into a cohesive network of research repositories, at the same time taking steps to equip Australian research data managers with the skills to become expert in creating, managing and sharing research data under well formed and well maintained data management policies. The concept of research data manager is here an inclusive notion, in which the ANDS programme seeks to address the broad issues of research data ownership and the roles and responsibilities associated with ownership and maintenance. An ambitious platform engineered for the nationwide promotion of best practice in the curation of experimental, research and published data.

ANDS is a top-down government-sponsored programme, initially proposed in 2007 by the Department of Education, Science and Training (Australian Government, 2007) and introduced in 2008 by the Federal Department of Industry, Innovation, Science and Research (DIISR), which entered into an agreement with Monash University to establish ANDS under the National Collaborative Research Infrastructure Strategy (NCRIS). Funding of A\$48 million (£30.4/\$47 million) over two years was agreed in 2009 'to create and develop an Australian Research Data Commons (ARDC) infrastructure' (ANDS, 2011). A more detailed discussion of national strategies for research data management in Australia and in the USA is provided in Chapter 9 of this book.

But however forward-looking and well intentioned, can such national strategies expect to be successful in coaxing or cajoling the traditionally independent researcher to participate in and support them? A good deal of positive advocacy will have to be rolled out before that bond can be secured, coupled with a sound demonstration of the benefits to all potential stakeholders, particularly those for whom signing up to the concept of systematically managed data may represent a new and burdensome workload. For some this new interest in their research data may even be perceived as a threat to traditional rights and practices, for notwithstanding the intellectual property rights asserted by employing institutions, the data produced and assembled by university researchers is regarded as their intellectual capital, the basis of their credentials as effective researchers and the stuff on which career progression is built. Whether real or imagined, any fears that their perceived ownership of that data is in peril will have to be assuaged before progress can be made.

After Doomsday

Such a conundrum returns us to the role of the modern data practitioner or information professional; still to be born perhaps from the ashes of an outmoded perception of the librarian or information scientist but the most likely candidate for the role of standard-bearer when national or institutional strategies are to be rolled out. There is no question that the Doomsday Scenario for librarians painted in 1979 has proved to be wrong. The profession has continued to adapt and change as it always had, finding and developing new roles as the digital age advanced, and we began to hear about media librarians and systems librarians, witnessed the introduction of e-libraries and more recently watched the implementation of information repositories. There has been a succession of changed and changing roles.

Yet nearly all of this flux and change has been seen in the context of published information, not data. True, there is a handful of data librarians employed in our more iconoclastic institutions – it was estimated not so long ago that there were five in the UK, principally individuals 'originating from the library community, trained and specializing in the curation, preservation and archiving of data' (Key Perspectives, 2008) – but the library world has yet to commit wholeheartedly to the transition. The library schools in our universities may provide a sound education in what is broadly described as knowledge management or information management, but training in the intricacies of web search engines, information systems and database design does not properly equip the new professionals with an outlook that will fit them for a role as data manager in a research intensive university. This is despite the profession having unrivalled occupation of the high ground when it comes to owning a long list of fundamentally appropriate skills in classifying, organizing, appraising, selecting, annotating, preserving, storing, retrieving, distributing, sharing and managing access to information – some list indeed, worth repeating here, and one that closely reflects the activities implicit to the DCC's data curation lifecycle model!

The following chapters in this book address in greater detail many of the issues raised in this introduction, and more, adding practical advice on such topical themes as data management planning and the sustainability of digital curation, with analyses of national policies and strategies in the Old and the New World. All start from the premise that we have answered the question 'Why manage research data?' We hope readers of this book will as quickly be convinced and that, on good argument, it will inspire them also to become committed advocates of the research data management cause.

References

ANDS (2011) *Overview of Funding Processes*, Australian National Data Service, http://ands.org.au/funded/funding-overview.html.

Australian Government (2007) *Towards the Australian Data Commons*, Department of Education, Science and Training, www.pfc.org.au/pub/Main/Data/TowardstheAustralianDataCommons.pdf.

Britt, R. (2010) *NSF Science Resources Statistics*, National Science Foundation, www.nsf.gov/statistics/infbrief/nsf10329/.

DCC (2009) *Curation Lifecycle Model*, Digital Curation Centre, www.dcc.ac.uk/resources/curation-lifecycle-model.

DCC (2011) *Overview of Funders' Data Policies*, Digital Curation Centre, www.dcc.ac.uk/resources/policy-and-legal/overview-funders-data-policies.

EPSRC (2009) *EPSRC Landscapes*, Engineering and Physical Sciences Research Council, www.epsrc.ac.uk/research/landscapes/Documents/LandscapeIntro.pdf.

ESRC (2010) *Research Data Policy*, Economic and Social Research Council,
www.esrc.ac.uk/about-esrc/information/data-policy.aspx.

Incremental (2010) *Scoping Study Report and Implementation Plan*,
www.lib.cam.ac.uk/preservation/incremental/docs.html.

JISC (2010) *Research Data Management Infrastructure Projects (RDMI)*, Joint Information Systems
Committee, www.jisc.ac.uk/whatwedo/programmes/mrd/rdmi.aspx.

Key Perspectives (2008) *Skills, Role and Career Structure of Data Scientists and Curators: assessment of
current practice and future needs*, Joint Information Systems Committee,
www.jisc.ac.uk/publications/publications/dataskillscareersfinalreport.aspx.

MacArthur, D. (2008) *How Much Data is a Human Genome?*, www.genetic-
future.com/2008/06/how-much-data-is-human-genome-it.html.

NSF (2010) *Dissemination and Sharing of Research Results*, National Science Foundation,
www.nsf.gov/bfa/dias/policy/dmp.jsp.

Pryor, G. (2006) *Project StORe Survey Report Part 1: cross-discipline report*,
http://hdl.handle.net/1842/1419.

RCUK (2011) *Common Principles on Data Policy*, Research Councils UK,
www.rcuk.ac.uk/research/Pages/DataPolicy.aspx.

RIN (2009) *Patterns of Information Use and Exchange*, Research Information Network.

University of Minnesota (2007) *Understanding Researcher Behaviors, Information Resources and Service
Needs of Scientists at the University of Minnesota*,
www1.lib.umn.edu/about/scieval/documents.html.

University of Virginia Library (2011) *Scientific Data Consulting*,
www2.lib.virginia.edu/brown/data.

CHAPTER 2

The lifecycle of data management

Sarah Higgins

Introduction

Digital materials are inherently fragile and need to be managed from the outset if they are to remain retrievable, identifiable and usable for the community that needs to access, use and reuse the information they contain. The set of activities required to manage data, known collectively as digital curation, aims to ensure that not only is the bit-stream maintained but that the data can be discovered and rendered throughout its lifecycle. Such lifecycle management ensures that documented policies and processes are developed, roles and responsibilities are defined, and the technical framework is in place to create, store and manage research data collections while delivering user access.

Drivers for lifecycle management of data

The science of archives and records management has long adopted a lifecycle approach to managing information. The imperative of an archivist is to ensure that information created in the course of a business or activity is adequately managed so that it can be identified, located and used when required, to support future activities. In the analogue world, paper or photographic materials may deteriorate over time through bad handling or poor storage conditions, allowing damp, mould, insect infestation or vermin damage to accrue. The context of their creation may be lost through divorce from their original environment, or poor documentation. The ability to find them may be hampered through inadequate cataloguing or misplacement. Capable management throughout the lifecycle ensures that these problems are minimized. The threats to digital material and the techniques for managing them may differ, but the underlying principles and the underpinning processes and policies, originally developed for dealing with the mountains of paper created in the pre-digital world, remain applicable to the digital paradigm.

The necessity of adopting the lifecycle approach to the management of data is discussed by Pennock (2007). Digital materials rely on a combination of hardware, software and storage media to create, store, access and render them. From the moment they are created they are vulnerable to the speed with which technology advances and the possibility of the failure of these technologies, so data can rapidly become inaccessible, or even completely lost. Additionally, the ease with which data can be moved, copied, edited and deleted may make its integrity and reliability questionable and its provenance dubious, with consequent repercussions for reuse. A lack of metadata may make it unidentifiable, irretrievable and unusable. If data is not managed from the point of creation onwards, and the correct activities undertaken at the relevant points in the data's lifecycle, the ability to look after it successfully may be greatly diminished. Tremendous time and effort may be required just to make it possible to open the files. It may never be possible to make them understandable. In the worst case scenario they may need to be re-created, assuming this is even possible. It is therefore in the best interests of all stakeholders to ensure that the relevant activities are undertaken at the right time to enable the survival of the data, and maximize the initial investment made in its creation or collection.

The lifecycle of research

Academic research activity has two main outputs, both of which need to be managed: published papers that analyse data collected to test stated hypotheses and the data collected or created in the course of the study (which is the basis and the verification of the published results). Historically, the public face of research is embodied in the final publication, with robust processes for the management, preservation, discovery and citation of these embedded into information management. The current movement for open access to these research papers is exemplified by the open repositories movement, which aims to increase accessibility to research results through organizational or domain-specific self-publication. The data generated throughout the research lifecycle has, until recently, been regarded as a by-product of the publication process, only for the consumption of the researchers and their associates. Data could be managed in isolation, using personal methodologies, with all the resulting variations and eccentricities of practice. However, it is now increasingly acknowledged that the data resulting from and supporting research is a valuable product in its own right, since it serves to verify results, enable experiments to be repeated and forms the basis of new research (UKRDS, 2009; Fry, et al. 2008).

The research lifecycle is modelled in Figure 1.1. This identifies six sequential phases of research in which data is central to the process. Three of the phases result in the creation of data: the *research phase* collects or creates the raw data on which the research is founded; the *synthesize phase* uses modelling or statistical techniques to make sense of the data collected in the research phase, ultimately leading to a new dataset; while the *reuse phase* takes data created in both phases to create new datasets that can be the foundation of new hypotheses to test. Throughout the research lifecycle documents that assist the core research activity are also created. These include documents that support and explain the research activity, for instance sampling procedures, code lists and workflows; administrative data such as copies of research bids, minutes of meetings and team wikis; and dissemination such as items for newsletters and Web 2.0 activity. All this data requires to be managed throughout the research lifecycle if accessibility and understandability are to be maximized, and if reuse is to be facilitated.

The nature of data

Data produced throughout the research lifecycle includes any information in binary digital form that is created, stored, accessed and rendered with the use of computer technology. Data can encompass both digital objects and databases. There are two kinds of digital object created in the course of research activity. The first is a simple digital object; a discrete item such as an individual text, image file or sound file. These are the simplest kind of digital material to curate as they stand alone, consisting of a single file that has only one format. Only one software package is required to render them and they can be described with a single catalogue entry. A number of software packages have been designed to manage simple digital objects, often referred to as digital object management systems.

The second is a complex digital object, a discrete digital object that is made by combining a number of separate digital objects. These are harder to curate as a combination of software packages may be needed to render them. Additionally the constituent parts need to be conceptually linked together if their relationship to each other is to be explicitly understood. Three different types of complex digital objects are shown in Figure 2.1, each of which presents a different set of curation challenges.

The first is a digitized book (Figure 2.1a). This object consists of a digitized image of each page of the book, each created in the same file format. The second shows an

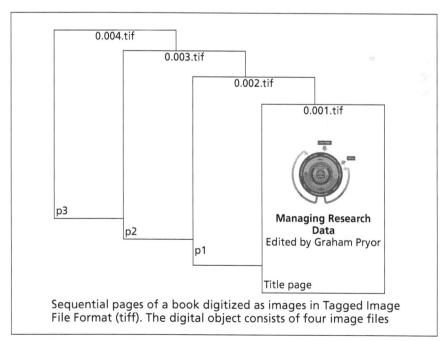

Sequential pages of a book digitized as images in Tagged Image File Format (tiff). The digital object consists of four image files

Figure 2.1a *Examples of complex digital objects*

office document which is made up of a text file with an embedded image (Figure 2.1b). Two formats are combined to make this object. The third shows a website, which is a combination of a number of files, each with a different format: the source code in hypertext markup language (HTML), an embedded image in Joint Photographic Experts Group (JPEG) format, a linked document in Portable Document Format (PDF), and a Cascading Style-sheet file (CSS) to create the formatting (Figure 2.1c).

Databases consist of structured information, which is organized to facilitate machine searching and sorting, and is organized into sets of fields which together make up the record. A set of records constitute a file. Databases are used ubiquitously in research, and the results of quantitative data collection are normally stored in a database to enable their analysis.

Research data constitutes the *record* of the research activity: 'data or information in a fixed form that is created or received in the course of individual or institutional activity and set aside (preserved) as evidence of that activity for future reference' (Pearce-Moses, 2005). The International Standard for Records Management defines four characteristics of an authoritative record that digital curation activities must ensure are maintained throughout the record's lifecycle, if their value is to be retained. Records must be:

- *authentic* – be what the record purports to be, be created or sent by the purported person, and be created or sent at the purported time
- *reliable* – have trusted contents which accurately reflect the business transaction documented
- *have integrity* – be complete and unaltered
- *usable* – can be located, retrieved, presented and interpreted (ISO 15489-1, 2001).

The inherent nature of digital materials, with their ability to be readily copied, moved, edited and shared, makes this task increasingly complex.

The data policy environment

Data management is best facilitated by a series of documented policies, strategies and procedures, and may not in fact be viable without them. Policies at organizational level, or research funder level, underpin the activities required, ensuring that they are embedded into a research organization or university's workflow. A high-level policy environment can be critical in ensuring that digital curation is given the support it requires through strategic and financial planning. It can be vital for ensuring that funding, staffing and equipment is available to undertake the required tasks. The wider policy environment and the benefits of organizational buy-in are considered in later chapters. This chapter will concentrate on the more detailed activities that must be planned, staffed and documented throughout the data's lifecycle.

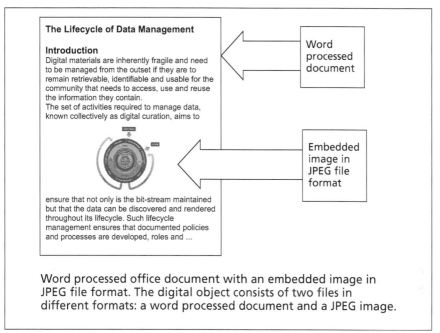

Word processed office document with an embedded image in JPEG file format. The digital object consists of two files in different formats: a word processed document and a JPEG image.

Figure 2.1b *Examples of complex digital objects*

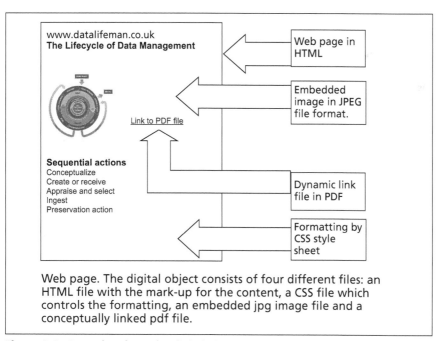

Web page. The digital object consists of four different files: an HTML file with the mark-up for the content, a CSS file which controls the formatting, an embedded jpg image file and a conceptually linked pdf file.

Figure 2.1c *Examples of complex digital objects*

Data management styles

There are three styles of data management that may be followed within a research organization:

1   Data management is undertaken by the research team throughout the curation lifecycle and the data remains within their custodianship when the research is completed.
2   An overview of data management activities within an organization, along with advice on best practice, is maintained by an information professional such as a librarian, while the data is managed and retained by the research team. For large organizations such as universities there may be a departmental level intermediary who liaises between the researcher and the information professional.
3   Data management is undertaken by the research team while the research is in progress and the data is then transferred to a custodian such as an organizational library, a domain-specific repository or a data library.

The method being followed, which is determined by high-level policy, will dictate how the workflow and capabilities are addressed to best ensure the curation of research data.

The curation lifecycle

The Digital Curation Centre's (DCC) Curation Lifecycle Model (Higgins, 2008) (Figure 1.2) identifies the activities required for the successful curation of data from the original conception of the research that will generate the data, to either the data's disposal or selection for reuse and long-term preservation. This high-level graphical overview is generic in nature, being applicable to the data output of any research domain. The model identifies and defines three sets of activities: those which support curation throughout the data's lifecycle; those which need to be undertaken sequentially to ensure successful curation; and those which may be undertaken occasionally if certain situations arise. Used by the DCC as a training tool to describe and discuss curation activities, it is increasingly being applied by digital curation professionals as an organizational tool to plan a coherent workflow and build the capability to deliver curation. Three areas of capability need to be developed to ensure that digital materials are curated successfully: the policies and procedures that underpin curation, the roles and responsibilities in delivering curation, and the framework of standards and technologies that support it.

The Model illustrates an idealized situation where data curation is thought out at the start of a research project and considered and planned for throughout. In practice this is often not the case, with the need for curation identified while the project is ongoing, or even at the end when staff are tidying up loose ends. But the Curation Lifecycle Model allows one to start at any point, to identify gaps in planning and undertake mitigating actions.

In the rest of this chapter detailed consideration will be given to each of the activities identified by the DCC Curation Lifecycle Model, with observations on how the capabilities to support them can be developed throughout the research lifecycle and within different data management styles. The activities that should be undertaken sequentially will be considered first, followed by the activities that pervade the entire lifecycle. Those required only occasionally will be considered at the appropriate stage in the lifecycle.

Conceptualize

The conceptualize stage of the curation lifecycle is where research is planned with digital curation in mind. Digital curation should be factored into a research project at the earliest point possible, preferably at the point of conceptualization, with curation planning undertaken during the hypothesize stage of the research lifecycle, where a research project is designed and the researcher defines the raw data that will be collected to prove or disprove the developed hypothesis. This is one of the most important stages for digital curation, as the practical considerations made at the very beginning will resonate throughout the project and affect the possibility of long-term access and use. At this stage the researcher should identify which of the data management styles outlined above will be followed and make the relevant contacts. It is not sufficient to create data that is fit for the purpose of an individual research project over the short term; good practice ensures that the needs of future users are also addressed.

The conceptualize stage is the point where technical and workflow issues should be addressed and roles and responsibilities identified and documented. Practical considerations for digital curation at the conceptualize stage include: how the data will be captured; how it will be identified and described; and how the data and its descriptions will be stored and recovered when required. These will be influenced by the legal and ethical framework within which the project operates, so this should also be clearly identified at the conceptualize stage. This includes the intellectual property rights surrounding the planned data, which should be established and documented from the outset to ensure difficulties do not arise as the project progresses. A funding body may impose particular requirements, such as deposit in a particular data repository or use of a defined technical framework. Changing tack once the project is under way can be costly in time and effort, and early decisions should keep these issues in mind from the outset.

Interoperability across communities of practice (and future users of the data) is a major consideration at the conceptualize stage. Interoperability has been defined as the 'Ability of a system or product to work with other systems or products without special effort on the part of the customer' (IEEE, 2010). It is achieved through the use of common standards, and these should be chosen carefully at this stage to ensure that short-term and long-term interoperability goals can be achieved.

Two levels of interoperability are needed to ensure that data can be exchanged and interpreted. Syntactic interoperability ensures that the technical infrastructure such as the hardware, software and data formats used to create and discover the data are able to communicate with each other. Semantic interoperability ensures that the data can be interpreted once exchanged, through the use of common data and metadata structures and content. Best practice demands interoperability across a domain of activity to enable data to be shared or integrated across the community. Semantic interoperability is made possible by structuring data and its descriptions according to the standards that have currency within the researcher's domain of operation. An example is the Flexible Image Transport System (FITS) file format used in astronomy. It supports the collection of scientific specific structured metadata such as provenance, context and equipment calibrations in conjunction with image capture.

At the conceptualize stage liaison between the researcher and an information professional or data repository staff should ensure that data will be created that can readily be curated. A designated information professional should have an overview of the organization they represent and, through awareness raising and tailored advice, can ensure that relevant technologies are employed. An institutional or domain-specific data repository may mandate the use of certain technologies such as data capture tools, file formats or metadata standards, so data is readily integrated into existing systems. Many data repositories have a documented interoperability framework defining the technologies to which submissions must conform; for example, the Archaeology Data Service specifies the file formats it prefers for deposit and those it will accept with additional discussion and documentation (Archaeology Data Service, 2008). The development of an international interoperability framework to support digital preservation is being considered (Chang, 2010). There may be some mismatch between the data requirements of the project, the dominant standards used in the project's domain and the chosen repository's abilities to care for the data. These should be addressed at the earliest possible point to ensure that data is not created which cannot be used by all possible current stakeholders or curated to ensure access for future users.

Curation is best supported by the use of open file formats rather than closed or proprietary ones. Open file formats guard against the dangers of digital obsolescence, a situation that arises when the media, hardware or software required to read the files is no longer available. The specifications for open file formats are publicly available, making it possible to decode them in the future, should software which supports their rendering be discontinued. The differences between open and closed file formats are summarized in Table 2.1.

Planning to create data that will be curation ready reduces work at a later stage and can limit the possibility of data integrity and usability being compromised by, for instance, file format transformations, loss of metadata, or ethical problems.

Create or receive

The create and receive stage of the curation lifecycle focuses on ensuring that data

Table 2.1 *Comparison of open and closed file formats*	
Open file formats	**Closed (proprietary) file formats**
Full documentation available	Full documentation usually not available
No licence fees or patent owners	Licence and patent rules may apply
Generally free to use	Licence fees may apply with agreements subject to change
Code made available and open for self-modifications	Code not available and cannot be modified (except for example through user group pressure)
User-led development and upgrade	Vendor-led development and upgrade
Multiple software packages, which can render them	Limited software packages, which can render them

created is fit for purpose and ready for curation. Relationships developed between the researcher and the information professional during the conceptualize stage should continue during the nitty-gritty of planning a research data creation methodology. Each of these has a different role, the former being concerned with creating the data and the latter being concerned with receiving the data from the creator for ongoing management. These roles will be considered in turn.

Create

For the researcher, this stage is concerned with identifying how data will be created and by whom, and the documentation of this, as much as the actual creation activity. The research phase of the research lifecycle sees the creation of the raw data and the descriptions of that data, which will form the basis of the rest of the project. The technologies and standards to be used should have been identified in the conceptualize stage of the curation lifecycle, when interoperability issues were considered and the final custodian decided. In the create stage detailed specifications for using these technologies and standards are developed to ensure that the data can be used to test the research hypothesis and, more practically, make co-ordinated data capture and storage possible. These specifications should be documented as technical metadata (see the section 'Describe and represent information', below) to ensure continuity across related projects, or changes in personnel, and may include:

- calibrations for scientific instruments
- file formats to be used
- profiles of chosen metadata standards
- specifications for ensuring quality of data and metadata content
- ontologies, thesauri or authority files to be applied.

The application of metadata standards is an aspect of curation that has to be considered throughout the whole lifecycle. Its role will be considered in more detail in the section

'Describe and represent information', below.

Workflow for the creation of data and associated metadata needs to be specified and documented at the create stage of the lifecycle, and roles and responsibilities for research and support staff should be identified. Specifics will depend on the project being undertaken and the data capture and storage methods to be adopted. Data management workflow should include roles and responsibilities, as well as identify any training requirements for the following tasks:

- data creation
- assignment of persistent identifiers
- metadata creation
- attaching or linking the metadata to the data
- indexing or tagging
- quality assurance procedures for data, metadata and indexing
- ensuring legal and ethical metadata is collected
- appraisal and disposal procedures
- procedures for transfer to storage media.

These tasks may not be discrete activities but rather functions that must be included. For example, the assignment of a persistent identifier, metadata creation and linkage of the metadata and a digital object might all be undertaken as a single data entry function.

Receive

For the information manager this stage is concerned with ensuring that policies are in place for the type and structure of data that can be accepted for deposit, as well as the structure and content of the metadata that should accompany it. The task of keeping research data can be made more efficient if a data repository limits what can be accepted into custodianship in the first instance. The management of large, multifaceted and heterogeneous datasets generated by some research domains and processes can represent a considerable technical problem. Accommodating a diverse range of data structures, file formats and metadata standards suggests a complex technical endeavour, which may not be scalable in efficiency, budget and staffing. Accepting a broad range of subject matter may further compound these technical issues, because of the domain-specific data models on which the data are built, with the result that by trying to cater for too many needs the repository's authority could be diluted.

A collection development policy specifies the scope of the data that will be accepted by a repository, by theme and topic of the data and the technical specifications to be managed. Such policies support the development of a collection by giving the repository manager the authority to select data suitable for deposit and reject data that is not suitable. The elements required in an archives collection development policy have been specified by The UK's National Archives (National Archives (UK), 2004). Data collection includes some additional elements and is summarized in Table 2.2. Good examples of collection development policies have been produced by the UK Data Archive and the US National Geospatial Digital Archive. The former evolved over ten years and is now in its fourth edition (UK Data Archive, 2008). The latter elaborates detailed collection development policies for different collaborators in the Project (National Geospatial Digital Archive (USA), 2005–2009).

Restricting the file formats and technical standards that will be accepted into a repository, through implementation of a data model, can avert problems of data management, as researchers will be prevented from creating data that cannot be technically integrated into a repository without significant data transformations or cleaning. Furthermore, data managers would be able to refuse datasets that they are technically unable to manage.

Regular communication between the researcher and the information professional, during the conceptualize and the create stages, can help to ensure that the data created is curation ready when transferred into custodianship. Curation ready data must be:

Table 2.2 *Elements of a collections development policy*	
Repository identification	Name and address of the repository and governing body information
Legal status of the collection and authority to collect	• the repository's statutory situation and obligations • official recognition of the repository • service standards adopted.
Scope of the collection	• overall priorities and mission statement • co-operation with other collecting bodies • statement of scope of materials collected, e.g.:–Geographical area–Subject area–Chronological period–Genre or media.
Collection process	Method of acquisition and technical requirements: • technical standards to which the data should conform • what accompanying metadata is required • the acceptable quality of the data and metadata • data transfer methods. Selection and de-accessioning policies
Access to the collection	• intellectual property rights and their management • designated community to which access will be enabled, and their use and reuse rights.

- fit for purpose or potential purposes
- well structured, conforming to any relevant data model
- adequately documented through accompanying metadata, created to documented profiles of relevant standards
- complete – all required information is included in the correct fields
- created in a format that best ensures its longevity
- interoperable with other appropriate datasets
- authentic: what it claims to be
- accurate: not tampered with
- renderable (used in the ways for which it was intended, or viewed as originally intended).

Appraise and select

Appraisal and selection is the process of evaluating material in order to decide which to retain over the long term, which to retain for the meantime and which to discard. It is a fallacy that digital material can all be kept and does not need appraising because storage is cheap and continues to become cheaper (Wright and Miller, 2009). Whyte and Wilson (2010, 1) found that the growth of content can fairly quickly outstrip any benefits from cheaper storage and that the requirement to back up or mirror digital material immediately doubles the cost of storage. Storage is only one aspect of managing digital material and it is unviable to maintain and manage large amounts of redundant data. Data quickly becomes unusable, unless adequately documented, and metadata creation and maintenance can be one of the most time consuming and expensive aspects of data management (Geisler et al., 2002, 213). Maintaining logical links between digital materials can also be a complex and expensive activity.

There are five main reasons for undertaking the appraisal of research data and the associated records which research generates:

1 It reduces the amount of material that has to be managed or curated over the long term, so resources can be directed to material which has long-term value.
2 It facilitates the ability to maintain intellectual access to the material, to create and attach metadata, index and to store logically, so the data can be searched and retrieved quickly and efficiently.
3 It ensures that preservation activities can be undertaken in a timely and organized fashion to best ensure the data's longevity.
4 It limits the costs of storing and managing the material.
5 It ensures that legal obligations for data storage and access are discharged.

Data should be appraised, selected and disposed of in an organized, regular and documented fashion. Appraisal can be a very subjective process: 'one man's trash is another man's treasure'; it is not sufficient to rely on an individual's decisions, taken *ad hoc.* An appraisal policy should be developed and implemented in conjunction with relevant information professionals, to ensure that, as far as possible, the appraisal and selection process remains objective. This should identify the long-term value of the data and associated metadata, depending on what a researcher or repository *wants* to keep, and also what they *need* to keep for legal or evidential purposes. For instance, a research project will need to consider whether the raw data collected during the research phase and the processed data resulting from the synthesize phase need to be retained, and whether there is a legal and evidential imperative to retain the administrative data created during the course of the project. An appraisal policy should:

- support the collection development policy
- support the goals of the research and host organizations and any data repository
- support the research requirements of the user community
- consider whether accessibility needs to be maintained through changes of technology
- identify the benefits and risks of either keeping or disposing of the data
- ensure that any legal obligations for the data are identified and provision made to ensure compliance, e.g. relevant freedom of information or data protection laws
- ensure a methodology is in place for recording appraisal decisions for evidential and audit purposes
- specify a testable quality threshold for retaining data.

Appraisal is an iterative process: the value of maintaining data needs to be reassessed over time to ensure that collections remain relevant. This process can be supported by the development of retention schedules, which specify from the outset how long data should be kept, or a date for reappraisal. This is a particularly helpful tool for managing data that has been identified as having short-term value, or where it is difficult to determine long-term value in a first assessment.

Dispose

Data that is not selected for retention should be disposed of in accordance with the appraisal policy. Destruction may be appropriate and this should be undertaken securely to ensure that personal or sensitive information cannot be accessed by unauthorized persons. BS EN 15713:2009 defines a code of practice for the secure destruction of confidential material and covers a wide range of data management issues such as security, confidentiality, media shredding and disposal (British Standards Institute, 2009). It is a compliance standard against which professional data destruction companies can be accredited.

Ingest

Ingest is the process of formally submitting data to a curation environment. This can be through deposit in a domain-specific archive, an institutional repository or a data centre. For self-managing projects the process may be as simple as moving it, in an organized fashion, to a dedicated folder in a shared drive that someone has been given the responsibility to maintain. The term ingest, which is now ubiquitous, originated as a functional entity of the OAIS Reference Model (ISO 14721, 2003, 4–5), which identifies model requirements for the technical and organizational activities required to manage research data.

The formal accession of data into an archive should be supported by a deposit or accession agreement made at the point of ingest and retained throughout the custodianship. The administrative metadata collected during the ingest procedure ensure that physical and intellectual control of the data can be established, record the terms and conditions under which the data is held and managed, and can be used to identify any legal issues that may need to be considered (Carnell, 2004). An accession agreement should ensure that the data can be unequivocally identified within the repository and establish who owns the data, who created the data and any legal obligations. It should also give the information professional authority for reuse, re-purposing and any required preservation actions. Responsibilities for a number of tasks required at ingest should also be made clear by the accessions policy. It should identify who will be responsible for tasks such as transforming data to acceptable formats and the creation of administrative metadata or links between the data and metadata. The minimum information required in an accession or deposit agreement is listed in Table 2.3.

Table 2.3 The minimum information to collect at accession	
Data ownership and legal requirements	• data and metadata creator(s) • data and metadata owner(s) • contact details for the depositor • who to contact when ingest is completed • date acquired • intellectual property rights • legal restrictions and terms of use and reuse • the location and management details of originals or copies.
Data management	• assignation of a persistent identifier • date(s) of data creation • name of the dataset(s) • scope and content of the data and the metadata • quantity of the data and metadata – number of files and total server space required for storage • file formats of the data and the metadata • responsibilities for ensuring data and metadata quality • responsibilities for additional metadata required by the management environment • responsibilities for supplying representation information • assigned storage location • appraisal schedule • define preservation activities which can be performed.

A number of activities need to be undertaken before new data is incorporated into a repository. As a first step it should be quarantined, scanned and cleaned, to prevent any possible infection of the repository from viruses, trojans, malicious spyware or malware. This will prevent devastating cross-infection between the files being introduced and those already being curated. Security measures such as locally devised and stored passwords or encryption will need to be removed so that they do not render the data inaccessible.

The ingest stage is also the point in the curation lifecycle where quality assurance procedures should be enacted. The retention of poor quality data can confuse research results and reduce trust in the resource. Poor quality metadata can render the data unusable. Design and documentation of a quality assurance policy makes explicit the acceptable quality of data and metadata and ensures that this remains high, through documented processes to identify and rectify data that don't pass the test. The characteristics of quality data have been identified by the UK Audit Commission and are listed in Table 2.4. The ISO 8000 suite of standards also addresses Data Quality (ISO 8000:2009), with standards to address provenance, accuracy, conformance to specification and completeness.

Clear associations between the data and the metadata should be made at the point of ingest. Necessary links may have been established by the researcher before deposit but changes to the linkage methodology may be required for integration into a repository storage environment, to ensure the data can be identified and discovered in its new management environment. This is often automated during the deposit process (e.g. through a web based upload form) so no additional activity is required but some manual intervention may be needed by the information professional. Links to representation information (see below) may also need to be established at ingest.

If the custodianship of digital material changes at this stage of the lifecycle, enhancements to discovery metadata may be required to enable the data to be integrated

Table 2.4 *The characteristics of quality data (Audit Commission, 2007, 7–8)*	
Accuracy	Data should be accurate for its intended purpose. It may have multiple purposes but should only be captured once, at the point of activity.
Validity	Should be captured and used in compliance with relevant standards, rules or definitions. This ensures consistency across applications and interoperability between organizations.
Reliability	Stable and consistent data collection processes should be used so variations reflect real changes rather than differences in data collection methods.
Timeliness	Data should be captured as quickly as possible after an activity and made available for its intended use within a reasonable time limit.
Relevance	Data should be relevant for the purpose it will be used for, and periodic review of requirements should reflect changing needs.
Completeness	Data should be complete and valid when measured against a clear specification of information needs, without missing, incomplete or invalid entries.

into the new storage environment, and be accessed by the search and discovery tools it provides. These might include ensuring that the same metadata elements are used, confirming that a consistent methodology is used for access points or indexing, or the addition of specific metadata fields required for access tools.

Ingest also involves a number of preservation-specific activities, which are required to ensure the longevity of the data. These are described in the following section.

Preservation planning and action

A number of preservation actions are required before material is integrated into the curation environment to ensure that their authoritative characteristics, as identified by ISO 15489-1, can be retained over the long term. Activities that support the preservation process should be planned in a structured and organized manner through the maintenance of a preservation plan, which is to be reviewed and revised at regular intervals. (To take account of rapid changes in technology and preservation requirements, a review of the plan should be undertaken annually.) The plan should document the actual activities that will be undertaken to ensure the longevity of data, rather than a statement of commitment to curation. A preservation plan should include the administrative procedures required before undertaking preservation activities and the technical requirements of preservation.

Any administrative or technical activities undertaken should be recorded as preservation metadata. This is specialist administrative metadata defined as 'the information a repository uses to support the digital preservation process' (PREMIS Editorial Committee, 2011, 3). Its purpose is to document transparently any activities that are undertaken to help ensure the longevity of data, or maintain access to it over time. The varied purposes of metadata are described in the later section on metadata and representation information; but among other things, preservation metadata would normally record the activities discussed below.

No preservation activities should be undertaken unless explicit permission has been obtained and the legal right to alter data is established. Planned preservation activities should be notified to the researcher(s) who created the data and the recognized owner of the data. It is possible that planned preservation actions will affect the future use of the data and the wider effects of these should be carefully considered.

A persistent identifier should be applied, if not already assigned during data creation, to ensure efficient and persistent discovery and to support the sustained usability of the data. This preservation action ensures that data can be robustly identified, and that links between data, metadata and the component parts of complex digital objects can be maintained. It also provides a unique citation to the data for use in later publications.

There are a number of different strategies available for creating persistent identifiers. Erpanet (2004) gives an overview of the application of the four most prominent strategies, including case studies from different domains, covering the Handle System; the Digital Object Identifier (DOI), an implementation of the Handle System for intellectual property; the Persistent Uniform Resource Locator (PURL); and the Archival Resource Key (ARK). There is ongoing discussion over the pros and cons of these systems, particularly the Handle System, which is a commercial undertaking.

The authenticity and integrity of digital materials can readily be compromised as a result of the ease with which they can be copied, altered, shared and manipulated. To determine whether material has altered between two points in time, the fixity needs to be determined. Calculation of a hash value or checksum on ingest can enable comparisons to be made at a later date, in order to determine if any changes have been made. These fixity values can also be used to determine whether there is any corruption to data, through bit rot or decay, over time.

Accessibility to digital materials over time is determined by the availability of the hardware and software required to access and render (open and read) it. Knowing the file format is a prerequisite for managing obsolescence, thereby ensuring that processes are in place for dealing with changes to the availability of hardware and software. Identifying and recording file formats is an important preservation activity, which is not as straightforward as reading the suffix appended to the file. There are huge discrepancies in how these are assigned, which can be misleading, and file content analysis is the only foolproof method.

There are a number of methods of undertaking this, which is itself an area of active research in digital forensics. The UK's National Archives has developed PRONOM (National Archives (UK), n.d.) a freely available database of file formats and the software required to render them. This can be used in conjunction with Digital Record Object Identification (DROID), an open source automatic file format identification tool (Brown, 2006). Validation of a file format is the next stage in preservation, ensuring that a file format actually conforms to the identified format specification, so it can be correctly rendered by the identified software before being integrated into a curation environment. Automatic identification and validation of a number of digital file formats can be undertaken automatically using the open source JHOVE tool developed by Harvard College (JSTOR and the President and Fellows of Harvard College, 2003–2009). This identifies syntactic validity (whether the file is well formed) and semantic validity (whether the file is valid).

Obsolescence of hardware and software can mean that although the bit-stream of digital materials is available, it cannot be rendered or used. A curation environment normally uses one of two strategies to ensure that accessibility is maintained: migration of materials to a new file format as technologies change, or emulation of the original environment. Migration is the more frequently used strategy and is an occasional activity described by the DCC Curation Lifecycle Model. It is perceived as being more straightforward than emulation, but it is not without its problems. Rothenberg identified as early as 1998 that migration requires a case-by-case solution, being 'labor-intensive, time-consuming, expensive, error-prone, and fraught with the danger of losing or corrupting information' (1998, chapter 6). Best practice is to maintain the original bit-stream as a back-up for future migrations and the possibility of better methodologies evolving as research develops.

Migration may also be used to normalize materials as they are accessioned to ensure they can be adequately cared for in the storage and access environment.

The key point when planning migration strategies is that information or functionality will be lost during the process, so it is very important to consider what the significant properties of the digital material that needs to be maintained through the migration are. These are 'the characteristics of an information object that must be maintained to ensure that object's continued access, use, and meaning over time as it is moved to new technologies' (Knight and Pennock, 2008, 160). The main considerations for migration are the maintenance of:

- *Look and feel* – Does the migration need to retain formatting which gives it a specific appearance or is it sufficient to maintain the contents?
- *Structure* – Are there relationships between constituent parts which need to be retained?
- *Functionality* – Does certain functionality such as hyperlinks to other material, or embedded comments need to be retained?
- *Interoperability* – Does the data need to retain interoperability with other datasets?

Migrations should take account of not only future accessibility of the content of the material, but also the function it is expected to perform, while ensuring that links to associated metadata or representation information are maintained. These considerations will determine the approach taken to migration. Conversion of textual documents to PDF format (or even better the preservation version PDF/A) is routine for institutional repositories, as this maintains the original structure and look and feel and only one format needs to be managed. The Netherlands Data Archiving and Networked Services (DANS) normalize structured data, created in a selection of spreadsheet and database software, to EXtensible Markup Language (XML). This is performed on ingest to negate subsequent obsolescence (Roorda, 2007; Data Archiving and Networked Services (NL), n.d.), a strategy that is suitable where the content is considered to be more important than the look and feel.

Dynamic documents, those with embedded functionality, may require emulation strategies to ensure their usability. Emulation is 'to access or run original data/software on a new/current platform by running software on the new/current platform that emulates the original platform' (Granger, 2000). This strategy was demonstrated to good effect in the CAMiLEON Project, which used the rescue of the BBC Domesday Project as its main proof of concept (CAMiLEON, n.d.) and is one of the preservation strategies being developed for the e-Depot at the National Library of the Netherlands (Koninklijke Bibliotheek, n.d.).

Store

Storage does not need to be a function managed centrally by a research organization, or an official place of deposit such as a data library. It may be as simple as the project's centralized shared drive space on an institutionally managed server, as mentioned above. Consideration may also be given to storage 'in the cloud' by a third party provider. Whichever solution is used it is important that the storage environment is actively managed, secure and reliable over time and that it enables the level of control and accessibility required by the researcher and others who need access, use and reuse of the data. There are two aspects to take into account when considering options for the long-term storage of digital material: the actual storage facilities provided and the administration environment of these facilities.

The longevity of research data relies on storage facilities offering comprehensive backup policies and disaster recovery plans. Timely refreshment of storage media is required to protect data against obsolescence. Storage media become obsolete at a remarkable rate and data may quickly become inaccessible when there is no hardware suitable for accessing the storage medium. Floppy disk drives are the obvious example of this phenomenon; they are disappearing fast and are no longer supplied as standard on new computing equipment. A rolling programme of media refreshment should be undertaken, copying data to new storage media as it wears out or becomes obsolete. Refreshment is not to be confused with migration, discussed above, where the actual file format of the data is changed.

Refreshment also guards against the gradual physical decay, or bit rot, of the storage media over time. Portable media are designed for convenience rather than a long-term storage solution and are prone to decay through the effects of temperature, humidity, light and poor handling among others. A study by the Library of Congress and the National Institute of Standards and Technology (2007, 17) established that if optical discs are kept in ideal ambient conditions 70% of recordable CDs will last for over 45 years, with less favourable results for recordable DVDs. The survival rate is much reduced if ideal conditions cannot be maintained and a period of ten years is often quoted for CDs. Hash tags or checksums generated at ingest can be cross-checked against a newly generated set to examine the integrity of storage at designated intervals.

The security and therefore the authenticity, reliability and integrity of data is more likely to be guaranteed if storage facilities are audited against ISO/IEC 27001 and certified for compliance (ISO/IEC 27001, 2005). This international standard specifies a complete information security management system, which is continuously monitored for quality control and improvement through implementation of the iterative Plan–Do–Check–Act Model (Shewhart, 1939). The strengths of systems that comply with ISO/IEC 27001 are that they follow a defined and structured approach, which documents organizational commitment to information security, so processes and procedures are documented and embedded in process. Independent verification through certification can ensure that relevant legislations are being complied to, for instance 'in England and Wales the standard is recognized by the Information Commissioner as an appropriate source of advice for ensuring compliance with the Data Protection Act 1998' (Higgins, 2009).

The administration environment of the data storage service is as important as the range of facilities provided. Key attributes and responsibilities for achieving the status of trusted digital repository have been identified by the OCLC and RLG Working Group on Digital Archive Attributes (Research Libraries Group, 2002) and are listed below. They relate to the overall management infrastructure and are built around the activities required for conformance to the OAIS Reference Model (ISO 14721, 2003). The obligations of a trusted digital repository should be discharged within an effective and efficient policy framework, one that has been designed according to a strategic programme for preservation planning and activity. At a practical level, appropriate and adequate staffing and the discharge of legal responsibilities are as important for effective management as the provision of sufficient funds, with significant risk factors attaching to the level of responsibility that a repository will take for data stewardship and whether any activities are outsourced.

The OCLC and RLG report identified the need for an audit and certification methodology. Two self-audit methodologies were developed in response: Trusted Repositories Audit and Certification (TRAC), a checklist of criteria for a trustworthy repository, and DRAMBORA, an audit methodology based on risk assessment. These will soon be superseded by the International Standard ISO 16363. At the time of writing this is in draft form as a Consultative Committee for Space Data Systems (CCSDS) Red Book (CCSDS 652.0-R-1, 2009):

- Accept responsibility for the long-term maintenance of digital resources on behalf of its depositors and for the benefit of current and future users;
- Have an organizational system that supports not only long-term viability of the repository, but also the digital information for which it has responsibility;
- Demonstrate fiscal responsibility and sustainability;
- Design its system(s) in accordance with commonly accepted conventions and standards to ensure the ongoing management, access, and security of materials deposited within it;
- Establish methodologies for system evaluation that meet community expectations of trustworthiness;
- Be depended on to carry out its long-term responsibilities to depositors and users openly and explicitly;
- Have policies, practices, and performance that can be audited and measured;
- Meet organizational and curatorial responsibilities with regard to: the data's scope; preservation and lifecycle management; stakeholder issues; legal responsibilities; and cost implications;
- Meet operational responsibilities with regard to: negotiating appropriate information from content providers; obtaining sufficient control of the information; determining the designated community and making the data understandable and available to them; documenting and following policies and procedures; advocating good data creation practices.

(Research Libraries Group, 2002, 5)

Access, use and reuse

The aim of digital curation is the access use and reuse of data, and careful consideration should be given, from the conceptualize stage, to defining what the OAIS Reference Model (ISO 14721, 2003, 31) calls the designated community – who or what the data is for. This is a user base that procedures and tools to facilitate access should be aimed at. Analysis of the data should also be undertaken to ensure that relevant legislations regarding freedom of information and data protection are adhered to when allowing others to access it. Registration of data with the relevant authorities may be required to comply with such legislation, as may redaction or anonymization of sensitive or personal data before making it available to users.

Policies should be developed that establish who will be authorized to view, edit, download, upload or reuse the research data. The implementation of authority control procedures, which allow only those with relevant permissions to access materials, can guard against illegitimate access and use. The application of authentication requires a layer of administrative metadata, sometimes created as part of the preservation metadata and concerning access rights, permissions to download and permissions to upload materials. For in-project management, authentication can be as simple as applying password protection and user privileges to a project's storage and management environment. Information professionals in research organizations and higher education institutions manage federated authentication through subscription to authentication management services such as OpenAthens (Eduserv, n.d.), or the implementation of middleware such as Shibboleth (Internet2Sites, 2011). A co-ordinated approach across an organization represents best practice and reduces the effort and cost of authentication.

The provision of search and discovery tools should also be appropriate for the designated community and consideration should be given to how searches will be undertaken and how the data will be delivered. Provision of appropriate and consistent discovery, through searching and browsing, can be facilitated by using domain specific metadata standards and paying attention to interoperability issues.

Transform

Research data is collected in the research phase to enable it to be synthesized, analysed, selected or queried. This synthesize phase of the research project inevitably transforms the raw dataset to create a new one. As mentioned above, the appraisal policy should determine which of these transformations need to be curated as datasets in their own right. Transformed datasets can perform a variety of roles such as verifying the results obtained from the analysis of the raw data, forming the basis of further experiments, or forming the basis of a new hypothesis. The transformation of data finds the curation and research lifecycles restarted through the creation of new derived datasets and the imaginative reuse of data to underpin new research.

Data migrated to combat obsolescence or for normalization has also been transformed. An effective curation environment stores the transformed and the original bit-stream to enable a return to the original if required for evidential purposes and to guard against loss.

Description and representational information

The description of research data, otherwise known as metadata, is the 'backbone of digital curation' (Higgins, 2007a). Creating metadata is time-consuming and perceived as unrewarding (Treloar and Wilkinson, 2008, 784–85), but it ensures that data can be discovered, identified, managed and retrieved, and it is vital to successful curation. Inadequate or incomplete metadata can make digital material unusable in a short space of time as it may become undiscoverable, or the context of its creation may be lost. Descriptive, administrative, technical and preservation metadata all need to be recorded; relying on memory is not a sustainable strategy as details are easily forgotten as a consequence of technical and personnel changes.

To support the condition of interoperability metadata standards rather than bespoke solutions should be used. Standards are usually developed and controlled by a particular community, with a particular domain in mind, so it is important to choose those most applicable to the data being described, the identified designated community and the storage and access method to be used. Choices can be complex, and to guide such decisions Riley (2009) has mapped metadata standards according to the domain community and the function they perform. A metadata standard may support some or all of these functions:

- *descriptive metadata* – ensures identification, location and retrieval of information resources; includes classification, indexing and links to related resources
- *technical metadata* – records the technical infrastructure used to create, or required to access data, such as the file format, calibrations of equipment, associated representation information and the software or hardware used
- *administrative metadata* – manages acquisition and accession information, appraisal decisions, intellectual property rights and legal obligations
- *use metadata* – manages access rights and tracks usage
- *preservation metadata* – documents preservation actions such as checksum calculations and migrations. (Based on Higgins, 2007b)

Metadata standards tend to take into account every eventuality, so normal practice is to develop a profile through the creation of use cases, which include the mandatory elements and those specific to the data being managed. Interoperability across metadata standards demands that the minimum set of information required for the adequate control of data is recorded. This is embodied in the Dublin Core Metadata Element Set (ISO 15836:2009). Any developed metadata standard profile should include the fields which correspond to the 15 elements defined in Dublin Core. These are also required for creating search facilities and indexes, as well as for enabling the aggregation of metadata sets through harvesting, using the Open Archives Initiative Protocol for Metadata Harvesting (Open Archives Initiative, 2008b). A number of cross-walks, which map the elements between metadata standards, are available online, with automated tools being developed by OCLC (2010).

Sometimes a metadata standard will encompass all the functions required to manage data adequately, but this is not usually the case. It is likely that a framework of complementary metadata standards will have to be implemented to ensure that all the functions are satisfactorily performed. For instance, elements encompassing preservation metadata and use metadata are usually not included in domain specific standards; specialist standards may have to be employed in addition to the chosen descriptive standard. PREMIS is a technically neutral preservation metadata standard, which was developed in the light of the OAIS Reference Model to support the 'viability, renderability, understandability, authenticity, and identity of digital objects in a preservation context' (PREMIS Editorial Committee, 2011, 1). It includes elements for recording the information required for most long-term data curation requirements.

The time-consuming aspect of metadata capture can make it an expensive part of any data curation activity. Capture methodology should be devised to limit the amount of work required while ensuring the consistency of the data. Metadata content rules that define the semantics and syntax of entries in individual elements, used in conjunction with domain appropriate classifications, vocabularies, ontologies or thesauri, can help to ensure consistency, improve discovery, and increase the speed of data capture. It may be possible to create certain metadata automatically, thereby saving on time and resources. Examples of this include technical metadata that are routinely captured along with digital images, or descriptive metadata being extracted from documents in PDF format. XML markup has become the *de facto* standard for ensuring that standardized digital formats of metadata are created and for facilitating technical delivery. Most metadata standards have an associated XML schema to help ensure consistency and facilitate interoperability. Time and effort can be saved if metadata creation and XML markup are undertaken simultaneously.

Representation information goes hand-in-hand with metadata. This is information required to ensure that data can be understood, interpreted and rendered over the long term and is defined in the OAIS Reference Model's information definition (ISO 14721:2003, 2–3). The depth and amount of representation information that is collected and maintained is dependent on the designated community for which it has been defined and the technological framework in which it operates.

It is important to be aware that the needs and knowledge base of any designated community, as well as the equipment available to them, will change over time. Representation information that supports the ability to understand data over time must therefore include semantic information such as code books used to define the meaning of the data in its original context, calibrations used for the data collecting equipment, full definitions of database fields and descriptive definitions of the weights and measures used. There may be a common professional understanding over the use of these at the time data is created but it should not be assumed that these will be understood implicitly at a later date. Representation information that supports renderability includes structural information such as file format documentation and XML schema definitions, giving a clear profile of those used.

A curation environment should ensure that structured links between the constituent parts of data, their metadata and their representation information are maintained. These links would normally be defined and described as part of the ingest process, so that conceptual packages hold all the components together. Packaging standards can be used to ensure that this is done in a consistent and organized manner. Figure 2.2 shows the conceptual links that packaging standards maintain between a simple digital object, its metadata and its representation information. A number of methodologies have been designed to enable this.

The Metadata and Encoding Transmission Standard 'describes, anchors, and organizes the components of a digital object so that the integrity of the digital object may be retained even when its components are stored in different places' (Digital Library Federation, 2010, 15). It was created specifically to address the increasing complexity of digital materials and the metadata required to manage them and uses an XML schema to describe links between digital materials and their metadata. Similarly the Open Archives Initiative Object Reuse and Exchange (OAI-ORE) 'defines standards for the description and exchange of aggregations of Web resources' (Open Archives Initiative, 2008a) using semantic web concepts. The international industry standard MPEG-21 Digital Item Declaration (ISO/IEC 21000-2:2005) designed to 'define a multimedia framework to enable transparent and augmented use of multimedia resources across a wide range of networks and devices used by different communities' has also been used successfully by the digital library community to define relationships (Bekaert, Hochstenbach and Van de Sompel, 2003).

Community watch and participation

All researchers will naturally keep up with developments in their field through the identification of other members of the relevant research community and by reading their publications; they will routinely collaborate with others in the field and attend pertinent meetings and conferences. Data management is a professional and intellectual domain in its own right, and those who create and manage research data need to maintain a watch on appropriate community activities to ensure that they remain up to date with developments and activities in this area.

Collaborative effort can be highly advantageous to effective data management, enabling the development and implementation of shared policy environments and documentation, workflows, tools and technical frameworks, staffing and costs. The benefits of collaboration for preserving data have been identified by UNESCO as:

Packaging information
Conceptually links together all constituent parts

Digital object and metadata

Archive quality (tiff image)

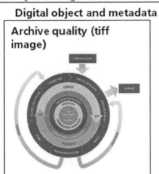

Descriptive metadata (Dublin Core)

Title	DCC Curation Lifecycle Model
Creator	Higgins, S.
Contributor	DCC staff and others
Coverage	International
Date	2008
Description	A model which describes the activities required for successful digital curation
Format	Digital still image
Identifier	DOI: dcc3456365
Etc…	

Technical metadata (Niso Mix)

file format	tiff
date	20110703
size	15 x 10
dpi	300
Etc…	

Preservation metadata (PREMIS)

preservationLevel	1
SignificantProperties	content
fixity	Checksum value= 23liy43t3kk43
Etc…	

Representation information

TIFF™
Revision 6.0
Final — June 3, 1992

Dublin Core Metadata Element Set Version 1.1

Niso Metadata for Images in XML Schema

PREMIS Data Dictionary for Preservation Metadata Version 2.1

Figure 2.2 *Metadata and representation information required to support the long-term management of a digital image*

- having access to a wider range of expertise
- sharing development costs
- having access to tools and systems that might otherwise be unavailable
- sharing learning opportunities
- increasing coverage of preserved materials
- better planning to reduce wasted effort
- encouraging for other influential stakeholders to take preservation seriously
- sharing influence on agreements with producers
- sharing influence on research and development of standards and practices
- attracting resources and other support for well co-ordinated programmes at a regional, national or sectoral level (National Library of Australia, 2003, 63).

Conclusion

The final action in the DCC Curation Lifecycle Model is curate and preserve. This action reminds us that for data to remain accessible over the long term, curation techniques need to be considered throughout the data lifecycle. It is not sufficient to be aware of the problem; it also has to be addressed through action. The Model provides an idealistic view where activities are addressed sequentially and the necessary policies and procedures, roles and responsibilities and framework of standards and technologies can be readily developed and implemented. The reality is of course less holistic and takes managerial support, time, effort and collaboration. Addressing the activities one step at a time can eventually lead to a comprehensive data management environment. While this is developing, incremental improvements in practice can mitigate the problem. 'Waiting for comprehensive, reliable solutions to appear before taking responsible action will probably mean material is lost' (National Library of Australia, 2003, 23).

References

Archaeology Data Service (2008) *Guidelines for Depositors*, Version 1.3, University of York, http://archaeologydataservice.ac.uk/advice/depositCreate.

Audit Commission for Local Authorities and the National Health Service in England (2007) *Improving Information to Support Decision Making: standards for better quality data*, www.wao.gov.uk/assets/englishdocuments/ImprovingInformationToSupportDecisionMaking.pdf.

Bekaert, J., Hochstenbach, P. and Van de Sompel, H. (2003) Using MPEG-21 DIDL to Represent Complex Digital Objects in the Los Alamos National Laboratory Digital Library, *D-Lib Magazine*, **9** (11), www.dlib.org/dlib/november03/bekaert/11bekaert.html.

British Standards Institute (2009) *Secure Destruction of Confidential Material*, Code of Practice BS EN 15713.

Brown, A. (2006) *Digital Preservation Technical Paper 1: automatic format identification using*

PRONOM and DROID, The National Archives,
www.nationalarchives.gov.uk/aboutapps/fileformat/pdf/automatic_format_identification.
pdf.

CAMiLEON (n.d.) *BBC Domesday*,
www2.si.umich.edu/CAMILEON/domesday/domesday.html.

Carnell, B. (2004) *Accession Forms: representative samples*, Library of Congress,
www.loc.gov/rr/print/tp/Accession Form Samples.pdf.

CCSDS 652.0-R-1:2009 *Audit and Certification of Trustworthy Digital Repositories: draft recommended practice: red book*, Consultative Committee for Space Data Systems,
http://public.ccsds.org/sites/cwe/rids/Lists/CCSDS%206520R1/Attachments/652x0r1.
pdf.

Chang, W. (2010) *Digital Preservation Interoperability Framework (DPIF) Summary*, National
Institute of Standards and Technology, www.jtc1dcmp.org/Doc/2010DCMPm005_1
DPIF_Events_Summary.pdf.

Data Archiving and Networked Services (NL) (n.d.) *Mixed: documentation*,
https://sites.google.com/a/datanetworkservice.nl/mixed/documentation.

Digital Library Federation (2010) *<METS>: metadata encoding and transmission standard: primer and reference manual*, version 1.6 revised,
www.loc.gov/standards/mets/METSPrimerRevised.pdf.

Eduserv (n.d.) *OpenAthens*, www.openathens.net.

Erpanet (2004) *ErpaSeminar: persistent identifiers*, University College, Cork, Ireland, 17–18 June
2004, www.erpanet.org/events/2004/cork/Cork Report.pdf.

Fry, J., Houghton, J., Lockyer, S., Oppenheim, C. and Rasmussen, B. (2008) *Identifying the Benefits Arising from the Curation and Open Sharing of Research Data*, UK Higher Education and
Research Institutes, Centre for Strategic Economic Studies and Loughborough University,
http://ie-repository.jisc.ac.uk/279/2/JISC_data_sharing_finalreport.pdf.

Geisler, G., Giersch, S., McArthur, D. and McClelland, M. (2002) Creating Virtual Collections
in Digital Libraries: benefits and implementation issues. In *Proceedings of the 2nd Joint
Conference on Digital Libraries (JCDL) held on 13–17 July 2002*, organized by the Association
for Computing Machinery and the Institute for Electrical and Electronics Engineers
Computer Society (ACM/IEEE-CS), ACM Digital Library.

Granger, S. (2000) Emulation as a Digital Preservation Strategy, *D-Lib Magazine*, **6** (10),
www.dlib.org/dlib/october00/granger/10granger.html.

Higgins, S. (2007a) *Using Metadata Standards*, Digital Curation Centre,
www.dcc.ac.uk/resources/briefing-papers/standards-watch-papers/using-metadata-
standards.

Higgins, S. (2007b) *What are Metadata Standards?* Digital Curation Centre,
www.dcc.ac.uk/resources/briefing-papers/standards-watch-papers/what-are-metadata-
standards.

Higgins, S. (2008) The DCC Curation Lifecycle Model, *International Journal of Digital Curation*, **3**
(1), 134–40.

Higgins, S. (2009) *Information Security Management: the ISO 27000 (ISO 27K) series*, Digital

Curation Centre, www.dcc.ac.uk/resources/briefing-papers/standards-watch-papers/information-security-management-iso-27000-iso-27k-s.

IEEE (2010) Standards Glossary,
www.ieee.org/education_careers/education/standards/standards_glossary.html.

Internet2Sites (2011) *Shibboleth: a project of the Internet Middleware Initiative*,
http://shibboleth.internet2.edu.

ISO 14721:2003 *Space Data and Information Transfer Systems: open archival information system, reference model*, International Organization for Standardization.

ISO 15489-1:2001 *Information and Documentation: records management, part 1: general*, International Organization for Standardization.

ISO 15836:2009 *Information and Documentation: the Dublin Core metadata element set*, International Organization for Standardization.

ISO 8000:2009 *Data Quality*, International Organization for Standardization.

ISO/IEC 21000-2:2005 *Information Technology: multimedia framework (MPEG-21), part 2: digital item declaration*, International Organization for Standardization.

ISO/IEC 27001:2005 *Information Technology: security techniques: information security management systems – requirements*, International Organization for Standardization.

JSTOR and the President and Fellows of Harvard College (2003–2009) *JHOVE: JSTOR/Harvard object validation environment*, http://hul.harvard.edu/jhove/index.html.

Knight, G. and Pennock, M. (2008) Data Without Meaning: establishing the significant properties of digital research, *International Journal of Digital Curation*, **4** (1), 159–174, www.ijdc.net/index.php/ijdc/article/viewFile/110/87.

Koninklijke Bibliotheek (NL) (n.d.) *Emulation*,
www.kb.nl/hrd/dd/dd_projecten/projecten_emulatie-en.html.

Library of Congress and National Institute of Standards and Technology (US) (2007) *NIST/Library of Congress (LC) Optical Disc Longevity Study: final report*, www.loc.gov/preservation/resources/rt/NIST_LC_OpticalDiscLongevity.pdf.

National Archives (UK) (n.d.) *The Technical Registry PRONOM*,
www.nationalarchives.gov.uk/PRONOM/Default.aspx.

National Archives (UK) (2004) *Archive Collection Policy Statements: checklist of suggested content*, www.nationalarchives.gov.uk/documents/information-management/archive_collection_policy.pdf.

National Geospatial Digital Archive (USA) (2005–2009) *Collection Development Policies*, University of California, Santa Barbara, www.ngda.org/policies.html.

National Library of Australia (2003) *Guidelines for the Preservation of Digital Information*, Information Society Division, United Nations Educational, Scientific and Cultural Organization, http://unesdoc.unesco.org/images/0013/001300/130071e.pdf.

OCLC (2010) *Metadata Schema Transformation Services*, Online Computer Library Center, www.oclc.org/research/activities/schematrans/default.htm.

Open Archives Initiative (2008a) *Open Archives Initiative Object Reuse and Exchange: ORE user guide – primer*, www.openarchives.org/ore/1.0/primer.

Open Archives Initiative (2008b) *The Open Archives Initiative Protocol for Metadata Harvesting:*

version 2, www.openarchives.org/OAI/2.0/openarchivesprotocol.htm.

Pearce-Moses, R. (2005) *A Glossary of Archival and Records Terminology*, Society of American Archivists, www.archivists.org/glossary.

Pennock, M. (2007) Digital Curation: a life-cycle approach to managing and preserving usable digital information, *Library & Archives*, January, www.ukoln.ac.uk/ukoln/staff/m.pennock/publications/docs/lib-arch_curation.pdf.

PREMIS Editorial Committee (2011) *PREMIS Data Dictionary for Preservation Metadata*, version 2.1, Library of Congress, www.loc.gov/standards/premis/v2/premis-2-1.pdf.

Research Libraries Group (2002) *Trusted Digital Repositories: attributes and responsibilities; an RLG-OCLC report*, Online Computer Library Center, www.oclc.org/research/activities/past/rlg/trustedrep/repositories.pdf.

Riley, J. (2009) *Seeing Standards: a visualization of the metadata universe*, www.dlib.indiana.edu/~jenlrile/metadatamap/seeingstandards.pdf.

Roorda, D. (2007) *MIXED: migration to intermediate XML for electronic data*, http://homepages.inf.ed.ac.uk/hmueller/presdb07/papers/WDP-Edinburgh-position-DANS.pdf.

Rothenberg, J. (1998) *Avoiding Technological Quicksand: finding a viable technical foundation for digital preservation*, Council for Library and Information Resources, www.clir.org/pubs/reports/rothenberg/inadequacy.html.

Shewhart, W. (1939) *Statistical Method from the Viewpoint of Quality Control*, Dover.

Treloar, A. and Wilkinson, R. (2008) Rethinking Metadata Creation and Management in a Data-Driven Research World, *Proceedings of the Fourth IEEE International Conference on eScience held on 10–12 December 2008*, organized by the Institute for Electrical and Electronics Engineers, http://doi.ieeecomputersociety.org/10.1109/eScience.2008.41.

UK Data Archive (2008) UK Data Archive Collections Development Policy: public version, www.data-archive.ac.uk/media/54773/ukda067-rms-collectionsdevelopmentpolicy.pdf.

UKRDS (2009) *The Data Imperative: managing the UK's research data for future use*, UK Research Data Service, www.ukrds.ac.uk/resources/download/id/14.

Whyte, A. and Wilson, A. (2010) *How to Appraise and Select Research Data for Curation*, Digital Curation Centre, www.dcc.ac.uk/sites/default/files/documents/publications/guides/How to Appraisefor Final.pdf.

Wright, R. and Miller, A. (2009) The Significance of Storage in the 'Cost of Risk' of Digital Preservation, *International Journal of Digital Curation*, **4** (3), 104–22, www.ijdc.net/index.php/ijdc/article/viewFile/138/173.

CHAPTER 3

Research data policies: principles, requirements and trends

Sarah Jones

The UK data policy landscape

Data management drivers

The open access movement underpins many of the drivers for research data management. In 2007, the 30 member countries that form the Organisation for Economic Co-operation and Development (OECD) issued *Principles and Guidelines for Access to Research Data from Public Funding* (2007). Central to these 13 principles is the notion that publicly funded research data is a public good, produced in the public interest, and should be openly available to the maximum extent possible. This expectation of public access to publicly funded research data is apparent in the rhetoric of most ensuing data policies.

Co-ordinating bodies such as Research Councils UK (RCUK) have issued similar codes and principles to inform research governance. In its publication *Expectations for Societal and Economic Impact* RCUK notes that those who receive funding are expected to 'take responsibility for the curation, management and exploitation of data for future use' (RCUK, 2008). More detailed requirements are noted in the *Policy and Code of Conduct on the Governance of Good Research Conduct* (RCUK, 2009). This states that researchers and their research organizations are jointly responsible for the proper management and preservation of data and primary materials, and have a duty to:

- keep clear and accurate records of the research procedures followed and the results obtained, including interim results
- hold records securely in paper or electronic form
- make relevant primary data and research evidence accessible to others for reasonable periods after the completion of the research: data should normally be preserved and accessible for ten years, but for projects of clinical or major social, environmental or heritage importance, for 20 years or longer
- manage data according to the research funder's data policy and all relevant legislation
- wherever possible, deposit data permanently within a national collection.

Similar requirements are put forward in the *Code of Practice for Research* issued by the UK Research Integrity Office (UKRIO, 2009). This puts forward the notion of planning data management at an early stage of the design of the project, stating that researchers should consider how data will be gathered, analysed, managed and made available to others. The Code also offers a helpful one-page checklist for researchers to support good practice.

A signal development in UK research data policy is RCUK's *Common Principles on Data Policy* (2011). These provide some harmonization across the research councils akin to the joint *Position Statement on Access to Research Outputs* (RCUK, 2006), which covers access to publications. The *Common Principles on Data Policy* reiterate the OECD declaration that data is a public good and should be openly available where possible. The importance of policies and planning to ensure that data of long-term value is retained and made available is also noted. The *Common Principles* put forward a number of additional points for researchers and research organizations to consider: discoverability of data; legal, ethical and commercial constraints on data release; the right of first-use for data creators; data citation; and cost-effective methods for data management and sharing. Three principles to highlight, which are likely to have a marked effect on practice in coming years, are that:

- published results should always include information on how to access the supporting data
- all users of research data should acknowledge the sources of their data
- it is appropriate to use public funds to support the management and sharing of publicly funded research data.

Broader legal frameworks also act as drivers for effective data management. Cases at the University of East Anglia and Queen's University Belfast in 2009/10 showed that unpublished research data is subject to the Freedom of Information Act and Environmental Information Regulations, demonstrating the need for effective data management (Fearne, 2010). Subsequent guidance from the Joint Information Systems Committee (JISC) (2010) points to the value of formally documented publication plans, as they could support a decision not to release data.

These overarching requirements have influenced the specific data policies released by research funders and journal publishers. The following sections will describe these policies in greater detail.

Research funders' data policies

Most of the UK research councils and several health funders have issued data policies. The earliest of these were released in the mid to late 1990s and came from funders that had established data centres: the Arts and Humanities Research Council (AHRC), the Economic and Social Research Council (ESRC) and the Natural Environment

Research Council (NERC). Data policies were issued by the Biotechnology and Biological Sciences Research Council (BBSRC), Cancer Research UK (CRUK), the Medical Research Council (MRC) and the Wellcome Trust during 2006 and 2007, when the findings of the OECD report on promoting access to public research data were developed into a set of formal principles and guidelines.

Some time later than the majority of UK research councils, the Engineering and Physical Sciences Research Council (EPSRC) released its data policy in 2011. Unlike those earlier data policies, this places the onus on research organizations to provide appropriate policies and infrastructure, and to ensure that their researchers are aware of their individual responsibilities regarding data management and sharing. But the EPSRC has decided against requiring that individual researchers submit data management and sharing plans; assessing institutional capacity may prove easier to administer and monitor.

Some funders have a few clauses in their guidance relating to data management and dissemination, rather than anything that can be termed a formal data policy. The British Academy, for example, states that 'data and documentation should be offered for deposit at the Arts and Humanities Data Service or Economic and Social Data Service within a reasonable time after the completion of the project' (2006, 1). Other funders' requirements focus solely on publications and dissemination, as is the case for the British Heart Foundation, the Science and Technology Facilities Council (STFC) and the European Commission's FP7 programme. Such examples are not included in the detailed synthesis and summary in this chapter.

Eight UK research funders have formal data policies, which are summarized in Table 3.1. Further details can be found on the DCC policy web pages (www.dcc.ac.uk/resources/policy-and-legal), which present the UK funders' specific policy stipulations, or at Sherpa JULIET (www.sherpa.ac.uk/juliet), which provides an international listing of research funders' open access policies for publications and data archiving.

Data management and sharing plan requirements

A key requirement in most UK research funders' data policy is the submission of a data management and sharing plan at the grant application stage. The expected format, coverage and specifics relating to these plans vary by funder. Guidelines typically ask for a succinct summary (often one or two pages), submitted as part of the 'Case for Support' or in an allocated section of the application form. The AHRC specifies the contents of the plan, providing six sections which ask set questions, while all other funders propose several themes and questions which researchers should consider as appropriate to their proposal.

Table 3.1 *A comparative summary of UK research funders' data policies*

Arts and Humanities Research Council	
Policy details	Research Funding Guide, v1.4 (AHRC, 2011). See section 'Deposit of resources or datasets' (81) and 'Technical appendix' (37). Two pages.
Data plan requirements	Submit a 'technical appendix' – a section of the Joint electronic Submission (Je-S) form. Six predefined sections with set questions. Each question has a strict character limit ranging from 1000 to 2000 words.
Timeframe on data sharing	Archaeology data must be offered to ADS for deposit within three months of project completion.
Maintenance of data post-grant or project	Significant datasets are to be made available in an accessible depository for at least three years after the end of the grant.
Meeting the costs of data management and sharing	The Archaeology Data Service (ADS) is supported by the AHRC until 2012. ADS will apply charges for all AHRC projects due to finish during or after 2012 (ADS, 2007).
Key additional points	Former AHRC-funded data centres offer relevant services. Charges may apply. Visual Arts Data Service (http://vads.ac.uk/services/index.html). Oxford Text Archive (http://ota.ahds.ac.uk). History Data Service at the UKDA (www.data-archive.ac.uk/deposit).
Biotechnology and Biological Sciences Research Council	
Policy details	Data Sharing Policy, v1.1 (BBSRC, 2010). 15 pages.
Data plan requirements	Submit a 'statement on data sharing' as part of grant proposals. One page in case for support. Eight themes are suggested that applicants may wish to incorporate.
Timeframe on data sharing	To be in line with best practice in field, but generally no later than publication of main findings. Within three years of generation of the dataset, as a guide.
Maintenance of data post-grant or project	Data are to be maintained for ten years in suitable accessible formats using established standards.
Meeting the costs of data management and sharing	Funding to meet data management costs can be requested as part of full economic costs. Example costs given include staffing, storage and networking capability.
Key additional points	Adherence to the proposed data management and sharing strategies will be monitored through the final report assessment procedure. This information may be taken into account when assessing future proposals.
Cancer Research UK	
Policy details	Data Sharing Guidelines (Cancer Research UK, 2009). Four pages.
Data plan requirements	Submit a 'data management and sharing plan' at the application stage. The exact content and format is not specified for flexibility. Eight themes or questions are given that should be considered.

Table 3.1 *(continued)*

Cancer Research UK (continued)

Timeframe on data sharing	Data to be released no later than the acceptance for publication of the main findings (unless restrictions still apply), or data release can be on a timescale in line with the research area.
Maintenance of data post-grant or project	Data must be properly curated throughout its lifecycle and released with the appropriate high-quality metadata. This is the responsibility of the data custodians, who are usually those individuals or institutes that received Cancer Research UK funding to create or collect the data. Data to be preserved and available for sharing for a minimum period of five years.
Meeting the costs of data management and sharing	CRUK considers timely and appropriate data management and sharing an integral component of the research process so will not provide additional funds for these activities.
Key additional points	In most instances, sharing of data should be possible without compromising the confidentiality of participants. Reference is made to consent for sharing, anonymization and data enclaves.
Economic and Social Research Council	
Policy details	Research Data Policy (ESRC, 2010). Nine pages.
Data plan requirements	Submit a 'statement on data sharing' and a 'data management and sharing plan' as part of the application. Around two page data plan expected to include nine suggested themes. This updated requirement came into force in spring 2011.
Timeframe on data sharing	Research data should be made available to the scientific community in a timely and responsible manner. Data must be offered to the ESRC data service providers for reuse and/or archiving within three months of the end of the award.
Maintenance of data post-grant or project	The ESRC data service providers are responsible for ensuring long-term access to data. The UKDA's preservation policy defines long term as beyond the next round of technical change.
Meeting the costs of data management and sharing	The ESRC will review any costs associated with implementing the data plan as an integral part of the funding decision and based on this decision provide appropriate funding for data management. The ESRC is responsible for post-award data management and preservation via its data service providers.
Key additional points	The ESRC will withhold the final payment of an award if data have not been offered for archiving to the required standard within three months of the end of the award.
Engineering and Physical Sciences Research Council	
Policy details	Policy Framework on Research Data (EPSRC, 2011). Around nine pages.
Data plan requirements	None.
Timeframe on data sharing	Research organizations are expected to publish appropriately structured metadata describing the research data they hold online (normally within 12 months of data generation).

Table 3.1 *(continued)*

Engineering and Physical Sciences Research Council (continued)

Maintenance of data post-grant or project	Research organizations should ensure that EPSRC-funded research data is securely preserved for a minimum of ten years from the date that any researcher 'privileged access' period expires or, if others have accessed the data, from the last date on which access to the data was requested by a third party.
Meeting the costs of data management and sharing	It is reasonable and appropriate to use public funds to support data management costs. Research organizations are expected to ensure adequate resources are provided from within their existing public funding streams to support the curation of publicly funded research data.
Key additional points	Published research papers should include a short statement describing how and on what terms any supporting research data may be accessed. EPSRC will monitor progress and compliance by case. If it appears that proper sharing of research data is being obstructed, the EPSRC reserves the right to impose appropriate sanctions.

Medical Research Council

Policy details	Policy on data sharing and preservation (MRC, c.2006). Two pages. Also see the Good Research Practice guide (MRC, 2005).
Data plan requirements	Submit a 'data sharing and preservation strategy' as part of the case for support. Plans must be succinct and include a summary on three themes. Two additional questions are given for those planning to extend existing dataset(s).
Timeframe on data sharing	Data must be shared in a timely and responsible manner. A limited, defined period of exclusive use of data for primary research is reasonable.
Maintenance of data post-grant or project	Data must be properly curated throughout its lifecycle and released with the appropriate high-quality metadata. This is the responsibility of the data custodians, who are usually those individuals or institutes that received MRC funding to create or collect the data. Primary research data must be retained in their original form within the research establishment that generated them for a minimum of ten years (MRC, 2005).
Meeting the costs of data management and sharing	Not specified.
Key additional points	The MRC is currently reviewing its data policies and plans to release new versions in summer 2011.

Natural Environment Research Council

Policy details	Data policy (NERC, 2011). Three pages.
Data plan requirements	Submit an outline 'data management plan' at the application stage, then a full plan once funded. Plans must identify which of the datasets being produced are considered to be of long-term value. This new requirement for data management plans will be implemented in 2012.

Table 3.1 *(continued)*

Natural Environment Research Council (continued)

Timeframe on data sharing	Data should be offered for deposit as soon after the end of data collection as is possible. Researchers are entitled to exclusive access to data they generate, usually for a maximum of two years.
Maintenance of data post-grant or project	Data must be submitted to NERC designated data centres for long-term management and dissemination.
Meeting the costs of data management and sharing	The grant application must identify all resources needed to implement the data management plan. NERC will maintain environmental data centres for the management and dissemination of environmental data of long-term value.
Key additional points	All research publications arising from NERC funding must include a statement on how the supporting data and any other relevant research materials can be accessed. From 2011, NERC will supply the data it holds for free, apart from a few special cases. Those who do not meet these requirements risk having award payments withheld or becoming ineligible for future funding from NERC.

Wellcome Trust

Policy details	Policy on data management and sharing (Wellcome Trust, 2010). Two pages. Also see the guidelines on good research practice (Wellcome Trust, 2005).
Data plan requirements	Submit a 'data management and sharing plan' as part of the application. There is no set format or structure, but seven questions are given to consider and briefly address. Guidance on completing data management and sharing plans is available (Wellcome Trust, n.d.).
Timeframe on data sharing	As an absolute minimum, researchers should make relevant data available on publication of their research. Opportunities for timely and responsible prepublication data sharing should be maximized.
Maintenance of data post-grant or project	Research institutions are required to maintain data securely for a minimum of ten years. Researchers should deposit data in appropriate data repositories in a timely manner.
Meeting the costs of data management and sharing	The Trust considers that timely and appropriate data management and sharing should represent an integral component of the research process. Applicants may therefore include any costs associated with their proposed approach as part of their proposal.
Key additional points	The Trust advises that while timely publication in peer reviewed journals and presentations at scientific meetings are key forms of dissemination, they are not equivalent to data sharing and do not in themselves constitute a data management and sharing plan.

The DCC provides a summary of UK research funders' expectations (Jones, 2011). The four most common themes across these are:

- development of data and documentation
- legal and/or ethical restrictions
- data sharing
- long-term access and preservation.

Some guidance on completing the plan is typically offered, particularly in the case of biomedical funders. The BBSRC, for example, includes detailed notes within its policy, while the Wellcome Trust provides an FAQ on developing a data management and sharing plan (n.d.).

The BBSRC, ESRC and MRC ask questions about the relationship of the proposed dataset to existing data and the potential for reuse instead of creating new data. The AHRC and ESRC are the only funders to ask for specific details of data management arrangements during a proposed project, such as back-up strategies, responsibilities and skills within the team. Resourcing has also been introduced in the 2010/11 updates to NERC and Wellcome Trust requirements, with a request to submit appropriate costs in the application. NERC will also require those funded to produce a full data management plan in conjunction with the relevant NERC data centre, as it considers details submitted at the application stage to be an outline plan.

Biomedical and health funders place more focus on data sharing than data management. Recent updates to existing data policies show a general shift in this direction. The ESRC, for example, asks all applicants to include a statement on data sharing, providing ample justification if data cannot be shared and showing engagement with how the challenges could be overcome. In a similar vein, NERC and the EPSRC now require that all research publications include a statement on how the supporting data and any other relevant research materials can be accessed. It seems that focusing on sharing and reuse of data is quickly becoming the preferred rhetoric.

More detailed discussion of data management plans and planning, including information about the tools that are available, is to be found in Chapter 5.

Data sharing and preservation

Most funders state their expected timeframes for data release and periods for preservation. The AHRC and ESRC expect data to be offered to their designated data centres within three months of the end of the award. Several funders focus on publication as the determining factor, expecting data to be released at this point, or on acceptance for publication. There is, however, a common recognition that timescales for data sharing are best determined by the discipline, and a recommendation is made that researchers abide by the accepted practice for their area if different to the periods stated. In addition, researchers are often permitted a limited period of exclusive use.

The RCUK guidelines on good research conduct state that data should be available for ten years or longer from the point of completion. Although this is the timescale typically stated, some funders specify shorter, more realistic periods in their individual policies. The AHRC, for example, expects significant datasets to remain accessible for three years, while Cancer Research UK states that data should be preserved for a minimum of five years. A similar degree of pragmatism is evident in the UK Data Archive's preservation policy, which defines long-term as 'beyond the next round of technical change' (2010, 3). In contrast, the EPSRC data policy extends the period to ten years from the date that any researcher 'privileged access' period expires or from the last date on which access to the data was requested by a third party. For clinical data or that of major social, environmental or heritage importance, the expected period of preservation can be 20 years or longer.

The preservation of data requires active management and so is best performed by specialist repositories and data centres. Some funders, such as the ESRC and NERC, have established their own designated data centres. The health funders in contrast have contributed to joint initiatives such as the European Bioinformatics Institute, which curates various databases and tools. An overview of the role of the national data centres is provided in Chapter 8.

The evolution of funders' data policies

Data policies are becoming more explicit about roles and responsibilities. The 2010 ESRC policy, for example, makes clear the responsibilities of grant applicants, grant holders, the ERSC and its data service providers. Each stakeholder is tasked with various activities in the implementation guidance. Cancer Research UK and the MRC note that curation is the responsibility of the data custodians, who are usually those individuals or institutes that received funding to create or collect the data, and the EPSRC policy very clearly outlines the key role that institutions should play.

Concerns about meeting the cost of data management and sharing are also starting to be addressed. Five funders (BBSRC, EPSRC, ESRC, NERC and the Wellcome Trust) note that costs associated with data management and sharing can be supported where justified. Moreover, the RCUK *Common Principles on Data Policy* confirm that it is appropriate to use public funds to support the management and sharing of publicly funded research data. Only Cancer Research UK explicitly states that it will not provide additional funds for these activities, as it considers timely and appropriate data management and sharing to be an integral component of the research process.

Funders' data policies are tempering data management requirements with cost/benefit considerations, as there is an acceptance that investment in data management and sharing is not appropriate in all cases. The BBSRC policy states that data sharing should be cost-effective and driven by scientific need, while the Wellcome Trust specifies that data management and sharing plans are only required where a proposal involves the generation of datasets that have clear scope for wider research use and hold significant long-term value. Determining when and to what extent investment in data management and sharing is appropriate is a moot point. The NERC is introducing a 'data value checklist' to identify data of long-term value and to help set criteria that inform the selection and appraisal decisions made by its designated data centres, while the EPSRC expects the period of preservation to extend based on third party access requests.

This trend for cost-effectiveness is reinforced by the shift in language from data management to data sharing, as noted earlier. Reuse, as opposed to preservation, is perceived to deliver greater value. The NERC was the first research funder to require that publications include a statement on how the underlying data can be accessed so that the integrity of the research it funds can be validated. Coupled with its decision to make all data held by its designated data centres open access, this seems certain to boost research impact. Indeed, the 2011 NERC data policy takes a forward-thinking stance on many hot topics, such as data selection, citation and open data, and is therefore likely to set a precedent that others will follow.

Journal data policies

As with funders' data policies, requirements from journal publishers to share associated data began to emerge in the 1990s. An early study (McCain, 1995) found that 132 (16%) out of the c.850 natural science, medical and engineering journals assessed made some statement on the sharing of associated research data and materials in their guidelines to authors. In the subsequent years, other publishers have released similar requirements. When comparing the findings of two more recent studies (Piwowar and Chapman, 2008; Weber et al., 2010) it seems that policies are more prevalent in disciplines with established mechanisms for sharing certain types of data. A register of journal open data policies is under construction in the Open Access Directory wiki (http://oad.simmons.edu/oadwiki/Main_Page).

The coverage of journal policies varies: some policies require data sharing while others merely suggest it; some specify the use of a particular data repository or public database; and some require evidence of data sharing as a precondition to publication (e.g. the accession number provided on deposit in community databases). A high-profile and influential example of a journal data policy is that of the Nature Publishing Group, which requires authors to 'make materials, data and associated protocols promptly available to readers without undue qualifications in material transfer agreements' (www.nature.com/authors/policies/availability.html). Restrictions must be disclosed to the editors at the time of submission, and also be noted in the manuscript with guidance on how readers can access the data. A number of community databases and public repositories are suggested as places of deposit, and in cases where existing mechanisms for data sharing are in place, an accession number is a precondition of publication.

Not all journal policies are as thorough as *Nature*'s: several only apply to certain types of data rather than requiring data sharing in general, and many journals do not check the level of compliance with their policies.

Research has been undertaken into the correlation between policy requirements and author behaviour. Piwowar and Chapman (2008) investigated the policies of journals that publish studies about gene expression microarray data. Of the 70 journals studied, 53 (76%) had data sharing policies, 40 of which applied to microarrays. They classified 17 of these policies as relatively weak as they were suggestions rather than requirements so were unenforceable, and 23 as strong policies as an accession number was required before publication. Journals with the strongest policies had the highest compliance rates; those journals with no data sharing policy, a weak policy, and a strong policy had a median data sharing prevalence of 8%, 20% and 25% respectively.

Another study (Piwowar, Day and Fridsma, 2007) positively linked data sharing with increased citation rates. Studying publications from a sample of 85 cancer trials showed that publicly available data was significantly associated with a 69% increase in citations, independent of other factors. Such findings demonstrate tangible benefits that have real currency with researchers. Indeed, the greatest uptake of data sharing has occurred where a community sees a direct benefit or where there is appropriate infrastructure in place. A study by Brown shows how journals in such fields have strengthened their policies as data sharing becomes the norm (Piwowar and Chapman, 2008, 12).

Developing policies and infrastructure in unison is a model adopted by the Dryad data archive and its partner journals. They released a joint data archiving policy (www.datadryad.org/jdap) in January 2011, which makes it a condition of publication that data supporting the results in the paper should be archived in an appropriate public archive. Dryad is collaborating with its partner journals to embed data submission prompts into existing publication workflows to facilitate compliance. They also assign persistent identifiers to deposited data to enable citation. Co-ordination of this kind removes barriers to uptake and is a useful means of adding weight to policies.

Institutional policies and infrastructure

Higher education institutions (HEIs) typically issue institutional codes governing good research conduct based on the RCUK and UKRIO policies mentioned earlier. The Russell Group, which represents 20 leading UK universities committed to maintaining the very best research, stated its commitment to developing institutional data policies in a code it released in 2005 and signalled a preference for data management to take place at a more centralized level than that of the individual researcher (Ruusalepp, 2008, 41). In 2008/09, the JISC funded a number of studies to encourage data policy development. One such study investigated existing digital preservation policies to show how these can be tied into existing business drivers (Beagrie et al., 2008), while another tackled the practicalities of developing policies for curating research data in repositories (Green, Macdonald and Rice, 2009).

Institutional data policies and statements of commitment to research data management started to emerge in the UK around 2010. A series of JISC projects helped the University of Oxford to advance its approach. The Embedding Institutional Data

Curation Services in Research (EIDCSR) project involved collaborating with the University of Melbourne to learn their lessons on developing, supporting and implementing data policies. This resulted in an institutional statement of commitment to research data management at Oxford (www.admin.ox.ac.uk/rdm).

The University of Edinburgh is also making rapid progress in this area under the leadership of the Vice Principal for Knowledge Management, who has convened complementary working groups to explore the University's requirements for research data storage and research data management. An 'aspirational' research data management policy was approved and released in May 2011 (www.ed.ac.uk/is/research-data-policy). It is interesting to note that Edinburgh's policy has been introduced with the observation that implementation will take some years.

Elsewhere, the University of Southampton has been addressing data policy development through the Institutional Data Management Blueprint (IDMB) project, which designed a ten-year roadmap for the University to develop and embed data management as an institutional business routine; the University of Bristol has also developed a draft institutional data policy. At the time of writing it is expected that both policies will be released in 2011. Meanwhile, the DCC is collecting examples to assist other institutions to develop data policies (www.dcc.ac.uk/resources/policy-and-legal/institutional-data-policies).

The £4.3 million Joint Information Systems Committee Managing Research Data (JISC MRD) programme (www.jisc.ac.uk/whatwedo/programmes/mrd.aspx), which ran from October 2009 to July 2011, has been instrumental in promoting the advancement of data management strategies in UK higher education. The five strands of the programme addressed: infrastructure development; data management planning; programme support and tools; citing, linking, integrating and publishing data; and research data management training.

A second JISC MRD programme is being planned, which will continue to support the development of data management infrastructure, tools and training. It is likely that projects funded under the next infrastructure strand will be expected to deliver institutional data policies.

Further investment in data management is being made through the Shared Services and the Cloud Programme (www.jisc.ac.uk/whatwedo/programmes/umf.aspx). A shared IT infrastructure will be set up to offer cost-effective data management and storage services to HEIs. Data management tools will be deployed as services in a shared online 'cloud' environment to allow institutions to benefit from reduced implementation and hosting costs.

The UK in context: the international data policy landscape

Research data management is high on the agendas of other countries, particularly those within the OECD. Some countries, such as the USA, have comparable research funder requirements for data management and sharing plans, while others, such as Australia, are further forward in developing national co-ordination. A brief overview of data policies and developments to implement those in some OECD member countries is provided for comparison.

Australia

The Australian Research Council and National Health and Medical Research Council have policies encouraging the archiving and sharing of research data. The most influential policy in the Australian context is the *Australian Code for the Responsible Conduct of Research* (Australian Government, 2007), which is jointly issued by the Australian Research Council, the National Health and Medical Research Council and Universities Australia. It sets out how data should be managed, the need for institutions to acknowledge their responsibilities, and the value of institutional mandates for policies on data retention, ownership and storage. Institutions are also expected to provide appropriate facilities to store data safely and securely.

The Code has driven universities to take a leading role in developing institutional policies and support to address data management challenges. Useful examples are in place at several institutions, such as the Queensland University of Technology (www.tils.qut.edu.au/initiatives/researchsupport/datamanage), the University of Melbourne (www.eresearch.unimelb.edu.au/activities/research_data_management_ for_researchers) and Monash University (www.researchdata.monash.edu.au). As described in Chapter 9, the government has invested in the Australian National Data Service (http://ands.org.au) to provide a national infrastructure to co-ordinate access to Australia's research output. ANDS is working with Australian universities to share their expertise at a national level.

Canada

In Canada, a research data strategy working group was established in 2008, bringing together universities, institutes, libraries, funding agencies, and individual researchers (http://rds-sdr.cisti-icist.nrc-cnrc.gc.ca). An initial gap analysis was undertaken to inform work in this area, and recent developments include a gateway to scientific resources, supported by the National Research Council Canada, which provides access to datasets and good practice guidance for data management. Some health funders also have data sharing policies, for example the Canadian Institutes of Health Research (CIHR, 2007). Genome Canada (2008) also requires that grant applicants provide a data and resource sharing plan.

Finland

In light of the OECD declaration, the Ministry of Education in Finland allocated resources to the Finnish Social Science Data Archive (FSD) to chart national and international practices related to open access to research data (Kuula and Borg, 2008). This study found that there was little long-term planning and that most data remained in the hands of the original researchers. In 2008, the Academy of Finland, under which four research councils sit, brought in a requirement for research plans to include a section on 'research methods and material, ethical issues' providing details of how materials will be obtained, stored securely and shared (www.aka.fi/en-gb/A/For-researchers/How-to-apply/Appendices/Research-plan). More recently, the Finnish advocate for open access, FinnOA (www.finnoa.fi) expanded its remit from publications to encompass the whole spectrum of knowledge production. It started working on the issues surrounding open access to research data in 2010.

Germany

In 2009 the German Research Foundation Deutsche Forschungsgemeinschaft (DFG) issued *Recommendations for the Secure Storage and Availability of Digital Primary Research Data* (2009). The DFG promotes preservation and open access to the research it funds, and expects researchers to consider how data will be managed and shared. The DFG is also funding a round of projects to develop information infrastructures for research data, in a similar vein to the JISC MRD programme in the UK. The Alliance of German Science Organisations, which includes several research institutes and key funders, has adopted *Principles for the Handling of Research Data* (2010). These support the preservation of and access to publicly funded research data and note the value of developing interoperable infrastructures.

Netherlands

The Royal Netherlands Academy of Arts and Sciences (KNAW) and Netherlands Organisation for Scientific Research (NWO), two major research funders in the Netherlands, encourage open access to research data and publications. Together they support the Data Archiving and Networked Services (DANS) to preserve and provide access to research data. DANS (2009) produced the *Data Seal of Approval*, a well respected model used internationally, which specifies the roles and responsibilities of data producers, data repositories and data consumers (2009). The three technical universities in the Netherlands have also joined forces under the 3TU federation to establish a shared data centre (www.datacentrum.3tu.nl).

Additional tools and services are supported through the SURFfoundation. An organization similar to the JISC in the UK, SURFfoundation states its mission as initiating, orchestrating and driving innovation in information and communication technologies (ICTs) through knowledge-sharing, incentive programmes and partnerships (www.surffoundation.nl/en). One recent initiative has focused on enhanced publications, developing models for sharing datasets, images, audio and video alongside text-based publications (www.surffoundation.nl/en/themas/openonderzoek/verrijktepublicaties).

New Zealand

The Ministry of Research Science and Technology (MORST) is instrumental in shaping New Zealand's approach to data management. It held an event called Data Matters in July 2010, bringing together representatives from research institutes, libraries, archives, universities and the government to discuss what was needed to make the most of publicly funded research data. MORST is continuing this initiative by working with key stakeholders to develop and implement research data management policies (www.morst.govt.nz/current-work/Science-Infrastructure-and-Data-Management/Data-Management).

USA

In the USA, several major research funders require data management and sharing plans at the grant application stage. The most high-profile examples are those of the National Institutes for Health (NIH, 2003) and the National Science Foundation (NSF, 2011). Universities have been very proactive in developing support for researchers in response to these mandates. The California Digital Library, for example, has compiled a helpful list of funder policies (www.cdlib.org/services/uc3/datamanagement/funding.html). Many universities have produced excellent guidance on data management, for example MIT Libraries (http://libraries.mit.edu/guides/subjects/data-management), the University of Minnesota (www.lib.umn.edu/datamanagement) and the University of Wisconsin-Madison (http://researchdata.wisc.edu). The library community is taking a leading role, with the Association of Research Libraries (ARL) issuing guidance to help librarians understand the NSF data sharing policy so they can better assist researchers with data management plans (Hswe and Holt, 2010).

The NSF is supporting the Sustainable Digital Data Preservation and Access Network Partners (DataNet) programme to develop a set of exemplars for research data infrastructure. Two projects were funded in 2009: DataOne (www.dataone.org) and the Data Conservancy (http://dataconservancy.org). These DataNet projects aim to provide reliable long-term digital preservation, access, integration and analysis capabilities.

Cross-national initiatives

Initiatives such as the Knowledge Exchange (www.knowledge-exchange.info), which brings together Denmark's Electronic Research Library (DEFF), the DFG, the JISC and the SURFfoundation, are co-ordinating national strategies for making scientific content openly available. Its primary research data working group is investigating how policies might align and enabling the exchange of expertise in this area.

The Committee on Data for Science and Technology (CODATA) is an interdisciplinary scientific committee of the International Council for Science (ICSU). It was established in 1966 and has a membership of research funders, scientific unions and various representative bodies. The CODATA promotes improved scientific and technical data management and use. One of its four stated goals in support of this mission is to 'pursue the development of national and international data policies commensurate with the needs of the scientific and technical research communities as well as society as a whole' (CODATA, n.d.).

Other examples show co-ordination along disciplinary lines. An international group of 17 health research funders, for example, signed a joint statement encouraging the sharing of research data to improve public health (Walport and Brest, 2011). This policy statement also outlines planned areas of collaboration to enable implementation.

Emerging trends in research data policies

Weber et al. (2010) point to a data policy gap across funders, repositories and journals, as they lack explicit guidelines for sharing and citing data. Associated infrastructure is crucial if policies are to be feasible to implement, and this is increasingly being addressed in the UK. Several research funders already support data centres and clarification that appropriate costs will be met through research grants is on the increase. Some UK HEIs are also starting to develop data management services. Insights from others will be crucial during this development phase.

Lessons on translating policies into practice were shared at the Research Information Network's event Research Data – Policies And Behaviours in November 2010. Reflecting on the SysMO-SEEK project, Carol Goble explained that researchers' distrust of systems and desire to retain control can prevent compliance, even when there are strong policies. Working alongside researchers is key to ensure that systems meet their needs, fit in with working practices and can be trusted. The NERC's introduction of a data value checklist reminds us that not all data have long-term value, so selections need to be made. Their collaborative approach between data creators and curators is a useful model to adopt. Institutions should also acknowledge that they may not be able to support all data types, and avoid competing where there is more appropriate provision, such as a subject data centre. Knowing what data has been created and where it is held is most important, and initiatives like the ANDS Data Commons provide a means of achieving that.

As publication is the main vehicle for academic recognition, journals policies may have more influence than those of either research funders or the institutions themselves. Some publishers have rigorous processes of monitoring in place, requiring data accession numbers at the prepublication stage to demonstrate that supporting data have been made openly accessible. This approach could be useful to research funders and institutions, as few of their policies incorporate robust monitoring procedures. Where established mechanisms for data sharing are in place through repositories, data centres or community databases, it may be feasible to ask for such references to be included in the final reports or other internal documentation used to close projects.

Policy makers could advance the practice of effective data management and sharing by providing more recognition and rewards to encourage uptake. Institutions could be encouraged to return data in the Research Excellence Framework (REF), for example, and methods for linking data and publications would ensure that the academic researcher sees a direct return through increased citations. The new EPSRC and NERC policies seek to close the loop between publications and the underlying data in this way, and as the RCUK *Common Principles* state that published results should always include information on how to access the supporting data, it is likely other funders will add this requirement to their policies soon. More could also be done to promote reuse of existing data, as grant funding tends to support the creation of new data. The ESRC already requires researchers to check if there is existing data that could be used and other funders ask how new data will complement existing datasets. A considerable culture change is required to sustain the shift to sharing and reusing data, and more incentives are needed to speed this along. Policies are often seen as an imposition and are unlikely to inspire the widespread adoption of new practices. Recognition and rewards will arguably offer a far greater return.

By 2011 the rhetoric of data policies had changed in emphasis from data management to data sharing. Another shift is required to move away from simply issuing policies to engaging with questions of applicability, as it is short-sighted to argue for data management and data sharing for their own sake. Requirements are best applied only in those cases where there is a demonstrable and measurable return on the time and resources that need to be invested. Indeed, funders such as the BBSRC and Wellcome Trust make it clear that data sharing should be cost-effective and only planned where there is scope for wider research use. Without pragmatic implementation, policy makers run the risk of diminishing the strength of their mandates and inviting lip service to be paid where implementation is undesirable or impractical.

Data policies are undoubtedly useful and well advanced in the UK, but supporting tools, services and infrastructure that match researchers' needs and evoke their trust are crucial if effective data management and sharing is to occur. Data policies are only the first step in the process. Determining the cases in which they should be applied and enabling implementation through the provision of relevant support services, sustained by appropriate mechanisms of recognition and reward, is the key to ensuring their adoption.

References

ADS (2007) *Charging Policy*, 4th edn, Archaeology Data Service,
    http://archaeologydataservice.ac.uk/advice/chargingPolicy.
AHRC (2011) *Research Funding Guide*, v1.4, Arts and Humanities Research Council,
    www.ahrc.ac.uk/FundingOpportunities/Documents/Research%20Funding%20Guide.pdf.
Alliance of German Science Organisations (2010) *Principles for the Handling of Research Data*,
    www.allianzinitiative.de/en/core_activities/research_data/principles.

Australian Government (2007) *Australian Code for the Responsible Conduct of Research*, www.nhmrc.gov.au/guidelines/publications/r39.

BBSRC (2010) *Data Sharing Policy*, v1.1, Biotechnology and Biological Sciences Research Council, www.bbsrc.ac.uk/organisation/policies/position/policy/data-sharing-policy.aspx.

Beagrie, N. et al. (2008) *Digital Preservation Policies Study*, Charles Beagrie Ltd, www.jisc.ac.uk/media/documents/programmes/preservation/jiscpolicy_p1finalreport.pdf.

British Academy (2006) *Larger Research Grants: conditions of award*, www.britac.ac.uk/form/condits.cfm.

Cancer Research UK (2009) *Data Sharing Guidelines*, http://science.cancerresearchuk.org/funding/terms-conditions-and-policies/policy-data-sharing.

CIHR (2007) *Policy on Access to Research Outputs*, Canadian Institutes of Health Research, www.cihr-irsc.gc.ca/e/34846.htm.

CODATA (n.d.) *Constitution (Statutes and By-laws)*, Committee on Data for Science and Technology, International Council for Science.

DANS (2009) *Data Seal of Approval: quality guidelines for digital research data*, www.datasealofapproval.org.

Deutsche Forschungsgemeinshaft (2009) *Recommendations for Secure Storage and Availability of Digital Primary Research Data*, www.dfg.de/download/pdf/foerderung/programme/lis/ua_inf_empfehlungen_200901_en.pdf.

EPSRC (2011) *Policy Framework on Research Data*, www.epsrc.ac.uk/about/standards/researchdata/Pages/default.aspx.

ESRC (2010) *Research Data Policy*, Economic and Social Research Council, www.esrc.ac.uk/about-esrc/information/data-policy.aspx.

Fearne, H. (2010) Research Intelligence: request hits a raw spot, *Times Higher*, (15 July), www.timeshighereducation.co.uk/story.asp?storycode=412475.

Genome Canada (2008) *Data Release and Resource Sharing Policy*, www.genomecanada.ca/medias/PDF/EN/DataReleaseandResourceSharingPolicy.pdf.

Green, A., Macdonald, S. and Rice, R. (2009) *Policy-making for Research Data in Repositories: a guide*, Data Information Specialists Committee UK, www.disc-uk.org/docs/guide.pdf.

Hswe, P. and Holt, A. (2010) *Guide for Research Libraries: the NSF data sharing policy*, Association for Research Libraries, www.arl.org/rtl/eresearch/escien/nsf/index.shtml.

JISC (2010) *Freedom of Information and Research Data: questions and answers*, Joint Information Systems Committee, www.jisc.ac.uk/publications/programmerelated/2010/foiresearchdata.aspx.

Jones, S. (2011) *Summary of Research Funders' Expectation for Data Management and Sharing Plans*, Digital Curation Centre, www.dcc.ac.uk/webfm_send/358.

Kuula, A. and Borg, S. (2008) *Open Access to and Reuse of Research Data: the state of the art in Finland*, Finnish Social Science Data Archive, www.fsd.uta.fi/julkaisut/julkaisusarja/FSDjs07_OECD_en.pdf.

McCain, K. (1995) Mandating Sharing: journal policies in the natural sciences, *Science Communication*, **16**, 403–31, http://scx.sagepub.com/content/16/4/403.abstract.

MRC (2005) *Good Research Practice*, Medical Research Council,
www.mrc.ac.uk/Utilities/Documentrecord/index.htm?d=MRC002415.

MRC (c.2006) *Policy on Data Sharing and Preservation*, Medical Research Council,
www.mrc.ac.uk/Ourresearch/Ethicsresearchguidance/Datasharinginitiative/Policy/index.
htm.

NERC (2011) *Data policy*, Natural Environment Research Council,
www.nerc.ac.uk/research/sites/data/policy2011.asp.

NIH (2003) *Final NIH Statement on Sharing Research Data*, National Institutes of Health,
http://grants.nih.gov/grants/policy/data_sharing.

NSF (2011) *Dissemination and Sharing of Research Results*, National Science Foundation,
www.nsf.gov/bfa/dias/policy/dmp.jsp.

OECD (2007) *Principles and Guidelines for Access to Research Data from Public Funding*,
www.oecd.org/dataoecd/9/61/38500813.pdf.

Piwowar, H. and Chapman, W. (2008) A Review of Journal Policies for Sharing Research Data.
In *Proceedings ELPUB 2008 Conference on Electronic Publishing*, Toronto, Canada,
http://elpub.scix.net/data/works/att/001_elpub2008.content.pdf.

Piwowar, H., Day, R. and Fridsma D. (2007) Sharing Detailed Research Data is Associated
with Increased Citation Rate, *PLoS ONE*, **2** (3), e308,
www.plosone.org/article/info:doi%2F10.1371%2Fjournal.pone.0000308.

RCUK (2006) *Position Statement on Access to Research Outputs*, Research Councils UK,
www.rcuk.ac.uk/documents/documents/2006statement.pdf.

RCUK (2008) *Expectations for Societal and Economic Impact*, Research Councils UK,
www.rcuk.ac.uk/documents/innovation/expectationssei.pdf.

RCUK (2009) *Policy and Code of Conduct on the Governance of Good Research Conduct*, Research
Councils UK, www.rcuk.ac.uk/documents/reviews/grc/goodresearchconductcode.pdf.

RCUK (2011) *Common Principles on Data Policy*, Research Councils UK,
www.rcuk.ac.uk/research/Pages/DataPolicy.aspx.

Ruusalepp, R. (2008) *A Comparative Study of International Approaches to the Sharing of Research
Data*, Joint Information Systems Committee, www.jisc.ac.uk/media/documents/
programmes/preservation/national_data_sharing_report_final.pdf.

UK Data Archive (2010) *Preservation Policy*, www.data-archive.ac.uk/media/54776/ukda062-
dps-preservationpolicy.pdf.

UKRIO (2009) *Code of Practice for Research: promoting good practice and preventing misconduct*, UK
Research Integrity Office, www.ukrio.org/sites/ukrio2/the_programme_of_work/
code_of_practice_for_research.cfm.

Walport, M. and Brest, P. (2011) Sharing Research Data to Improve Public Health, *The Lancet*,
377 (9765), 537–39, (12 February).

Weber, N. et al. (2010) Evaluating Data Citation and Sharing Policies in the Environmental
Sciences, *ASIST Conference Proceedings*, www.asis.org/asist2010/proceedings/proceedings/
ASIST_AM10/submissions/445_Final_Submission.pdf.

Wellcome Trust (n.d.) *Guidance for Researchers: developing a data management and sharing plan*,
www.wellcome.ac.uk/About-us/Policy/Spotlight-issues/Data-sharing/Guidance-for-

researchers/index.htm.

Wellcome Trust (2005) *Guidelines on Good Research Practice*, www.wellcome.ac.uk/About-us/Policy/Policy-and-position-statements/WTD002753.htm.

Wellcome Trust (2010) *Policy on Data Management and Sharing*, www.wellcome.ac.uk/About-us/Policy/Policy-and-position-statements/WTX035043.htm.

CHAPTER 4

Sustainable research data

Brian F. Lavoie

Introduction

It is common these days to speak of sustainable resources in areas such as energy, forests, fisheries or water. Sustainability is crucial because these resources are the raw materials that fuel economic growth and prosperity. Libraries, archives and other stewardship organizations also manage resources that we hope will be sustainable over the long term. These resources are the raw materials of research, learning and creative expression. The long-term sustainability of information resources is not a new problem, yet it is one that is complicated by the fact that an increasing proportion of the scholarly and cultural record is now manifested in digital form.

Digital research data, along with other digital products of the research process (e.g. digital laboratory notebooks) has emerged as a significant component of both the process and output of scientific inquiry. Microsoft researcher Jim Gray identified the development of a 'fourth paradigm' of scientific discovery, marked by the application of intensive computing resources and sophisticated computational techniques to massive datasets (Hey et al., 2009). Support is gathering around the proposition that creating and sharing an important dataset – one that could catalyze new strands of inquiry – should be considered a first-order scientific contribution, on a par with a published article or book. The importance of datasets is evident even in the realm of commerce: Hal Varian, Chief Economist for Google, has observed that successful businesses will be those that can mine their data for useful intelligence to inform business decision making (Levy, 2009).

As discussed in the previous chapter, the importance of research datasets is reflected in the emergence of policy measures designed to secure their long-term persistence. For example, the National Science Foundation (NSF) has imposed a requirement that grant applications include a data management plan, the merits of which would be considered as part of the overall evaluation of the application. In addition, a number of repositories, such as the UK Data Archive, the Inter-university Consortium for Political and Social Research (ICPSR) and Dryad have been established to provide long-term curation capacity for valuable research data.

If research datasets are to persist over the long term and continue to release value through access and reuse – in short, if they are to remain a sustainable resource – it is necessary to ensure that the activities entrusted with their curation are themselves sustainable over the long term. Sustainability is a term to which a variety of interpretations can be attached. In the context of digital preservation, one can speak of sustainability from a technical perspective, in the sense of developing repository architectures, workflows, tools and preservation techniques that are robust, flexible and scalable. Social sustainability, on the other hand, might involve cultivating a shared commitment to preservation among groups of stakeholders with a common interest in long-term access to a particular set of digital materials. Lastly, sustainability can be interpreted in an economic sense, addressing the issues and challenges of ensuring that digital preservation activities are adequately provisioned with ongoing funding and other resources, sufficient to achieve their long-term preservation goals. It is this form of sustainability – *economic sustainability* – that is the focus of this chapter. Topics discussed include the definition of economic sustainability in a digital preservation context; the key challenges associated with economically sustainable preservation of research datasets; and some current approaches to developing sustainability strategies for research data.

In this chapter the terms preservation, curation, archiving and stewardship are used interchangeably (and no doubt imprecisely). All are intended to be synonyms for the digital lifecycle management process. The terms selection and appraisal are formally defined concepts in the archival science lexicon. We use these terms 'informally' in this chapter, in the context of their standard dictionary meanings of evaluation and choice. However, it should be emphasized that archivists have devoted a great deal of thought to issues of appraisal and selection in print and digital contexts, and their expertise has obvious application to the selection of research datasets for preservation.

Economic sustainability: a definition

Before considering the issues and challenges of achieving economic sustainability in the context of research data, it is useful to spend a moment considering the concept of economic sustainability as it pertains to long-term digital curation generally. The report *Sustainable Economics for a Digital Planet* (Blue Ribbon Task Force, 2010) provides a list of conditions that must be met in order to maximize the prospects of achieving economic sustainability:

- recognition of the benefits of preservation by decision makers
- a process of selecting digital materials with long-term value
- incentives for decision makers to preserve in the public interest
- mechanisms to secure an ongoing, efficient allocation of resources to digital preservation activities
- appropriate organization and governance of digital preservation activities.

Recognition of benefits

The first condition – recognition of benefits – is fundamental to any preservation effort: a sustainable investment of resources in the long-term preservation of a set of digital materials must be predicated on a clearly articulated value proposition describing the nature of the benefits that are expected to be returned from the investment. Too often the rationale for preservation activities seems to be preservation for the sake of preservation itself; in other circumstances, the benefit from preservation is assumed to be self-apparent and is not explicitly detailed or stated only in very general terms. This is not sufficient to persuade funders, administrators and other decision makers to commit an ongoing stream of resources to long-term preservation, especially when there are many competing calls on a limited pool of resources. The value proposition for preserving a set of digital materials must be explicated as precisely as possible: for example, what kinds of scholarship would be made possible by the ongoing availability of a particular dataset? What costs would be avoided by eliminating the need to re-create the data at a later time? How would ongoing access to and use of the preserved data enhance the international reputation of the funding institution?

Selection of digital materials

The second condition – selection of digital materials – recognizes the basic economic principle that resources for any activity are finite; therefore, priorities have to be identified and choices made. It is not realistic – nor is it even desirable – to preserve all digital materials for all time. Therefore, any preservation activity must adopt a circumscribed view of the digital materials that will be in scope for the activity, and prioritize its efforts on the materials that are likely to generate the most value over the long term. A judicious selection policy, coupled with clearly defined, realistic preservation objectives, helps to align stakeholder expectations of what a preservation activity will deliver with what the repository can sustainability deliver, given available resources.

Incentives to preserve in the public interest

Incentives to preserve in the public interest constitute the third condition for sustainability. It is not enough simply to recognize the value of a preservation activity. Sustainability also requires appropriate decision makers to act in order to ensure that valuable digital materials are indeed brought under active stewardship. In other words, robust preservation incentives are needed, which implies willingness by certain organizations to accept responsibility for carrying out preservation activities. Articulating these incentives often means identifying and leveraging an institutional self-interest in preservation. This can take a variety of forms; for example, organizations can view preservation as a business opportunity, a mission-driven commitment, or an obligation related to policy compliance. Oftentimes a particular preservation context involves stakeholders with differing incentives to preserve; for example, a media company might perceive a revenue incentive to preserve a digital movie over a limited period while the asset has an economic value. When this period expires, mechanisms need to be in place to transfer the asset to another institution with a different preservation incentive, such as a library or archive. Sustainable digital stewardship requires orchestration of differing preservation incentives over the entire digital lifecycle.

Ongoing and efficient allocation of resources

The fourth sustainability condition calls for an ongoing and efficient allocation of resources. Oftentimes this consists in practice of developing mechanisms to transfer funding and other resources from those who benefit from and are willing to pay for digital preservation, to those who are willing to provide preservation services. There are a variety of market and non-market mechanisms for doing so, such as pricing strategies, donations and other forms of philanthropic support, and public fees and taxes. Whatever mechanism or mechanisms are chosen, they must be sufficient to generate an ongoing flow of funds sufficient for the preservation activity in question to meet its long-term goals. But it is not enough to simply make resources available for preservation. These resources must also be used as efficiently as possible. Efficiency in this sense does not mean 'cutting corners', or scaling down preservation objectives; instead it means extracting the most value out of the resources allocated to a preservation activity. For example, activities should be focused on leveraging economies of scale (spreading the fixed costs of digital preservation over higher volumes of preservation activity) and economies of scope (spreading the costs of preservation over different yet related services by, for example, locating preservation and end-user access services on the same repository platform). Developing mechanisms to support an ongoing and efficient allocation of resources to preservation activities leads to activities that not only are adequately resourced to meet long-term goals, but also use those resources as productively as possible.

Organizational form and governance

The last condition for economic sustainability involves choosing an appropriate means of organizational form and governance for digital preservation activities. Preservation activities can be managed through a variety of organizational forms: for example, an organization with no private interest in preservation but that preserves on behalf of others (e.g. a commercial digital archiving service); an organization that does have a private interest in preservation, and preserves on behalf of itself and others (e.g. a research library); or an organization operating under a mandate to preserve, to fulfill some stated public interest (e.g. a national archive). To the degree that there is discretion to choose, an organizational form for preservation activities should be selected that is appropriate given the conditions prevailing in a particular preservation context.

Of particular concern is the impact the organizational form will have on the ability to achieve the other four sustainability conditions. Once an organizational form is determined, it should be combined with a good governance mechanism to ensure that preservation goals are clearly articulated, a strategy is formulated for achieving these goals, preservation responsibilities are appropriately allocated, and metrics and benchmarks are in place to evaluate outcomes. Establishing the right organizational form and governance mechanism helps cultivate trust among stakeholders that the appropriate structures are in place to carry out a sustainable preservation activity and achieve long-term goals.

Summary

In summary, these are the conditions that a digital preservation activity must address if it is to maximize its prospects of achieving long-term economic sustainability. Conversely, if a preservation activity neglects to address one or more of these conditions, its chances for achieving sustainability are likely to be significantly diminished.

Challenges and approaches

With these sustainability conditions in hand, it is useful to examine each in the context of the preservation of research data, where achieving the condition of sustainability will entail different issues and challenges with respect to different digital preservation contexts. While the long-term stewardship of research data shares the same general requirements in regard to sustainability as other forms of digital content, actually meeting these requirements in practice often involves careful consideration of how sustainability manifests in the circumstances specific to the digital lifecycle of research data and its stakeholder community.

In this section, we review some of the nuances of sustainable long-term curation of research data that arise in the context of the conditions described in the previous section. In addition, some current work and exemplars related to these issues are referenced to supplement the discussion.

Value proposition

The value proposition for the long-term preservation of research data can be approached in several ways. One perspective focuses on the value of preserving data as a means of documenting the scientific process. There is a growing expectation that the byproducts of the process of scientific inquiry should become part of the permanent scholarly record along with published results. These byproducts include not only research data, but other materials such as digital laboratory notebooks and computer software or source code. Long-term stewardship of these byproducts of the research process leads to a deeper scholarly record and one that is more amenable to validation and replication. The value of replication has long been acknowledged in the physical sciences; more recently, the social sciences have taken an interest. For example, several studies have illustrated the difficulties of replicating the results of econometric research, because there is missing or incomplete data, lack of access to the functional code, or both (see for example McCullough, 2007).

Preservation of research data not only helps document the process by which the existing corpus of research was produced but also has the potential to catalyze new research. Ongoing access to important datasets can lead to advances within the bounds of the disciplines in which the data was created, or even entirely new uses in seemingly unrelated disciplines. It is not unusual that substantial resources are invested in the creation of a dataset; there is increasing concern that this investment is protected by ensuring ongoing accessibility of the data to future researchers.

Oftentimes a research dataset can be productively re-purposed over an extended time period: for example, a dataset describing survival patterns of sparrows caught in a snow storm, published in 1899 by the zoologist H. C. Bumpus, has been continuously reanalysed to the present day as an exemplar of natural selection in action. (The Bumpus data was brought to the author's attention in the presentation by Todd Vision of the Dryad project: www.oclc.org/us/en/community/presentations/guests/vision-20110425.pdf.)

The value of re-purposing was given further corroboration in a letter published in *Nature*, which estimated that the 2711 datasets deposited into the Gene Expression Omnibus database (GEO) in 2007 constituted 'substantive third-party contributions' to over 1150 published articles between 2007 and 2010 (Piwowar, Vision and Whitlock, 2011).

The Joint Information Systems Committee (JISC)-funded Keeping Research Data Safe (KRDS) project, part 2 (Beagrie, Lavoie and Woollard, 2010), has developed a benefits framework to aid in understanding the properties of benefits relevant for the long-term preservation of research data. The framework defines three dimensions along which benefits can be characterized: the outcome achieved, when the outcome is achieved and who benefits from the outcome. These dimensions comprise the basic components of a value proposition for preserving research data. Identifying the 'what', 'when' and 'who' of the value proposition is a key aspect of communicating the benefits of preserving research data to funders, administrators and other decision makers.

According to the KRDS benefits framework, outcomes can take the form of a direct, positive impact achieved through the preservation of a particular research dataset (e.g. fulfilling a mandate imposed by a funding agency). Benefits may also be indirect, in the sense of avoiding future costs; for example, investing resources in preservation early in the digital lifecycle may significantly diminish the likelihood of an even greater resource expenditure in the future, either to 'rescue' deteriorating datasets or to re-create corrupted, incomplete or otherwise missing data. The timing of benefits can be either near term (within five years) or long term (greater than five years); for example, the benefit of fulfilling a mandate attached to a grant award may be immediate, while avoiding the cost of re-creating damaged or missing data may be considered a long-term benefit. Lastly, the KRDS benefits framework suggests that the beneficiaries from preserving research data may be internal (in the sense of being affiliated with the organization responsible for the preservation; for example, an institutional data repository that provides long-term data curation services for affiliated faculty and students), or external (in the sense of being external to or unaffiliated with the preserving agency; for example, a data repository that offers free access to preserved datasets to researchers around the world).

The KRDS benefits framework was tested in the context of several operating data repositories and found to be a good fit as a tool for crafting statements of the value from preserving research datasets. Use of a model such as the benefits framework addresses one of the fundamental conditions for achieving sustainability: expressing a compelling value proposition for preservation that goes beyond the simple idea of 'preservation for preservation's sake'. In most cases, the value of preserving research data must be explicitly connected to expected future use and the types of valuable activities that would be supported by ongoing access to the data. It is only through the articulation of the key benefits from preservation that a sustained commitment of resources to the long-term stewardship of valuable research data can be obtained.

Selection

Vast amounts of research data are produced as a result of scientific inquiry worldwide. The value of preserving some datasets may be immediately apparent; the future value of other datasets, however, may be questionable. As discussed above, the resources available for preserving research data are finite; it is therefore unrealistic to suggest that a plausible preservation strategy is to retain all of it indefinitely. As with all economic activities, resource constraints will be binding and stakeholders will need to choose the subset of datasets on which preservation efforts will be focused.

An obvious criterion for selecting research data for long-term stewardship is expected future value. Unfortunately, this can be difficult to assess *a priori*. The long-term utility of a particular dataset may not become apparent for some time after creation, and its potential uses may arise in unexpected quarters. An interesting illustration of this was mentioned in Chapter 1 and can be found in the re-purposing of old Royal Navy ships' logbooks, which often contain detailed descriptions of weather patterns around the world. This data is now being employed in building climate models to better understand weather variability. Volunteers transcribe scanned images of the logbooks online; the transcriptions can then be used to compile a database of weather observations (www.oldweather.org).

While anticipated future use is one metric for selecting data for preservation, another key factor is the reproducibility of the data in question. Certain kinds of datasets – for example data produced from computer simulations – may often be reproduced fairly easily, with relatively little resource expenditure. In these circumstances, it may be more economical not to retain the data itself but instead preserve the means for re-creating the data (the simulation software). Other types of data may be reproducible but only at considerable expense and effort. Data produced from experiments might fall into this category: while it might be feasible to reassemble the necessary staff, equipment and laboratory conditions to reproduce the data, the cost of doing so may be prohibitively high. Finally, certain datasets may be impossible to reproduce, as is the case with survey data. Loss of survey datasets may be irreversible regardless of cost, in that the conditions under which the original data were collected can never be revisited. In general, all other things being equal, the greater the cost and effort required to reproduce a dataset, the stronger the case for preserving it.

Because resources are finite, selection will take place regardless of whether or not it is conducted deliberately. Put another way, decision makers can choose between accepting selection as a necessity and developing a systematic plan for managing it, or alternatively, letting it proceed in an unmanaged, *ad hoc* fashion where the corpus of datasets preserved is determined by happenstance. Some work has emerged which provides guidance for those adopting the first strategy. For example, Whyte and Wilson (2010) offer an overview of the rationale for appraisal and selection of research datasets, an enumeration of relevant stakeholders and decision makers, criteria for selection, and building an appraisal process around the criteria. More generally, the Digital Curation Centre provides a useful chapter in its *Curation Reference Manual* on appraising and selecting digital content (Harvey, 2007). The Digital Preservation Coalition has also developed an interactive Decision Tree tool to aid in selection decision making (Digital Preservation Coalition, 2009).

Another important issue to consider in regard to the selection of research data for preservation is to whom responsibility should fall for developing the criteria that forms the basis for selection policies. Clearly certain categories of data will be surrounded by communities of interest, such as academic disciplines, that hold a stake in long-term preservation. The Blue Ribbon Task Force on Sustainable Digital Preservation and Access, in considering sustainability issues in the context of research data, recommends that selection criteria be developed through a consensus-making process wherever identifiable constituencies can be brought together. Specifically, the report advises that '[e]ach domain, through professional societies or other consensus-making bodies, should set priorities for data selection, level of curation, and length of retention' (Blue Ribbon Task Force, 2010, 58). Shared agreement on preservation priorities across a particular stakeholder community diminishes the likelihood of a gap emerging between expectations and practice.

Sustainability requires decision makers to consider not just what they can do with the resources available but, equally importantly, what they should not do – or no longer do. This can entail halting a preservation effort if the value of continuing is not apparent. Preservation decisions are usually not once and for all commitments, but rather a series of decisions made over relatively short time horizons. These decisions should be revisited and re-evaluated and, in some cases, the 'de-selection' of archived content may be appropriate.

Incentives

The sustainable curation of research data is not possible without clearly understood responsibilities for undertaking preservation and compelling incentives for decision makers to act on those responsibilities. In a print-based environment, where the components of the scholarly record (e.g. books or journals) were generally owned by stewardship organizations like libraries, preservation responsibilities and incentives were for the most part straightforward. For example, when a library owns a print book as part of its collection the responsibility for preservation (and indeed the right to preserve) falls to the library by virtue of its ownership and custody of the book. The incentive to carry out this responsibility (to ensure the book is in fact preserved) is compelling to the library, in that it does not wish its collections (and by extension, its investment in its collections) to deteriorate and become unusable. Preservation of the book is also bolstered by the fact that many libraries probably own a copy of the book; so, assuming that at least some of them take action to preserve their copy, there is a high likelihood that the book will continue to be available indefinitely.

This scenario is altered considerably in a digital context. One key difference is that the roles of owner and user are often separated into two distinct entities. For example, rather than possessing physical custody of shelves of print journals, libraries now license access to electronic versions of the journals through the publisher or through third-party providers like JSTOR. In these circumstances, ownership and custody (and often the right to preserve) resides with entities like commercial publishers, which do not necessarily perceive a responsibility to secure the permanence of the scholarly record as part of their organizational mission. Additionally, the ease with which digital content can be shared and replicated from a single source diminishes the incentive for any particular organization to assume and carry out the responsibility of preserving a 'master copy' on behalf of society as a whole; instead, there is a strong incentive to let someone else incur this cost and 'free-ride' on the benefits. For a detailed discussion of the role of incentives in digital preservation, see the report *The Incentives to Preserve Digital Materials* (Lavoie, 2003).

These issues apply to research datasets as well as electronic journals and books. For example, those who own and have custody of research datasets – typically the scientists who create the data – often do not perceive a compelling incentive to invest funds and effort in their long-term curation. Academic reputation and credentials are built on published papers and it is to this end that scholars naturally direct their energy and resources. Consequently, too often little or no effort is made to secure the ongoing availability of research datasets. Those who would potentially benefit from future access to these data – current and future researchers throughout the scholarly community –

are not in a position to intervene in order to ensure that valuable datasets are indeed retained and curated as part of the permanent scholarly record.

The final report of the Blue Ribbon Task Force includes several recommendations that address incentive gaps arising from a diminished sense of the importance of devoting effort to the curation of valuable research data. The Task Force encourages funding agencies to impose preservation mandates where appropriate, requiring grant recipients to make arrangements to ensure that datasets produced under the auspices of funded research continue to be available after the term of the grant concludes (Blue Ribbon Task Force, 2010, 58). Preservation mandates will have their greatest impact on the incentive to preserve when endorsed by major funding agencies. In the USA, for example, the NSF announced in 2010 that grant applicants would in future be required to submit a data management plan with their funding applications. While not a preservation mandate *per se*, this requirement nevertheless strengthens the incentive to comply with the NSF's existing data sharing policies (www.nsf.gov/ bfa/dias/policy/dmp.jsp). The Task Force also recommends that 'funding agencies . . . explicitly recognize "data under curation" as a core indicator of scientific effort' (Blue Ribbon Task Force, 2010, 58–59). Historically, only the published results of research were generally considered worthy contributions to the scholarly record, which inevitably diminished researchers' incentives to curate research datasets. Elevating research data to the level of a first-class contribution to the scholarly record would strengthen the incentive for researchers to give data curation serious attention and effort. This view is beginning to take hold in some quarters; for example, DataCite, an international consortium of research libraries, data centres and other organizations, lists 'increas[ing] acceptance of research data as legitimate, citable contributions to the scientific record' as a key objective in its mission to make research data more visible and accessible (www.datacite.org).

Stewardship of research data can also suffer from the free-rider problem, in that many can benefit from the ongoing availability of important datasets, yet it is only necessary for one organization to incur the expense and effort involved in properly curating the data and making it available. It is usually in no single university or other research organization's interest to take on this responsibility on behalf of its peers, and this perhaps at least partially explains why many research data curation initiatives have gravitated toward public agencies, philanthropically funded projects, and third-party data centres. The Task Force report notes that '[e]ven with widespread recognition of long-term value and well defined selection criteria, data creators may lack strong incentives to preserve. A good rule of thumb is that the incentive to preserve diminishes as the decision-making unit becomes more granular – the most granular being the individual researcher' (Blue Ribbon Task Force, 2010, 58). Given this, it may be that a promising path toward sustainable preservation incentives and, by extension, sustainable data curation activities, lies through professional societies, public agencies, multi-institution collaborations, and other organizations operating at scale and acting on behalf of large communities of stakeholders. Issues relating to choices of organizational form are discussed in more detail below.

The incentive for some organization or group of organizations to step forward and assume responsibility for long-term curation is an essential prerequisite for sustainable research data, and therefore the importance of establishing and maintaining appropriate preservation incentives cannot be overstated. Research data will persist only as long as someone perceives a compelling incentive to take the necessary actions to preserve it; robust incentives to preserve therefore form the backbone of any credible sustainability strategy.

Resources

Any discussion of economic sustainability must of course address the issue of resources. Resources include the in-kind and monetary 'inputs' necessary to produce the desired 'output' of sustainable research data. Naturally, much of the attention focuses on the financial aspects of sustainability: how to create and sustain a flow of funds over time sufficient for a digital curation activity to meet its long-term goals. It has been well documented in many places that a chief concern about the sustainability of many digital curation activities is that they aspire to long-term goals on short-term funding. A commitment to the long-term availability of research data is an implicit commitment to a long-term allocation of resources.

Many questions can be explored in regard to resources and long-term sustainability but two are of particular interest: what resources are required in order to sustain a given curation activity – in other words, how much does it cost? – and how will those costs be shared across the activity's stakeholders? In this respect, research data is no different than any other form of digital content; however, there are some research and real-world exemplars that illuminate these questions in the context of research data.

The KRDS project has produced a cost framework designed specifically for projects engaged in the long-term curation of research data (Beagrie, Lavoie and Woollard, 2010). Every data curation activity is different, and therefore there can be no single answer to the question 'how much does it cost?'. However, it is possible to develop a cost framework that aids decision makers in determining the cost elements relevant to their particular circumstances. The KRDS Cost Framework includes an activity model, which enumerates the full range of activities required to support the long-term preservation of research data. Overlaid on the activity model is a list of cost variables that represent the various ways the activities can be 'adjusted' to conform to the circumstances of a particular digital preservation context. Service adjustments are adjustable aspects of the preservation process that impact costs: for example, the number of acceptable file formats, the volume and frequency of deposits, or the richness of metadata description. Economic adjustments spread the costs of digital preservation over time, and include the rates of inflation or deflation, and the rate of depreciation. In sum, the activity model identifies key cost allocations across the preservation process; the service adjustments adjust these costs to the specific requirements of a particular preservation activity; and the economic adjustments distribute these costs over time.

The practical utility of the KRDS Cost Framework was validated through a series of interviews with practitioners, along with four site visits to research data repositories. Feedback from these sources led to further refinements of the Cost Framework and the release of a second version. A benefits taxonomy was included with the second version of the Cost Framework (for a description of the benefits taxonomy, see the section 'Value proposition' above). In general, respondents felt that the Cost Framework was a useful tool for cost planning and analysis, and its flexibility in application, achieved through the service and economic adjustments, makes it of practical use for assessing the resource requirements of any research data preservation activity.

In addition to estimating the overall resource requirements of a preservation activity, it is also necessary to establish mechanisms to support an ongoing flow of resources to meet those requirements over time. Examination of the landscape of data preservation activities reveals a variety of funding mechanisms in place that could serve as potential models for new activities in the midst of shaping a sustainability strategy. For example the ICPSR, which manages more than 500,000 data files, earns revenue from a variety of sources including sponsored project awards, membership dues and education services (www.icpsr.umich.edu/icpsrweb/ICPSR/annualreport/financial.jsp). The RCSB Protein Data Bank, a collection of three-dimensional structural data for biological molecules, is jointly funded by the US National Science Foundation, the Department of Energy, and several agencies within the National Institutes of Health (www.rcsb.org/pdb/home/home.do). The Center for Research in Security Prices, part of the University of Chicago's Booth School of Business, manages collections of historical security price data; it is supported by fees from the more than 500 commercial and academic subscribers to the service (www.crsp.com).

A common thread among these examples is that sources of revenues – the mechanisms by which resources flow to the data repositories – are diversified, in that they do not rely on a single source. ICPSR spreads revenue over a variety of different sources, including project grants and membership fees. The Protein Data Bank receives support from a number of different federal agencies. The Center for Research in Security Prices spreads its revenues over a large subscriber base and further diversifies by including subscribers from both the commercial and academic sectors. The lesson is clear: diversifying revenue over as many sources as possible reduces the risk of catastrophic consequences, should the flow of resources from one source be temporarily or permanently interrupted. A case in point is the fate of the UK Arts and Humanities Data Service (AHDS), which until 2008 oversaw the operation of five subject-based data centres. In 2008, AHDS's primary funder, the Arts and Humanities Research Council, withdrew funding; AHDS's other funder, JISC, swiftly followed. This resulted in the demise of all but one of the data centres; the rest of the collections were forced to find homes in other repositories and some of the collections seem no longer to be available.

Assessing the amount of resources required to meet a particular data curation activity's long-term goals, as well as choosing appropriate mechanisms to support the ongoing allocation of these resources, are necessary conditions for achieving long-term sustainability. Of course, the circumstances surrounding each activity will be different, and therefore the amount of required resources and the best means of obtaining them will differ as well. But common to all scenarios is the premise that long-term data curation commitments must rest on long-term resource allocations if their sustainability is to be secured.

Organization and governance

The final condition for achieving long-term economic sustainability is organization and governance. The choice of organizational structure through which research data is collected, curated and made available for reuse – a public agency, a peer-based collaboration, a commercial archiving service, and so on – in turn impacts the strategies for meeting the other sustainability conditions. A sustainable organizational structure should assist in co-ordinating the various interests of stakeholders associated with the digital materials in question. To the degree there is discretion to choose, an organizational form for preserving research data should be selected that is appropriate given the conditions prevailing in a particular preservation context, and with a full understanding of its impact on the other conditions necessary for economic sustainability. Doing so will reinforce confidence among stakeholders that the appropriate structures are in place to sustain the data curation activity in achieving its desired long-term goals.

A key aspect of organizational structure in regard to the curation of research data is collaboration and scale. Although most higher education institutions, many public agencies and some private enterprises have a compelling interest in the long-term availability of research datasets, there seems to be little enthusiasm for reproducing curation capacity across many individual organizations. Instead, data curation efforts generally take the form of centralized services operating at scale and serving broad communities of potential users. For example, the UK Data Archive (www.data-archive.ac.uk/about/archive), operated by the University of Essex with funding from the Economic and Social Research Council and JISC, represents the largest collection of social science and humanities data in the UK. Similarly, the Worldwide Protein Data Bank declares its mission to be 'to maintain a single Protein Data Bank Archive of macromolecular structural data that is freely and publicly available to the global community' (www.wwpdb.org/faq.html). Dryad, an international repository that manages the research data underpinning peer-reviewed articles in the biosciences, operates under a governance structure that includes a consortium of more than a dozen journals (http://datadryad.org).

Organizational structures taking the form of large-scale, collaborative or centralized data curation services offer a number of advantages, including the opportunity to leverage economies of scale and reduce the per-unit cost of long-term data curation. Expertise in data curation (especially domain-specific expertise) is in limited supply and the long-term costs of data stewardship can be reduced if expertise is spread over large aggregations of data. Another factor supporting a centralized approach to organizing data curation activities is that ease of access can be improved when a collection of datasets relevant to a particular community of scholars is aggregated and accessible from a single source, rather than scattered over dozens of repositories and organizations. An alternative model to centralized services might be institutional repositories, where higher education institutions offer data storage and curation services to affiliated researchers. While there may be some scope for such localized services, it is likely that many of these repositories would not be able to achieve the necessary scale to place their service on a sustainable cost trajectory. Given this, large-scale, subject-specific repositories may prove to be a more sustainable way of organizing data curation activities.

In addition to organizational structure, governance should also be a chief concern for data curation activities. Governance should detail the distribution of responsibilities across stakeholders associated with the activity, describe the expected outcomes and the processes for achieving them, and incorporate a mechanism for periodically assessing whether or not objectives are indeed being met. Once a governance strategy has been agreed on, it should be formalized in policy statements, service-level agreements, memorandums of understanding, or some other appropriate means of documentation.

Two key aspects of a governance statement for data curation activity should be the period of retention and hand-off mechanisms. As the earlier discussion of selection indicates, it is unrealistic to expect that all datasets will be preserved forever. A variety of factors could lead to the de-accessioning of an archived dataset, for example, an extended period of non-use, the availability of an updated or enhanced version of the same dataset, or a change in economic conditions that forces a repository to scale back its preservation commitments. In circumstances where de-accessioning a dataset is necessary, a 'hand-off' to another repository may be appropriate, if one can be found that is willing to assume custody and stewardship of the data. This is especially important in cases where the value of the dataset is not in question, but the current repository simply does not have the resources or is otherwise unable to continue to preserve it. Transfers of stewardship responsibility are not uncommon over the course of the digital lifecycle, whether the material in question is research data or some other form of digital content. These transfers will be facilitated by planning for hand-offs well in advance of their occurrence.

Appropriate organization and governance are crucial elements for sustainable digital curation activities. They comprise the framework within which economic decision making is made and, in this way, impact all of the other sustainability conditions discussed in this chapter. Put another way, poorly conceived organizational structures and governance increase the difficulty of meeting the economic requirements for sustainability. However, when properly designed, they can serve to cultivate trust among stakeholders that the data curation activity can indeed fulfill its stated mission.

Conclusion

Research data is an integral component of society's permanent scholarly record. Properly curated research data can serve as a means of validating existing knowledge, and discovering new knowledge. In order for research data to continue to release value over the long term, it must be sustainable. As the discussion in this chapter suggests, sustainability is not some property inherent in the datasets themselves; instead, it is a property of the activity in which stewardship of datasets is embedded. In this sense, when we speak of 'sustainable research data', it is perhaps more accurate to say we are speaking of sustainable data curation activities.

Sustainability is inseparable from economics; therefore basic economic principles are a useful guide to understanding many of the issues involved in designing a sustainability strategy for research data. A key economic principle that comes into play time and time again in sustainability decision making is the notion of trade-offs, and the necessity of making difficult choices between competing ends. For example, those responsible for managing a data curation activity must decide whether access to the archived data will be available freely to all, or only to fee-paying subscribers. Open availability has the worthy outcome of spreading the benefits of the data as widely as possible, but charging for access might secure a reliable flow of revenues that would ensure the curation activity is provisioned with sufficient resources to carry out its stewardship responsibilities into the future. Choices of this kind are frequently encountered in addressing the sustainability conditions discussed in this chapter; a sustainability strategy will take its shape from the outcomes of the decision-making process that resolves them.

Of all the trade-offs associated with the long-term stewardship of research data, perhaps the most significant is the fundamental choice between allocating resources to the creation of new data (new scholarship) and the preservation of existing data (the scholarly record). As with all activities, the pool of resources available for the support of scholarly endeavour is finite. Trade-offs must therefore be evaluated and choices made.

It is natural that there will be a bias towards allocating resources to the creation of new data. Scholarship is, after all, motivated by a desire to discover the unknown. But while it is essential that we invest in creation, it is also necessary to invest in preserving what we have created. Sustainable research data will emerge from a judicious balancing of these priorities.

References

Beagrie, N., Lavoie, B. and Woollard, M. (2010) *Keeping Research Data Safe 2*, Joint Information

Systems Committee, www.jisc.ac.uk/media/documents/publications/reports/2010/
keepingresearchdatasafe2.pdf.

Blue Ribbon Task Force on Sustainable Digital Preservation and Access (2010) *Sustainable Economics for a Digital Planet: ensuring long-term access to digital information,* *http://*brtf.sdsc.edu/biblio/BRTF_Final_Report.pdf.

Digital Preservation Coalition (2009) *Decision Tree Interactive Assessment,* www.dpconline.org/advice/preservationhandbook/decision-tree/decision-tree-interactive-assessment.

Harvey, R. (2007) Instalment on 'Appraisal and Selection'. In *DCC Digital Curation Manual,* Digital Curation Centre, www.dcc.ac.uk/sites/default/files/appraisal-and-selection%5B1%5D.pdf.

Hey, T., Tansley, S. and Tolle, K. (2009) *The Fourth Paradigm: data-intensive scientific discovery,* Microsoft Research.

Lavoie, B. (2003) *The Incentives to Preserve Digital Materials: roles, scenarios, and economic decision-making,* Online Computer Library Center, www.oclc.org/research/projects/digipres/incentives-dp.pdf.

Levy, S. (2009) Secret of Googlenomics: data-fueled recipe brews profitability, *Wired Magazine,* **17** (6), www.wired.com/culture/culturereviews/magazine/17-06/nep_googlenomics?currentPage=all.

McCullough, B. D. (2007) Got Replicability?, *Journal of Money, Credit and Banking* Archive, *Econ Journal Watch,* **4** (3), http://econjwatch.org/articles/got-replicability-the-journal-of-money-credit-and-banking-archive.

Piwowar, H. A., Vision, T. J. and Whitlock, M. C. (2011) Data Archiving is a Good Investment, *Nature,* **473** (7347), www.nature.com/nature/journal/v473/n7347/full/473285a.html.

Whyte, A. and Wilson, A. (2010) *How to Appraise and Select Research Data for Curation,* Digital Curation Centre, www.dcc.ac.uk/sites/default/files/documents/publications/guides/How%20to%20Appraisefor%20Final.pdf.

CHAPTER 5

Data management plans and planning

Martin Donnelly

Introduction

> I tell this story to illustrate the truth of the statement I heard long ago in the Army: plans are worthless, but planning is everything.
>
> Dwight D. Eisenhower

Research funders place increasing importance on data management planning as a mechanism for improving the longevity of research data and for enabling its widespread access and reuse. As explained in Chapter 3, the majority of public research funders in the UK ask that all grant applicants include a plan covering such aspects of data management as preservation, curation and future reuse, as appropriate to the needs of their scholarly domain.

This chapter discusses the various factors that have led to the upsurge of interest in data management planning, outlines the components that commonly make up a data management plan, and provides examples of tools and other resources that can help researchers and research support staff embarking on the round of planning activities.

Planning can be a misunderstood and underappreciated endeavour. At its heart, the purpose of planning is to make things better, to anticipate and make provision against risks, and to help communicate these preparations and agreements. But while plans may help to protect against under-performance, crucially they stop short of ensuring a good one. Specifically, in the case of data management plans they do not guarantee or deliver good data management practice; but they do serve to mitigate risks and help instil confidence and trust in the data and its stewards.

Planning is no stranger to the world of electronic data. Preservation planning is a function of the Open Archival Information System Reference Model (CCSDS, 2002), an influential framework for long-term preservation systems. It is also a stage in the Digital Curation Centre (DCC) Curation Lifecycle Model (Higgins, 2008), as explored in detail in Chapter 2. Data management is a facet of digital preservation, which is itself a facet of digital curation; so a data management plan will fit into a policy suite, matrix or framework alongside, *inter alia*, operational procedures, policies and risk registers. Consequently, data management planning can be considered a component of preservation planning, just as preservation planning can be considered a component of data management planning. In essence, both boil down to the challenge of enabling data accessibility, which essentially addresses the question of 'can I access what I want, when I want it, in the right format and with confidence in its integrity'? (See Harvey, 2010, Chapter 7, for a more detailed analysis of preservation planning and policy, in particular the relationships between risk, planning, policy, and curation and management.)

Planning for future accessibility and reuse also implies recognition of the transitory nature of some data generating situations. In certain disciplines, notably the social sciences, humanities and environmental sciences, it may be impossible to reproduce or replicate the environment and circumstances under which data are generated and captured. When data is produced from the observation of unrepeatable events, perhaps in the recording of climate data, or where they are gathered over a number of years, as with longitudinal studies of human behaviour, greater stress will be placed on the long-term preservation of data. But in situations where fast and easy data sharing is desirable, as in medicine and the biological sciences, or where experiments are easily repeated, more emphasis is given to discoverability and reuse.

An analysis of the data-related policies of major UK research funders (Jones, 2011) showed that not all funders had published policies governing the data outputs generated from research. Where policies exist, the approaches taken are diverse, with some funders applying different policies to different types of program and with the same requirements being expressed in different ways by different funders. The situation remains fluid, although a more co-ordinated approach has been emerging since April 2011, when Research Councils UK (RCUK), the umbrella body of the seven publicly funded research councils, released *Common Principles on Data Policy* (RCUK, 2011). For the first time these presented a shared view on 'institutional and project specific data management policies and plans'.

This insistence on data management planning is not exclusive to UK funders. In the USA, for example, since early 2011, the National Science Foundation (NSF) has decreed that all research proposals it receives must include a supplementary two-page data management plan describing 'how the proposal will conform to NSF policy on the dissemination and sharing of research results' (NSF, 2010). In the wake of such policy developments support services in the UK, USA, Australia and Europe have followed suit by developing tools and guidance to assist researchers in planning and implementing data management processes throughout the research lifecycle.

The relationship between policy and plan is similar to that between strategy and tactics: the success of a strategy depends on its execution, while tactics bring a strategy to life. But we also need to consider – and link into – operational procedures. As may be inferred from the Eisenhower quotation that opens this chapter, the planning process can be considered useful as an end in itself, since it presents an opportunity to think through the broad range of factors that will impact on the actual processes of data collection, management and sharing – and to do this well in advance of having to meet them.

Why plan?
Because you (and others) might want to know where you're going

Planning is an intuitive and fundamental activity in all strands of human endeavour. It enables us to prepare to meet challenges and cope with contingencies and, by systematizing a course of action, generates confidence in the work that is about to be undertaken, as well as in those about to undertake it. But having said already that the process of planning itself may be as important, potentially, as the plan it produces, it is still unavoidable that in the field of data management planning the emphasis will be more on the arrival than the journey. As noted in the final report of the Blue Ribbon Task Force, the journey in this case is very much a derived demand (Blue Ribbon Task Force, 2010).

Knowing where you want to go with the data is in some fields of research a notion indicative of considerable cultural change. For researchers accustomed to dealing with issues as they arise in an *ad hoc* manner, data management planning may well be regarded as an additional and unwelcome burden. Such an attitude is likely to be particularly prevalent when no specific resources are attached to the frequently 'orphaned' activity of data management. But this situation is changing. More research funders now encourage grant applicants to include data management as a separate cost within their project budgets, in reflection of their own burgeoning demands for the practice of effective data management.

But if planning is perceived as a burden, perhaps more persuasive than the simple desire to plot a course of action is the need to avoid or manage risk. Harvey (2010, 83) cites planning as a proactive preservation activity aimed at minimizing risk and the very existence of a project data management plan may be construed as a basic indicator of the reliability of the data produced by it. Knowledge of an issue must surely be the first step to tackling it.

Because they make you: funders, mandates and requirements

While there remains much room for improvement, the broad trend in research funding is towards more stringent data-related requirements, accompanied by a closer monitoring of compliance with funder expectations. This manifests itself in instructions to applicants for the submission of a data management plan as part of their funding proposal. There are numerous and complex drivers behind this trend:

- Governments and publicly funded bodies are under increasing pressure to demonstrate transparency and value for money. A coherent and public data management and sharing plan reduces the likelihood of the same research being funded twice, while research data stored in publicly searchable repositories facilitates its reuse.
- The existence of an unequivocal data management plan will help data managers comply with legislation and other regulations governing the retention of data,

including institutional policies. A data management plan may, for example, state that all data created within a project will be destroyed immediately after the project's active lifetime. This can be explained in the plan as the most appropriate course of action despite not facilitating reuse or data sharing.

• In an increasingly open society there is a need to identify areas of research where openness may breach the accepted norm for ethics. A research project that collects sensitive data, such as that relating to living human subjects, may require tight constraints to be placed on the release of data in order to protect the identity of the data subject and to preserve the level of trust required to sustain the research. Such consideration of the data subject is one of a number of ethical concerns that argue against the sharing of data, for which the well structured data management plan provides an opportunity to identify, explain and manage.

Because it saves money in the long run

The sooner good data management is established within research practice the more effective it will be and the less of a shock to the system. This has benefits in quality and cost; as Harvey notes, 'It is far cheaper to properly curate data at the creation stage; adding or changing "bad" metadata is prohibitively expensive after time has passed' (2010, 90). For certain datasets, it may even be impossible. The rationale for data management planning is most often put in financial terms: datasets may be 'valuable' or even 'invaluable'. Irreplaceable datasets are by their nature priceless, although their bare fiscal value may be low. Achieving a balance between worth and risk is what planners are often obliged to do.

Because it leads to better quality research and enables high quality curation and reuse

It is wise to avoid situations wherein cause chases effect. Advocates of data management repeatedly warn that starting to think about data sharing and preservation towards the end of a project is too late. The groundwork has to be laid early in the lifecycle to ensure that the data is created and stored in the right formats, that the appropriate metadata is created and attached in order to enable subsequent discovery and interpretation of the information contained within the data. Resources and responsibilities must also be allocated to ensure that ongoing preservation actions are not shunted to the side when something more pressing or rewarding comes along. Research funders are increasingly explicit on this topic: the RCUK Shared Principles (RCUK, 2011) note both that 'publicly funded research data are a public good' and that 'It is appropriate to use public funds to support the management and sharing of publicly-funded research data'. Grant applicants are therefore entitled and even encouraged to plan for effective data management within their research proposals. The trend since 2010 has been towards more structured and intentional practice in this respect.

The limits of planning: what does a data management plan cover?

The process of data management planning cannot be treated as a discrete exercise that is divorced from the activities it predicts and the two elements of planning and operationalization will necessarily go forward together. Hence, a data management plan should cover all the relevant data-related aspects of a project across its entire lifecycle, from conceptualization to long-term deposit and/or disposal. It may cover big picture attributes like the overall goal of the project and how it fits into disciplinary developments; it may also cover minutiae, such as the precise model of camera with which a series of images was captured and a textual record of the weather conditions under which the photographs were taken. It can embrace the subjective and the objective. But what is of key importance is that the plan is fit for purpose and genuinely considered, as opposed to simply being modified from previously 'successful' plans. Adapting the successful elements of another project's plan merely to meet a funder's requirements is of very limited utility and may, in the end, cause more harm than good. But a balance can be struck and benchmarking good practice is often worthwhile.

Preparatory work: conducting analyses of existing data sources

Data management planning need not only involve laying the groundwork for the creation of new datasets. Often there will be existing datasets that can be reused, and determining whether or not such resources exist and can be accessed and reused are facets of the planning process. Success breeds success: the more visible examples of good data reuse exist the greater the likelihood that new projects will reuse them and structure their own data in a readily reusable way.

Broadly speaking there are two kinds of data that can be used: those created by third parties who are content for (or obliged to allow!) you to reuse their work, and those created by yourself or others in your immediate vicinity (be this an institution, a laboratory, a research group or some other collection of similarly interested scholars). Automated 'harvesting' of descriptive metadata from online repositories supports the former type of use by assisting researchers in the discovery and appraisal of third-party data, but, historically, a large quantity of data has been held in inaccessible places, whether in archives that are kept closed deliberately because of the nature of their content or some other governing factor, or less formally on private disc space (such as the hard drive of a standalone PC). Most at risk are the data kept on degradable media such as CD-ROMs/DVD-ROMs or cheap and portable (losable) media like USB flash drives and memory sticks.

Those wishing to identify the data that might be available within an organization could use the Data Asset Framework (www.data-audit.eu), a tool that can be used to assemble a clear view of a data collection. It provides a methodology for establishing the extent of existing resources, their current state of management, and advice on how to create a register and a timetable to support good data management planning.

Creating a data management plan: influences and actors

Every data management plan is different, since they each reflect the different forces acting on them. These influences include the country in which the research is taking place, the body that is funding it, the expected outcomes of the research (whether it will feed into commercial applications or be released to the public domain), whether the work is reproducible or unique, and so on. Specifically:

- *Funder requirements* – Funder requirements may stipulate a preferred place of long-term storage, a timeframe for deposit and sharing, file formats and storage standards.
- *Place of deposit* – The place of deposit (data centre, archive and so on) may only accept data in certain formats and on certain media.
- *Internal requirements* – Similarly, internal requirements may mandate that datasets and perhaps related publications are deposited (either in whole, in part or metadata only) in some kind of institutional repository and that data is collected and held according to self-imposed ethics policies.
- *Research groups* – Research groups may have storage systems and other hardware-related issues that affect the way in which data is created and stored. Laboratory equipment often comes with proprietary file formats as standard, so challenges to data sharing may arise unwittingly.
- *Softer influences* – There may also be softer influences such as disciplinary norms and trends. Even personal preference (e.g. Windows vs Mac vs Linux) will have an effect.
- *Publishers* – Publishers may require that datasets underpinning research papers are deposited with them; some request that the ownership of copyright and database rights are signed over to them as part of their default conditions, which may not be compatible with institutional policies.
- *Legal requirements* – Finally, there may be legal requirements pertaining to the data, such as a requirement to make publicly funded data available to any interested party (in the UK this is called freedom of information) or a responsibility to meet certain obligations with regard to information which could be used to identify a living person (in the UK, the Data Protection Act.)

Each of the above will exert different degrees of influence under different circumstances but most projects will have to consider more than one aspect when developing plans and strategies.

Dependencies and interactions: who needs to be involved?

Data management planning is a joint endeavour involving multiple drivers and stakeholders spanning all stages of the research data lifecycle. Each of these has to follow the same map in order to mitigate the risk of not arriving at the same destination. A paradigmatic example is the $125 million NASA Mars probe, which was lost in 1999 because a contractor used imperial measurements while the Agency's standard was the metric system.

First and foremost in this collaborative endeavour are the researchers themselves. Without direct involvement from the scientists and scholars who capture or create the data, a plan will be compromised and unlikely to be effective. Next in importance may be the people responsible for the long-term preservation and management of data, namely data librarians and data centre or repository managers. Not all datasets are appropriate for long-term preservation but in many cases the usefulness of a dataset will outlive the career span of its original creator. It is essential in these cases to involve long-term custodians in the development of a data management plan, particularly in its latter stages.

Other stakeholders in the process may include support staff such as research policy officers and grants officers. Policy officers develop and often oversee adherence to institutional mandates and other relevant policies on topics like ethics. Other specialists may also be consulted, such as archivists, records managers, and freedom of information and data protection officers.

Finally, technical and laboratory staff will be best placed to record the precise technical details relevant to some scientific projects. The make and model of laboratory equipment can have a considerable bearing on many facets of data management, from the calibration of recording equipment to processes for automated metadata capture, and specialist staff should in such instances be involved in the creation and maintenance of data management plans.

It is important to remember that the human challenges in data management are often more difficult to meet than the technological ones. Communication is vital.

When should I prepare a plan?

The DCC recommends three stages or versions for a data management plan: minimal, core and full.

1   A minimal data management plan is created at the conceptualization or grant application stage and addresses only the bare minimum necessary to secure funding. There is no sense in spending large amounts of time developing a detailed plan for a project that may not see the light of day. These plans differ in length and focus according to the specific requirements of the funder (or institution, or academic discipline). The minimal plan is by its nature promissory, 'We will do this . . .'

2   A core plan is developed once funding is in place and addresses a wider range of matters in considerably more detail. The DCC suggestion is for the core plan to address all relevant data management issues up to the point of those involving long-term management and preservation. This is the in-project 'working' plan, to be used in conjunction with on-the-ground data management procedures. 'We do this for these reasons . . .'

3   A full plan adds issues of longer-term data management. This would be prepared towards the end of a project and may be retained (and maintained) long after the project has been completed by individuals who were not necessarily involved in the data's capture or creation. The value of data outliving its originators is a key argument for data preservation.

Each stage builds on the one before and multiple versions may be created at each stage depending on the length of time over which the research is being carried out. It should be borne in mind that planning at its best is a process that reacts to change, and that no plan benefits from being set in stone or blindly adhered to regardless of changing circumstances. Key people must know when to follow the plan and when to change it, as well as how and when to communicate these changes successfully.

Horses for courses, or, how much planning is appropriate?

I referred earlier to a widespread preference in some quarters for *ad hoc* decisions over the labour of advance planning. On the flipside, it is also the case that some people prefer planning to action and one of the complaints most often heard about the increasing obligation to undertake data management planning is that time spent on this activity is time that could more profitably be spent 'doing science'.

It is no accident that these three types of data management plan occur in the order and schedule given, for there is little sense in a hard-pressed researcher thinking through every last detail of a project's data management plan before it is certain that the research it predicts will see the light of day. Similarly, thinking about longer-term preservation is often best kept for the latter stages of a project, by which time many of the in-project changes will have settled down; although it is usually wise to lay the groundwork for long-term preservation from the very outset by thinking about adherence to standards, the likely needs of future users, and other measures of future-proofing.

What does a data management plan look like?

The most common question asked about data management plans is 'Where can I find examples?' A quick web search will return several hits, which will be of varying degrees of usefulness depending on whether the results correspond to the discipline to which the searcher belongs, together with other such factors as whether the projects to which they refer are similarly budgeted and if their application is in related areas of research.

Within the UK data management community of funders and service providers there has been energetic discussion about the desirability of a central registry of data management plans. Such a facility would enable the wider sharing of plans, with the consequence that funding applicants could inform their own responses by gaining insight to examples of good practice. Notwithstanding an underlying pressure from freedom of information legislation, which promotes its own agenda for openness, researchers themselves are keen to see examples of successful data management plans as a means of achieving benchmarking. But there remain a number of arguments for and against the introduction of such a facility. Possible advantages include an increase in the transparency of publicly funded research, new options for the sharing of good practice and a reduction to the risk of 'reinventing the wheel' by undertaking duplicate investigations. But the primary disadvantage is more fundamental and merits a paragraph of its own.

Anecdotal evidence holds that many data creators see the development and maintenance of data management plans as a purely administrative overhead, a hurdle that must be cleared or a box that must be ticked in order to secure the desired funding. Researchers with this attitude will look for shortcuts but providing them with easy access to a store of successful data management plans comes complete with the risk that principal investigators and their research teams may not truly engage with the planning endeavour. Further, the temptation to replicate a model or exemplar could lead to lapses into a 'box-ticking' frame of mind with, typically, a failure to engage adequately with the job at hand. Anyone taking this mechanical route will say what needs to be said in order to win the funding but an inadequate analysis of the particular nature of a project's anticipated data output will mean that its longevity and shareability will very likely suffer as a result.

It is therefore important to strike a balance between offering appropriate levels of support and guidance without going so far as to render the exercise of planning meaningless and the words hollow.

Nonetheless, the argument put forward on the basis of improvements to transparency or with reference to the freedom of information legislation is a compelling one and, while acknowledging the above caveats, examples of data management plans that can be freely accessed online include 'Guidelines for Effective Data Management Plans' of the Inter-University Consortium for Political and Social Research (ICPSR): (www.icpsr.umich.edu/icpsrweb/ICPSR/dmp/index.jsp) and 'Data Management Plans' of MIT Libraries (http://libraries.mit.edu/guides/subjects/data-management/plans.html).

Checklist for a data management plan

It is hard, particularly for non-specialists, to bear in mind all the multifarious factors that pertain to achieving effective data management, to determine which are particularly relevant to a given project and then to express them in a plan, while at the same time adhering to good practice. In order to support researchers and other data management stakeholders in the development and maintenance of plans, the DCC created a checklist for a data management plan (first version Donnelly and Jones, 2010; the most recent version is available via www.dcc.ac.uk/dmponline). The development of this checklist followed an analysis that compared the requirements of the main UK research funders with the explicit data-related statements expected from their grant applicants (Jones, 2008).

There has been a longstanding expectation within some research councils – notably the Arts and Humanities Research Council (AHRC) and the Economic and Social Research Council (ESRC) – that researchers should consider the sustainability and future use of digital outputs from the outset of a research undertaking, and both councils provide specific questions to be answered in a dedicated section of the Joint electronic Submission (Je-S) system. The Biotechnology and Biological Sciences Research Council (BBSRC), Medical Research Council (MRC) and Wellcome Trust have introduced requirements to produce a data management and sharing plan. In contrast to the AHRC and ESRC, these funders ask for a broad statement to be submitted alongside the grant proposal. Suggestions and guidance are provided for topics that could be addressed in the statement; however, applicants can define the content based on the themes most relevant to their own research proposal.

The DCC Checklist has undergone multiple stages of consultation, with interested and expert parties invited to comment on the wording, suggest alternatives and propose useful guidance to accompany each question. The principal change between the first and subsequent iterations of the Checklist was a move towards simpler questions in which each addresses only a single issue, with closed and active phrasing designed to encourage the respondent to think in concrete terms about what they themselves would need to do to make data management happen.

As already noted, the Checklist is intended to work as a comprehensive and generic *aide mémoire* for all stakeholders across the entire data lifecycle. The downside of this comprehensiveness has been the length of the document, which with in excess of one hundred questions and headings risks discouraging researchers who would not necessarily have the time to address all of the issues identified. Of course, being generic they were not expected to answer all of the questions, but it became clear to the DCC that the length of the Checklist threatened to limit its operational usefulness and a more elegant and modern online solution was therefore the next and necessary step. That step produced DMP Online, which is discussed below in the section 'Other tools and resources'.

A representative structure for planning

Table 5.1 provides a more detailed analysis of the structure and content of an exemplar data management planning format, namely the DCC's Checklist for a Data Management Plan v3.0 (Donnelly and Jones, 2011). Other checklists are available but, according to an independent comparison (www.icpsr.umich.edu/icpsrweb/content/ICPSR/dmp/table.html), this is the most comprehensive. It was developed by way of 'crowdsourcing', with public consultation delivering responses from representatives of the major stakeholder groups: researchers, funders, long-term data storage facilities and support services.

Table 5.1 *Checklist for a data management plan (v3.0): structure and scope*			
§	Name	Contents and purpose	Relevance
1	Introduction and context	Sets the scene for the data management plan. Much of the early information is primarily administrative rather than data related. This section also addresses the aims of the project and the plan, and the likely or intended audiences for each, and asks for details of internal and external policies that apply to the data and its management.	Discovery
2	Data types, formats, standards and capture methods	Asks the researcher to describe the forms of data that the research will produce. It covers the data itself and the metadata which makes the data (re)usable. Access to this information is crucial for the bulk of data management and curation activities.	(Supporting) reuse Discovery Delivery
3	Ethics and intellectual property	Foregrounds issues of ethics and intellectual property. Some of the questions are concerned with meeting legal obligations, and refer specifically to pieces of UK legislation. Issues of licensing are raised here, which impacts on data sharing, but issues of embargo periods and release schedules are kept back until the next section on access, data sharing and reuse.	Shareability Compliance
4	Access, data sharing and reuse	Expands on its precursor, going beyond immediate issues of compliance and licensing to ask who would be the likely reusers of the data created and captured, and how and when the data might be accessed. This section is intended to be particularly useful in determining whether a given dataset is suitable for its intended reuse purposes.	Discovery Access
5	Short-term storage and data management	Concentrates on specifics about the management of the data during the project lifetime. The likelihood is that access to data will be constrained at this stage, and only available to those directly involved in the research. Specific questions about data volumes and formats assist data managers in planning resource requirements.	Shareability Preservation
6	Deposit and long-term preservation	Likely to be completed later in the research lifecycle, this section is most likely to be maintained with stakeholders unconnected with the original research. The usefulness of a dataset may long outlive the career (or interest) of its creator or capturer, and for this reason it is important that datasets of long-term value have clear and considered management plans in place and accessible by all those who stand to benefit from them. Consequently, this section supports a very broad range of activities, from underlying preservation to selection, appraisal, and discovery and access.	Preservation Access Shareability Appraisal Supporting reuse Discovery

(Continued overleaf)

Table 5.1 (continued)			
§	Name	Contents and purpose	Relevance
7	Resourcing	Data management has historically been something of an orphan activity, expected to be carried out but not explicitly funded. Ad hoc data management is risky, as activities that do not attract funding, reward or recognition will be the first to suffer when time or funds are tight. This section provides an invitation to address explicitly the human (time, expertise) and capital (finance, infrastructure) resources that will be required to meet both short-term and long-term commitments.	Infrastructure Finance
8	Adherence and review	Research funders are gradually moving towards more formal arrangements for the review and monitoring of data management plans. This section asks how the plan will be adhered to, how often it will be reviewed to ensure its ongoing suitability, and who will be responsible for these activities.	Preservation
9	Statement of agreement	Provides an opportunity to formalize the data management plan. It will not be relevant to all projects, but is felt to be useful in the case of multi-partner projects, and particularly academic or industrial partnerships where commercial interests are tied up in the data.	Administrative
10	Annexes	Provides a 'catch-all' opportunity to add/append any other details that may be relevant to the data management plan. Three examples are explicitly suggested: contact details and expertise of nominated data managers and named individuals, a glossary of terms, and previous versions of the plan (if relevant).	Miscellaneous

Other tools and resources
DMP Online

In order to overcome the inflexibility and potentially off-putting length of the one-dimensional DCC Checklist, a web-based tool was developed that would present only a subset of the questions included in the checklist, organized according to which funder the research was being submitted to and the stage (pre-funding, in-project, late- or post-project) that the research had reached.

DMP Online (http://dmponline.dcc.ac.uk) allows researchers, data custodians and other stakeholders to create, maintain and export data management plans. It was developed in order to help research teams meet increasingly prescriptive funder requirements and reflects the recommendation in the seminal report *Dealing with Data* (Lyon, 2007) that '[e]ach funded research project should submit a structured Data Management Plan for peer-review as an integral part of the application for funding'.

The tool is designed to help researchers by defining the roles and responsibilities pertaining to their data, by identifying risks that might arise at points of transition and by ensuring an appropriate and safe chain of custody for digital data as it passes from originator to subsequent stewards.

Researchers wishing to use DMP Online are first required to register, although use is free and open to anyone with an email address. The website and user interface were designed to enable the requirements of different funders to be mapped straightforwardly to the equivalent DCC clauses, with onscreen guidance and links provided to assist in the completion of plans.

For the technically minded, DMP Online was built using the Ruby on Rails web applications framework and runs on an Ubuntu GNU/Linux server via an Apache web server. Data is stored in a MySQL database and all technologies used in its development are free or open source. (See Donnelly, Jones and Pattenden-Fail, 2010, for more detail on the development of the first iteration of the tool, including technical detail.)

Where a researcher is applying to a funder that has expressed explicit data-related demands at the funding stage, DMP Online presents a 'template' made up of the DCC clauses that correspond most closely to that funder's specific requirements, the idea being that by answering the DCC clauses the researcher will *de facto* meet the funder's requirements. Where a researcher is applying to a funding council or other source that does not make explicit data-related demands at the application stage, DMP Online presents a generic template which users can modify as desired.

Users of DMP Online also have the ability to export their plans (or sub-sections thereof) in a variety of formats, including XML and comma separated values (CSVs), each of which assists in enabling links with research administration systems.

Resources in the USA

In the USA, in late 2010, a group of interested institutions began a collaboration to create a tool similar to DMP Online, with the specific purpose of supporting the creation of data management plans required by the NSF. Supported and informed by the Digital Curation Centre's pioneering work in this field, this group is taking a different approach. As a result of differing operational and cultural requirements, the eponymous DMP Tool will be capable of being deployed separately in each institution, as opposed to its delivery as a central, nationally co-ordinated resource. This approach has benefits in perceptions of ownership, with the payoff that it limits the amount of comparison that can be made between different institutions and disciplines.

Table 5.2 offers a high-level comparison of the two tools, their audiences and their functionalities.

As an indication of the level of interest that had been generated, the University of Minnesota Libraries also signalled an intention to develop an online tool along similar lines, and the Distributed Data Curation Center at Purdue Libraries has developed a documentary Data Management Plan Tool, which takes the form of a self-assessment questionnaire (http://d2c2.lib.purdue.edu/documents/dmp_self_questionnaire.pdf).

Table 5.2 *Comparison between DMP Online and DMP Tool*		
	DMP Online (UK)	DMP Tool (USA)
History	Developed by the Digital Curation Centre with funding from JISC. First version launched April 2010.	Multi-partner project involving University of California (UC) Curation Center at the California Digital Library, UC Los Angeles Library, UC San Diego Libraries, University of Virginia Library, University of Illinois at Urbana-Champaign, NSF's DataONE project and Smithsonian Institution, with support from the UK Digital Curation Centre. First version launch date in summer 2011.
Coverage	Initially covered the RCUK councils plus the Wellcome Trust. Subsequently expanded to allow institutional and disciplinary templates as well as funder templates, and used to create experimental templates for the NSF in the USA.	Developed to support applicants to the NSF only, although subsequent versions may support additional funders.
Functionality	Maps funder, and institutional and disciplinary requirements are added to a generic checklist. Applicants are presented with a three-column layout: the funder's questions, their checklist equivalents, and a text-input box for answers, and there are useful guidance and links in a separate pop-up box. Thus users do not answer the funders' questions directly, which improves flexibility and enables plans from different disciplines to be more readily compared.	Users answer the NSF requirements directly, assisted by their own institutionally defined guidance and links, and the NSF's guidance notes.
Export options	Various format options: PDF, HTML, CSV, XML and ASCII.	A two-page report designed to meet the NSF requirements.
Hosting	Centrally hosted by the DCC.	Installed separately at each of the partner institutions.
Guidance	Guidance materials were 'crowd sourced' from the user community, and can be customized for each template or funder. The generic set of guidance is routinely maintained and updated by the DCC.	Generic guidance from each NSF directorate is built into the tool. Institution-specific guidance is also provided by each institution, and not shared.

PLATTER

Developed by DigitalPreservationEurope (DPE), the Planning Tool for Trusted Electronic Repositories (PLATTER) is a methodological framework designed to assist repository managers in engendering trust in their repository's mechanisms for safeguarding digital materials. The tool is paper-based, although an electronic version is mooted in the PLATTER report, and comprises three stages:

- classifying the repository according to its function, implementation, operation and scale
- defining strategic objective plans for the repository linked to specific areas of operation
- an iterative planning cycle to ensure ongoing fitness for purpose and ultimately instilling trust in stakeholders; this stage produces continuously evolving plans linked to repository goals.

To minimize the risk of duplication of effort PLATTER (www.digital preservationeurope.eu/platter/) co-ordinates with and complements DRAMBORA (www.repositoryaudit.eu/), Network of Expertise in Long-term Storage of Digital Resources (nestor; http://files.d-nb.de/nestor/materialien/nestor_mat_08-eng.pdf) and Trusted Repositories Audit and Certification (TRAC; www.crl.edu/PDF/trac.pdf), three influential audit and certification tools and checklists. This is an important consideration given the commitment of time that is demanded by each of them. The use of tools such as PLATTER and DRAMBORA may fruitfully be cited in (and ideally linked to) wider-ranging data management plans, most likely in the post-project stage when the data has passed from the custody of its original creator or collector.

The data seal of approval

The data seal of approval (DSA) is another trust-focused mechanism where awarding the DSA indicates that an archive inspires confidence in its ability to store research data and make it available into the future.

It consists of 16 quality guidelines:

1 The data producer deposits the research data in a data repository with sufficient information for others to assess the scientific and scholarly quality of the research data and compliance with disciplinary and ethical norms.
2 The data producer provides the research data in formats recommended by the data repository.
3 The data producer provides the research data together with the metadata requested by the data repository.
4 The data repository has an explicit mission in the area of digital archiving and promulgates it.
5 The data repository uses due diligence to ensure compliance with legal regulations and contracts including, when applicable, regulations governing the protection of human subjects.

6 The data repository applies documented processes and procedures for managing data storage.

7 The data repository has a plan for long-term preservation of its digital assets.

8 Archiving takes place according to explicit workflows across the data life cycle.

9 The data repository assumes responsibility from the data producers for access and availability of the digital objects.

10 The data repository enables the users to utilize the research data and refer to them.

11 The data repository ensures the integrity of the digital objects and the metadata.

12 The data repository ensures the authenticity of the digital objects and the metadata.

13 The technical infrastructure explicitly supports the tasks and functions described in internationally accepted archival standards like OAIS.

14 The data consumer complies with access regulations set by the data repository.

15 The data consumer conforms to and agrees with any codes of conduct that are generally accepted in higher education and research for the exchange and proper use of knowledge and information.

16 The data consumer respects the applicable licenses of the data repository regarding the use of the research data.

Guidelines from the DSA website, www.datasealofapproval.org

The guidelines identify three types of stakeholder: data producer, data consumer and data archive, with the major focus being on the last of these. DSA compliance is assessed in two stages:

• an online self-assessment tool assists the process, prompting the repository to indicate how it meets each of the 16 guidelines

• a review of this assessment by a peer (either a board member or someone appointed by the board); if successful the DSA is awarded. Again, this decision is based on a measure of the level of trust rather than a more thorough audit or certification process.

DSA-awarded repositories must demonstrate ongoing development in order to maintain their status.

The DSA originated in the Netherlands but is now an international endeavour, with the DSA Board including members belonging to a variety of international data archives from Germany, France, the UK and the USA. The Board is responsible for an ongoing independent review process of DSA assessments and for the DSA's future development.

Plato

Plato (www.ifs.tuwien.ac.at/dp/plato/intro.html) is the Planets Preservation Planning Tool, developed by the EC-funded Planets project. This is more to do with preservation planning than data management planning *per se*, but it does fit with the broad and overarching 'why plan?' discussion.

Plato is pitched at a lower, more technological level than other tools described here. Specifically, it assists repository managers in deciding how and when to perform preservation actions such as migration and emulation by evaluating particular solutions against self-assessed requirements. Plato's aim is to automate these actions as much as possible according to an agreed plan.

Plato is open source software and is available for download from Sourceforge.

Guidance

It would be asking a lot to expect those who are new to data management and curation to come equipped with the plethora of jargon and vocabulary that is already legion. Most of the questions in the DCC's *Checklist for a Data Management Plan* are accompanied by default or generic guidance notes designed to assist in the completion of a plan. Guidance is provided in textual form, often accompanied by hyperlinks to useful resources on the web and originating from the DCC and other authoritative sources. It is intended to be as widely accessible and jargon-free as possible. As with the questions themselves, the guidance notes were crowd sourced from the digital preservation and data curation community. The DMP Online tool, a web-based successor to the Checklist, permits guidance specific to funders, disciplines and institutions to be attached to each question so the user experience is as intuitive and the barriers to uptake as low as possible.

The most mature collaborative relationship that the DCC has in matters pertaining to data management planning is with the UK Data Archive (UKDA). As 'curator of the largest collection of digital data in the social sciences and humanities in the United Kingdom' (www.data-archive.ac.uk), the UKDA is the trusted place of deposit for all research funded by the ESRC. UKDA staff work closely with social science researchers to provide guidance and advice on data management and sharing, with the consequent focus on guidance that is particularly strong on issues of compliance, ethics, anonymization and data sharing.

The case study below has been prepared for inclusion here as an example of one particular aspect of the UKDA guidance service.

Case study
UK Data Archive: helping researchers to share data
Prepared by Veerle Van den Eynden, UK Data Archive, University of Essex

Research funders increasingly require data management planning in research projects, to improve the longevity and quality of research data and make sure data can be shared beyond the primary research. The Economic and Social Research Council (ESRC) is at the forefront of data sharing in the UK and from spring 2011 has required data management and sharing plans as part of all research award applications where new data is being created. This is mandated in its research data policy (ESRC, 2010). A plan should detail planned data management activities, quality assurance and back-up procedures, expected difficulties in data sharing and plans to address them, and ethical measures to enable data sharing, and should allocate responsibilities.

ESRC has a longstanding arrangement with the UK Data Archive as a place of deposit for research data, with award holders required to offer data resulting from research grants to the Archive via the Economic and Social Data Service. The Archive enables data reuse by preserving data and making it available to the research and learning communities.

The UK Data Archive works closely with researchers and provides data management support through online guidance, a printed best practice guide (Van den Eynden et al., 2011) and regular training workshops. Data management support focuses on:

- ethical and legal aspects of data sharing and reuse
- documenting data and metadata
- quality control
- formatting data
- file formats for long-term preservation
- data security and storage
- ownership and data copyright
- roles and responsibilities of data management
- data management planning and costing
- data management strategies for research centres.

During the period 2008–2010 about 300 researchers attended training workshops, 3000 best practice guides were distributed among researchers and the online guidance received 3500 hits each month.

The Archive's guidance is based on expertise gained while working closely with numerous researchers around data management and sharing through services run by the Archive: the Data Support Service of the interdisciplinary Rural Economy and Land Use (RELU) Programme, the Economic and Social Data Service (ESDS) and the Data Management Planning for ESRC Research Data-rich Investments (DMP-ESRC) project. Via these initiatives Archive staff liaise with researchers on how data management and sharing can be addressed in a practical way as an integral part of research practices. Discussions with researchers during events, workshops and meetings have informed the development of the guidance over the years. At the same time the Archive exchanges experiences and expertise with data sharing expert agencies such as the Interuniversity Consortium for Political and Social Research (ICPSR), the Australian National Data Service (ANDS) and the Digital Curation Centre (DCC). Many stakeholders have also provided input into the Archive's published best practice guide.

The Archive also works closely with the ESRC and provided significant input for the development of the 2010 research data policy, which included requirements for data management and sharing plans, ensuring that policy and requirements are in line with researchers' practices. At the same time guidance for researchers completing a data management plan and for peer reviewers evaluating such plans was developed.

More recent collaborative effort between the DCC and UKDA has focused on integrating DMP Online more cleanly with the ESRC application form (the ESRC, in common with the other UK research councils, uses the online joint e-submission form), including the provision of new guidance for researchers and, in the case of peer reviewers, the means to evaluate the quality of these plans. A fresh aspect of this collaboration is the consideration of options for monitoring the way in which plans are put into practice and for measuring the extent to which good data management is being demonstrated. These are components of the planning process that were not included in the first tranche of data management and sharing policies to be published either in the UK or elsewhere. In the longer term, however, it is anticipated that this collaboration between the DCC and ESRC may provide a model for an integrated and comprehensive approach to data management planning across all the UK public funders of research.

Meanwhile, at a local level, numerous research-focused institutions and umbrella organizations have developed web-based data management resources. In the UK those in the vanguard include the University of Edinburgh, one of the first universities to sanction a research data policy (www.ed.ac.uk/is/research-data-policy), and the University of Southampton, which has designed a data management blueprint for export to other institutions (www.southamptondata.org). In the USA the lead has been taken by the research library community, with particular examples to be found at the University of Virginia (www2.lib.virginia.edu/brown/data/plan.html), the Massachusetts Institute of Technology (http://libraries.mit.edu/guides/subjects/data-management) and among the Association of Research Libraries (www.arl.org/rtl/eresearch/escien/nsf/nsfresources).

In the higher education environment, progress is rarely secured on the basis of a top-down decree alone, however formally it is prescribed. Consequently, as our models have demonstrated, it will be vital to the successful deployment of data management planning that the spirit of collaboration embraces policy makers, data practitioners and active researchers in the identification, promulgation and support to effective and advantageous practice.

Conclusion

Data management is a flow, a chain of events with multiple actors representing a variety of stakeholder groups. It is neither necessary nor appropriate for all stakeholders to become experts in every facet of the endeavour, but the planning process provides an opportunity to stake out clearly the roles and responsibilities for each stage of the process and to keep them up to date as requirements change over time. The next chapter provides a discussion of the place of libraries and librarians in setting out appropriate measures for supporting research data management, including proposals for education, training and careers.

Acknowledgements

I am indebted to Alex Ball of the DCC at UKOLN at the University of Bath for the section 'Checklist for a data management plan', which is influenced by the approach taken in his Erasmus Research Institute of Management (ERIM) report, cited above, and to Veerle Van den Eynden of the UK Data Archive at the University of Essex for the case study she prepared specifically for this publication.

References

Ball, A. (2010) *Thematic Analysis of Data Management Plan Tools and Exemplars*, Erasmus Research Institute of Management, http://opus.bath.ac.uk/21278/1/erim6rep100701ab10.pdf.

Blue Ribbon Task Force (2010) *Sustainable Economics for a Digital Planet: ensuring long-term access to digital information, final report of the Blue Ribbon Task Force on sustainable digital preservation and access*, http://brtf.sdsc.edu/biblio/BRTF_Final_Report.pdf.

CCDS (2002) *Reference Model for an Open Archival Information System (OAIS)*, Consultative Committee for Space Data Systems, http://public.ccsds.org/publications/archive/650x0b1.PDF.

Donnelly, M. and Jones, S. (2011) *Checklist for a Data Management Plan v3.0*, Digital Curation Centre, http://dmponline.dcc.ac.uk/system/attachments/8/original/DCC_Checklist_DMP_v3_md_sj.pdf?1300724157.

Donnelly, M., Jones, S. and Pattenden-Fail, J. W. (2010) DMP Online: a demonstration of the Digital Curation Centre's web-based tool for creating, maintaining and exporting data management plans. In Lalmas, M., Jose, J., Rauber, A., Sebastiani, F. and Frommholz, I. (eds), *Research and Advanced Technology for Digital Libraries*, Springer, 530–33.

ESRC (2010) *Research Data Policy*, Economic and Social Research Council, www.esrc.ac.uk/_images/Research_Data_Policy_2010_tcm8-4595.pdf.

Harvey, R. (2010) *Digital Curation: a how-to-do-it manual*, Facet Publishing.

Higgins, S. (2008) The DCC Curation Lifecycle Model, *International Journal of Digital Curation*, **3** (1), www.ijdc.net/index.php/ijdc/article/view/69/48.

Jones, S. (2008, rev. 2011) *Summary Of UK Research Funders' Expectations for the Content of Data Management and Sharing Plans*, www.dcc.ac.uk/webfm_send/358.

Jones, S. (2009, updated 2011) *Overview of Funders' Data Policies*, Digital Curation Centre, www.dcc.ac.uk/resources/policy-and-legal/overview-funders-data-policies.

Lyon, L. (2007) *Dealing with Data: roles, rights, responsibilities and relationships – Consultancy Report*, www.ukoln.ac.uk/ukoln/staff/e.j.lyon/reports/dealing with data report-final.pdf.

National Science Foundation (2010) *Dissemination and Sharing of Research Results: NSF Data Management Plan Requirements,* www.nsf.gov/bfa/dias/policy/dmp.jsp.

RCUK (2011) *Common Principles on Data Policy,* Research Councils UK, www.rcuk.ac.uk/research/Pages/DataPolicy.aspx

Van den Eynden, V., Corti, L., Woollard, M., Bishop, L. and Horton, L. (2011) *Managing and Sharing Data: best practice for researchers,* 3rd edn, UK Data Archive, University of Essex, www.data-archive.ac.uk/media/2894/managingsharing.pdf.

CHAPTER 6

Roles and responsibilities: libraries, librarians and data

Sheila Corrall

E-science has the potential to be transformational within research libraries by impacting their operations, functions, and possibly even their mission.

Lougee et al., 2007, 3

Introduction

The management of the research data generated by e-science and e-research has replaced open access to scholarly publications as the hot topic on the academic library and information services agenda. National and international bodies have issued a succession of reports, policies and guidance on dealing with the 'data deluge' that have flagged the need for concerted action by research organizations. Government and other official publications have often identified roles for library and information professionals in managing data alongside the other information and knowledge resources that libraries manage or provide for their communities. Professional associations in the library world have responded positively to such suggestions and university librarians are now starting to develop services or get involved in projects to explore what libraries can do to support researchers in meeting new requirements of funding agencies to facilitate access to their data.

Managing research data continues to be an emergent area of activity where responsibilities and practices within libraries are generally not yet firmly established, especially in the UK. However, there have been significant developments within the past few years, particularly in the USA, as a result of nationally funded project work and new requirements of research funding agencies for data management plans to be submitted with grant applications. Many libraries have seized these opportunities to form new partnerships and develop new services, which has in turn generated a growing body of literature on the subject offering insights and pointers for practitioners in other countries. In this chapter, we review the opportunities offered and the challenges presented for libraries and librarians in the research data arena, with particular reference to published reports and case studies of emerging practice, supplemented by evidence from university and library websites.

Some commentators have questioned whether library staff have the knowledge and skills needed to fulfil the roles suggested, so we look specifically at connections between research data management and established library roles and responsibilities to explore whether research data management represents another incremental step in professional practice or a true paradigm shift in collection development and service delivery requiring fundamental rethinking of roles, responsibilities and competencies to create 'next-generation librarianship', drawing where possible on the experiences and opinions of practitioners already involved in the field. Finally, we discuss professional education and continuing development needs for library engagement with research data, again referring particularly to initiatives already taken in the USA.

The case for library engagement

Several expert commentators in the information field have argued that the problems faced by institutions in managing research data offer an important and attractive opportunity for libraries to redefine their role in supporting research and to develop closer relationships with their research community. Hey and Hey (2006, 526) suggest that if librarians can respond effectively to the challenge, 'the e-Science revolution will put libraries and repositories centre stage in the development of the next generation research infrastructure'. Swan and Brown (2008, 2) in their report on workforce development for the UK Joint Information Systems Committee similarly see data management as a strategic issue for libraries and librarians:

> The role of the library in data-intensive research is important and a strategic repositioning of the library with respect to research support is now appropriate. We see three main potential roles for the library: increasing data-awareness amongst researchers; providing archiving and preservation services for data within the institution through institutional repositories; and developing a new professional strand of practice in the form of data librarianship.

Other reports have mentioned library involvement in managing research data, but often only in general terms or grouping librarians with other professionals without differentiating their respective roles. For example, the US National Science Board report *Long-Lived Digital Data Collections* categorizes librarians along with several other specialists (information and computer scientists, database and software engineers and programmers, disciplinary experts, curators and expert annotators, archivists) as 'data scientists' (NSB, 2005, 27). The NSF (2007, 38) also suggested that professional education for careers in data management and curation may need 'new, hybrid degree programs that marry the study of library science with a scientific discipline'.

Within the library world, the US Association of Research Libraries (ARL) has actively promoted the role of libraries in data management and e-science through a succession of reports on the subject that envisage a significantly expanded role in digital data stewardship for research libraries in collaboration with other stakeholders. Key themes highlighted by the ARL include the importance of partnerships, the challenge of working across disciplinary and institutional cultures and the need for education and outreach (Friedlander and Adler, 2006; Lougee et al., 2007). A survey in 2009 revealed overall enthusiasm among ARL members for new roles in the academic research process and identified 21 libraries (from 57 replies) already providing infrastructure or support services for e-science, with another 23 planning to do so. The findings confirmed the importance of collaboration, but also highlighted the relevance of library and information science (LIS) expertise (Soehner et al., 2010).

Within the UK, data-related library activity is largely represented by the local data libraries and support services established at the Universities of Edinburgh and Oxford in the 1980s and the London School of Economics in the 1990s, whose focus has been on social science data and geographical information systems (Macdonald and Martinez, 2005). There have been some studies exploring national and local approaches to the management of research data, including a feasibility study for a national research data management service instigated by Research Libraries UK and investigations of the use of repository technologies for data curation (Lewis, 2010; MacDonald and Uribe, 2008; Martinez-Uribe, 2007). A few libraries have been involved in data management projects funded by the Joint Information Systems Committee (JISC), such as the Institutional Data Management Blueprint at the University of Southampton (Takeda, 2010). There has also been significant debate on the roles of librarians and other stakeholders in the management of research data and on their skills, training and development needs (Lewis, 2010; Lyon, 2007; Pryor and Donnelly, 2009; Swan and Brown, 2008).

A more recent ARL report offers a bolder vision of new roles in digital curation, prefaced by the assertion that 'the strongest future for research libraries is one in which multi-institutional collaborations achieve evolvable cyberinfrastructures and services for digital curation' (Walters and Skinner, 2011, 5). This report anticipates a shift away from the traditional public (front-of-house) and technical (back-of-house) service mindset towards 'the trio of strong infrastructures, content, and services', where infrastructure is used to mean not only facilities and technologies, but also human expertise (Walters and Skinner, 2011, 5–6). These are the 'new roles' Walters and Skinner (2011) propose for research librarians in digital curation:

- acquisitions and rights advisers
- teachers and instructional partners in learning spaces
- observers and anthropologists of information users and producers
- systems builders
- content producers and disseminators
- organizational designers
- collaborative network creators and participants.

Some of these roles look novel, but others are more familiar, with the novelty derived from the context, rather than the focus of the role.

Data management and library practice

The debate about library involvement in data management has been conducted at both strategic and operational levels. Lewis (2010, 145) has previously argued that 'data from academic research projects represents an integral part of the global research knowledge base, and so managing it should be a natural extension of the university library's current role in providing access to the published part of that knowledge base', while also noting 'the scale of the challenge in terms of infrastructure, skills and culture' (Lewis, 2010, 145). Engaging with a completely new area of practice is clearly a challenging prospect, irrespective of the strategic case for getting involved, especially at a time when library budgets worldwide are under acute and continuing pressure as a result of the global economic downturn (Harper and Corrall, 2011; Nicholas et al., 2010). However, even though research datasets are in several ways very different from other library resources, practitioners working in the area have identified strong links and significant overlaps with existing library interests and activities.

First, the open data movement associated with e-science and e-research in general is the natural culmination of the open access movement, open source software and open standards, which all support the traditional commitment of libraries to the free flow of information and ideas (Corrado, 2005; Lougee et al., 2007; Macdonald and Uribe, 2008; Willinsky, 2005). Librarians are already active proponents of open access, typically taking the lead in establishing and developing institutional repositories within their universities, generally in collaboration with computing or IT services and other units (Rieh et al., 2007). The International Federation of Library Associations and Institutions (IFLA, 2011) has endorsed open access as an 'essential issue' within its information agenda, highlighting the work already done by librarians in building infrastructure, creating user-friendly services, educating research stakeholders, helping with deposit of outputs and securing long-term access.

Significantly, the IFLA statement explicitly includes 'research data curation and sharing' among the open access support provided by librarians (IFLA, 2011, 2). Walters (2009, 84) argues that data curation programmes represent a 'robust growth trajectory' for library institutional repository initiatives, which was the case for Georgia Tech Library and Information Center. Interestingly, Walters (2009) emphasizes that the programme initiated at Georgia Tech, and similar 'entrepreneurial steps' taken by like-minded colleagues at six peer organizations in the USA (Johns Hopkins University, University of California-San Diego, University of Illinois at Urbana-Champaign, University of Michigan, Cornell University and Massachusetts Institute of Technology) have essentially been bottom-up initiatives where individual library and technology professionals have reached out to faculty and research centres 'without the benefit of national mandates and high-level university policies'.

Secondly, the characterization of e-science as 'a new mode of 'collection-based' research' (Berman et al., 2002, 37) or 'collection-based science' (Beagrie, 2006, 5) also suggests a strong connection with library practice. Although institutional repositories are often established as distinct digital library or information management initiatives, Genoni (2004) argues that the management of repository content is essentially a collection management issue. Witt (2008) highlights the relevance for data curation of library expertise in classification and description through cataloguing and metadata, as well as experience in selecting, deselecting and presenting information in an appropriate context. He also notes that many research libraries have special collections staff with expertise in the appraisal and preservation of primary source material. He similarly sees parallels between new roles in managing research data and established responsibilities for preserving and curating special collections, suggesting that 'scientific datasets may be thought of as the "special collections" of the digital age'.

Similarly, the ARL E-Science Task Force notes that the dual focus of data curation on preservation and active management for access fits well with the mission and concerns of research libraries (Lougee et al., 2007). The ARL Task Force has also argued that library expertise in developing systems and standards for digital content and associated services can be exploited to create discovery and management systems for digital data, pointing to library experience with institutional and disciplinary repositories, integration and interoperability tools, and business and technical aspects of long-term archiving, though the report also points out that existing expertise and infrastructure 'will be seriously stretched by the new, more complex demands of e-science' (Lougee et al., 2007, 6). Salo (2010) usefully draws out both similarities and differences in the infrastructure (technological and human) needed to manage research data, warning against naïve re-purposing of systems and staff, but concluding positively: 'None of the challenges presented herein should discourage librarians from engaging with the research data challenge. Our unique expertise in metadata, digital preservation, public service, and technology translation will serve researchers well, as will our sturdy common sense and the domain expertise of our subject librarians.'

Education and training for specialist and non-specialist users of datasets is a recurring theme of official reports on digital data collections. The NSB (2005, 27) assigned responsibility to data scientists (including information scientists, librarians and archivists) for 'education and outreach programs that make the benefits of data collections and digital information science available to the broadest possible range of researchers, educators, students, and the general public'. Carlson et al. (2011, 630) suggest that the widespread involvement of academic libraries in information literacy education makes the development of an educational role in data management and curation 'a logical entry point into increasing libraries' role in supporting e-research' and Gabridge (2009, 17) similarly suggests that subject liaison librarians can easily extend their instruction roles 'to help student researchers understand what to do with their data and increase their awareness of library resources'.

Data-related reference and consultation services are also seen as 'a natural fit for subject librarians who provide similar services for other types of information' (Soehner et al., 2010, 16). Examples mentioned include identifying datasets to meet student or faculty needs, providing access to data resources and advising researchers on current standards for organization of data in specific subject areas, in addition to help with the specific task of developing data management plans and more general awareness raising through creation of special websites to describe services available. Recent policy decisions by research funding bodies to require researchers to submit plans for data management and sharing with their grant applications have given librarians a timely opportunity to offer information on funders' requirements and assistance with constructing a plan. The ARL has provided a set of web pages to help librarians make sense of the new National Science Foundation (NSF) requirement (Hswe and Holt, 2010). The UK Digital Curation Centre (DCC) has also provided a comprehensive set of resources for data management planning, which includes a summary of UK funders' data plan requirements, in addition to a checklist, guidance, examples and a web-based planning tool (DCC, 2010).

Strategies for engaging with data

Our review has shown how the management of research data resonates with library values (such as open access) and can be related to current operations and professional practices in several areas, including institutional repositories, collection management, systems development, information literacy and reference services. We have also pointed out a significant opportunity for librarians to offer valuable support for research in their institutions, by assisting investigators with data management planning and thus help them fulfil new requirements of funders to submit plans for data sharing with their grant proposals. Libraries that have not yet engaged with the research data agenda need to review possible areas of activity and decide where investment of effort is likely to have the most benefit for their particular institution, taking into account the local and national context. Working in partnership with other campus agencies to determine where to begin is recommended, notably computing and technology services, research offices and those responsible for research governance (such as a pro-vice chancellor or vice provost for research).

Lewis (2010, 154) previously suggested nine areas of strategic, tactical and operational engagement in research data management, grouped in a pyramid for ease of reference. We can now add data collection development as another area of activity discussed in recent library literature (Newton et al., 2010). Figure 6.1 shows the research data management pyramid for libraries supported by collection development and data resource management as a base layer of activity, represented here by the key processes of identifying, selecting, describing, preserving and presenting data resources for use. This list does not cover the complete set of 'full lifecycle', 'sequential' and 'occasional' actions specified by the DCC Curation Lifecycle Model (Higgins, 2008), which is often used to define the work involved in managing research data (Harvey, 2010; Lewis, 2010),

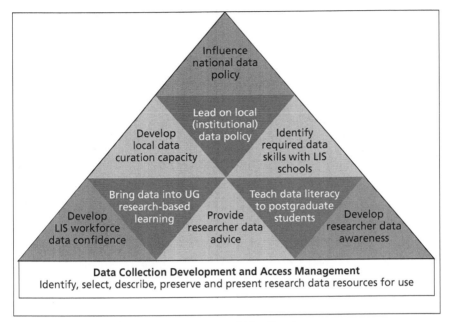

Figure 6.1 *Research data management pyramid for libraries*

but concentrates instead on areas where librarians already have skills and expertise that can be applied to research data curation (Witt, 2008).

Libraries engaging with research data for the first time can learn from the experiences and services of pioneers in the field, discussed in the growing body of academic and professional literature on the subject and also described on their institutional web pages. The websites of the ARL and DCC offer additional guidance. We highlight some prominent examples here.

Influence national data policy

Librarians in the USA have worked through the ARL to influence national developments in research data management. For example, the NSF not only funded the workshop organized by the ARL on long-term stewardship of digital datasets (Friedlander and Adler, 2006), but has also acted on key recommendations, by funding data curation projects involving libraries working in partnership with other stakeholders and by requiring data management plans to be included in grant proposals. In Canada, the research library community is strongly represented on the Government's Research Data Strategy Working Group (Government of Canada, 2011) and similarly in Australia, senior members of the library community have been appointed to the Steering Committee of the Australian National Data Service (ANDS, 2011). The European Union High Level Expert Group on Scientific Data also included the Head

Librarian of CERN, the European Organization for Nuclear Research, among its members (HLG, 2010).

Lead on local (institutional) data policy

Library directors and other senior library staff have a key role to play in helping senior administrators to understand the nature and importance of the data management challenge and develop an appropriate and coherent response. This will typically mean working with institutional research committees and other senior officers to achieve a joined-up approach. It may involve formulating a data management policy and/or making a business case for investment in research data management. For example, the University of Edinburgh has developed a policy statement on research data management, which is supported by a background document that includes links to a checklist and advice on data management planning available from the Information Services website (University of Edinburgh, 2011). Edinburgh's policy on management of research data was developed by a research data management working group convened by the Director of Library and Collections.

Develop local data curation capacity

Several libraries in the USA have used involvement in institutional repository management as the basis for exploring data curation via dataset deposit, notably Purdue University (Witt, 2008) and Georgia Tech (Walters, 2009), although extending repository services from publications to datasets is easier to conceptualize than to achieve technically (Salo, 2010). Financing scalable storage is another challenge: Georgia Tech and Purdue are looking at cost-recovery models in collaboration with their campus technology services. Three UK universities have also explored dataset repository development via the Data Information Specialists Committee UK (DISC-UK) DataShare project, experimenting with different software platforms (DSpace, ePrints and Fedora) and different architectures, with two incorporating datasets in their publications repository, the third developing a separate interoperable repository (Rice, 2009). The DataShare team has produced a comprehensive guide based on experience and research to inform local decision making and planning for expansion of repository services (Green et al., 2009).

Identify required data skills with LIS schools

National and international reports on research data management have flagged the need for development of education and training programmes for the professionals expected to take on responsibility for managing research data in their institutions (NSF, 2007; HLG, 2010). Swan and Brown (2008, 30) recommended that the UK research library community work with other stakeholders 'to develop a curriculum that ensures a suitable supply of librarians skilled in data handling', sensibly recognizing that educators need a steer from employers here on curriculum content and market demand. In the USA, a recommendation from ARL that the NSF and the Institute of Museum and Library Studies (IMLS) should fund training to prepare current and future library and information professionals for credible roles in data stewardship (Friedlander and Adler, 2006) has been followed through in a succession of innovative development projects funded by IMLS (Hank and Davidson, 2009; Ray, 2009). We discuss education and training more fully later in the chapter.

Develop LIS workforce data confidence

A survey of the UK academic library sector in autumn 2006 commissioned by a CURL and SCONUL task force on e-research found poor awareness of activities in the field among academic liaison and subject librarians, apart from institutional repository developments (Martinez, 2007). Research data have arguably gained a higher profile recently in the library community as a result of reports and events sponsored by the JISC and DCC, in addition to publications on the subject aimed at library practitioners (Lewis, 2010; Macdonald and Uribe, 2008; Salo, 2010; Westra, 2010), recommended readings on e-science (Szigeti and Wheeler, 2011) and a useful webliography on data curation, covering email lists, journals, guidelines, reports, organizations, directories, standards and software (Westra et al., 2010). The New England eScience Portal for Librarians is another useful educational resource offering overviews and primers (University of Massachusetts, 2011). However, managers may need to point library staff towards such sources to help them update their knowledge and gain the confidence needed to hold conversations on the subject with researchers.

Bring data into undergraduate research-based learning

American and European reports have called for data handling to be embedded in university and school curricula to support public understanding and participation in science (HLG, 2010; NSB, 2005). Carlson et al. (2011) argue that librarians should develop a data information literacy curriculum, working with disciplinary faculty to define the skill sets needed and to teach the skills identified. Ogburn (2010, 244) urges librarians to provide programmes for scientists and non-scientists 'that teach the interpretation of data and visual representations of research findings'. Many academic libraries provide specialist data resources and services to support research and teaching in social science disciplines (Czarnocki and Khouri, 2004; Read, 2007) and some have developed courses for undergraduates in the use of statistical data resources (Stephenson and Caravello, 2007). Extending provision to enable undergraduates to work with real research data fits well with problem-based and inquiry-based learning pedagogies favoured by research universities.

MacMillan (2010) provides a detailed case study showing how genetic data resources were incorporated into a third-year information literacy lab at Calgary University that simulated the working methods of experienced researchers. A structured step-by-step exercise based on tool-specific modules provided demonstration, practice and discussion of a set of resources, progressing from online encyclopedias and journal databases through Google Patents to gene and protein databanks and tools, which enabled the liaison librarian to highlight synergies and relationships among key resources. Macmillan (2010) argues that authentic assignments designed in collaboration with discipline faculty are the best way to foster student familiarity with key tools in the field and that 'faculty appreciate library partners who understand the structures of information in the discipline that complement more traditional bibliographic tools'. He provides full details of the questions set for each task and invites other librarians to use his resources to develop their undergraduate teaching.

Carlson et al. (2011, 633) use the term 'data information literacy' to distinguish their conception of the competencies needed for e-research from what they see as narrower prior concepts of literacy, explaining that their concept 'merges the concepts of researcher-as-producer and researcher-as-consumer of data products' and 'builds upon and reintegrates data, statistical, information, and science data literacy into an emerging skill set'. Based on interviews with research faculty at two universities, assessments of advanced undergraduate and graduate students on a geoinformatics course at Purdue, and comparison with the ACRL (2000) *Information Literacy Competency Standards for Higher Education*, they propose a set of thematically arranged core competencies as generic educational objectives for a data information literacy programme. They note that the balance between curriculum components and also between specific content elements will vary for different disciplines. Each theme consists of a heading supported by a description in two or more sentences (Carlson et al., 2011, 652–53). These are the 12 thematic headings:

- databases and data formats
- discovery and acquisition of data
- data management and organization
- data conversion and interoperability
- quality assurance
- metadata
- data curation and reuse
- cultures of practice
- data preservation
- data analysis
- data visualization
- ethics, including citation of data.

Teach data literacy to postgraduate students

Most UK university libraries have either formal or informal involvement in research skills training for postgraduate students, though few currently cover research data management (RIN, 2008). Postgraduate research training is a priority area for library efforts in supporting the management of research data as it presents an important opportunity to influence the behaviour of future researchers by developing their understanding of the generation, description, preservation, storage and use of data in line with good ethical and technical practice. UK information literacy practitioners have recognized the need to develop their teaching in this direction and have engaged with the postgraduate training agenda at a national level by influencing the information and data literacy content of the Researcher Development Framework, the new national competency tool for researchers (Vitae, 2010), and by developing a research lens that specifies data-related understanding and abilities for the revised and expanded version of the *Seven Pillars of Information Literacy* (SCONUL, 2011).

The Seven Pillars model is the most widely used information literacy framework in the UK and has been adopted by librarians and teachers around the world to support information skills training and information literacy development. The new format enables more detailed specification of information literacy attributes with explicit tailoring to the needs of different groups of information users. The introductory section of the research lens explains that information literacy 'encompasses concepts such as...data curation and data management' (SCONUL, 2011, 3). These are examples of data-related abilities included under each of the *Seven Pillars*:

- Identify – recognize a need for information and data to achieve a specific end and define limits to the information need.
- Scope – identify which types of information (e.g. data, people, videos, published information) will best meet the need.
- Plan – select the most appropriate search tools (people, search engines, databases and so on) and data collection techniques.
- Gather – access full text information, both print and digital, read and download online material and data.
- Evaluate – assess the credibility of the data gathered.
- Manage – identify data curation opportunities to ensure that research data is ethically stored for reuse in other projects.
- Present – see connections between sections of own data and the literature.

Provide researcher data advice

Many US librarians have extended their reference and consultation services to offer information and advice on issues related to data management, often building on existing offerings related to open access and other aspects of scholarly communication, including copyright and intellectual property, metadata and technical standards, data archiving and preservation. Several libraries provide curation services jointly with supercomputer or research computing centres, with the computer centre providing computation, storage and back-up services (for example, Cornell University and University of California-San Diego). Research data services for digital curation at the University of Wisconsin-Madison are provided by 'a group of librarians, IT staff, and graduate students in the School of Library and Information Studies' (UW-Madison, 2011a). Figure 6.2 shows the description of service offerings presented on the University of Wisconsin-Madison website.

Our services

All our services are free to UW-Madison faculty, researchers, staff, and graduate students.

Data management plan help
- We can help draft a plan to meet requirements from NSF and other funders.
- We can also review your plan and suggest improvements.

Consultations
- Data workflow and process improvement in your department, research unit, or laboratory.
- File-format and metadata standards that fit your research and your community.
- Digital preservation and archival concepts, to help you avoid losing your work.
- Advice on data sharing and reuse rights, to maximize your influence and credit.
- Database design advice and data modeling suggestions to get the most from your data.

Training and education
- We will train your trainers in data-management best practices.
- We also train you and your lab, customizing our approach to what you want to accomplish.
- We come to research-methods courses to train the next generation of researchers.
- We bring our expertise to your symposium, brown-bag, or meeting.

Referrals
- Storage and backup solutions, on campus and off.
- Data-security experts, particularly in the Office of Campus Information Security.

See something you need? Fill out the form below and we'll be in touch.

Figure 6.2 *Research Data Services at UW-Madison (UW-Madison, 2011b)*

Hswe and Holt (2011) report a huge surge of library activity around data management planning in the wake of the announced NSF requirement, in the form of web pages, templates, tutorials, webinars and workshops, though some libraries were already providing services in this area before the announcement. In a few cases, library data management planning web pages consist entirely of links to resources on other institution's websites, showing how easy it is now for libraries to develop a web presence in this area. Notable examples of US data management planning resources include:

- MIT Libraries' web page on data management plans (part of a set of a pages on data management and publishing), which lists recommended components for plans and provides links to external web-based resources, as well as offering an email address for help (MIT, 2011)

- University of Connecticut Libraries' web page on data management plans for grant funded projects (part of a scholarly communications website), which also lists typical elements of plans, but at a more detailed level, again providing links to additional web resources (University of Connecticut, 2011)

- Purdue Libraries' Data Management Plan Self-Assessment Questionnaire, which was developed by adapting data collection and curation tools already developed, and contains 31 questions under seven headings: Describing the research data, Data Standards, Metadata Standards, Data Sharing, Data Access, Intellectual Property and Re-Use, Data Archiving and Preservation (Purdue University Libraries, 2011)

- Duke University Libraries' LibGuide on research data planning, which is presented in the same format as their subject-based resource guides, enabling users either to navigate a comprehensive set of web pages to find specific information or to print the complete guide as a single document (Denniston, Herndon and Mangiafico, 2011).

Many other libraries have used the standard LibGuide template to provide guidance on data management planning and other data-related matters, for example on data curation and archiving or on finding data resources; other guides in this format provided by Duke University Libraries include *Scientific Data Repositories and Datasets* (Gray, 2011).

Develop researcher data awareness

In addition to providing specific information and advice, libraries can play an important role in general awareness-raising and advocacy around data management for their research communities, whose level of understanding and interest is likely to vary across campus. Shearer and Argáez (2010) advise that even general messages should ideally be tailored to particular groups, because of the different disciplinary cultures that often make the issues and challenges of data stewardship discipline-specific. Librarians with limited knowledge and experience of data management can draw on the array of web-based resources now available from centres of expertise to support this work, such as the DCC's series of introductory briefing papers and the Australian National Data Service (ANDS) awareness guides, as well as reviewing material on other libraries' websites.

Develop and manage access to data collections

Traditional conceptions of a library collection have been expanded over the past three decades to incorporate tangible physical and intangible digital objects that may be stored locally or remotely and owned by the library as a result of purchase, borrowed or managed by the library on behalf of others, accessed by library members under licence or selected for promotion to users from public domain resources (ARL, 2002; Gorman, 2000). Digital repositories and data resources (deposited in remote disciplinary or local institutional repositories) are recognized as part of this framework (Lynch, 2003), which has been variously depicted in concentric circles (Lee, 2003, 432) or a 'collections grid' (Dempsey, 2003, 124). Modern collection development is less about acquiring and hosting materials and more about negotiating and facilitating access to resources, but selecting and describing the information sources offered to users are still key activities for the library in the 21st century (Brophy, 2007).

Collection development and access management for data resources thus potentially includes building local data collections (which may be hosted by the library or stored in other institutional locations) and providing access to remote publicly available free, licensed or subscription-based data products and services. Many libraries already have experience of developing collections of externally sourced data that can inform policy and practice for data collection development based on locally produced datasets, for example through subscribing to statistical series (in hard copy and electronic services) and developing geospatial data collections based on government, commercial or academic data (Florance, 2006; Humphrey and Hamilton, 2004). The tasks involved in building locally and externally sourced collections are similar, such as identifying potential material for selection and describing the chosen resources for presentation to users; but the procedures are different, requiring application of knowledge and skills in new ways and/or development of new skills (Newton et al., 2010).

Several authors have suggested that libraries can play a particularly valuable role in collecting and archiving smaller-scale datasets generated by research groups or individual academics whose disciplines lack national or international repository infrastructure (Hey and Hey, 2006; Luce, 2008). Commentators also stress the need for librarians to reach out to academics proactively and become involved as partners 'in the early planning and data-modeling phases of eResearch' (Luce, 2008, 46) to ensure lifecycle management of data so that they can be preserved and used. Borgman also argues that 'early engagement is key to taking a temporal approach' and the need to reconfigure library organizations 'from being a reading room to a full research center' (2010, 4). As Newton et al. (2010) point out, methods such as publisher catalogues and feeds cannot be used to identify potential data acquisitions, so data selectors need to turn instead to faculty research profiles and grant announcements from academic departments and research offices.

The DCC and ANDS have provided a 'working level' guide to the appraisal and selection of research data for curation, which explicitly identifies a major role for information professionals in formulating a policy for their institutions (Whyte and Wilson, 2010). The guide identifies seven general criteria for assessing the value of a dataset, which are then elaborated as a checklist of bullet points under a series of questions. Newton et al. (2010, 67) provide a real-world example in a table of 'collection criteria' with supporting rationale developed at Purdue University Libraries, covering similar points, but adding an additional requirement for the data to have an 'Institutional association', defined as 'a clear institutional connection to Purdue University'. This point is more specific than Whyte and Wilson's (2010) 'Relevance to mission', a requirement that is covered separately by Purdue under the heading 'Value to Purdue's collection', which refers explicitly to the institution's 'research, teaching, and discovery missions'. Table 6.1 compares the two sets of criteria.

Table 6.1 *Comparison of the selection criteria used by DCC and ANDS and Purdue University Libraries for data collections*	
DCC and ANDS (Whyte and Wilson, 2010)	Purdue University Libraries (Newton et al., 2010)
	Institutional association
1 Relevance to mission	Value to Purdue's collection
2 Scientific or historical value	Value to research or education generally
3 Uniqueness	Uniqueness and availability of the data
4 Potential for redistribution	Degree of restrictions placed on the data
5 Non-replicability	Format of the data
6 Economic case	Cost
7 Full documentation	Condition of the data and its documentation

At a practical level, several libraries report the use of 'data interviews' to identify datasets for curation (Walters, 2009; Witt, 2008), which can be seen as an upstream re-purposing of the traditional library reference interview according to the process and skills used. Practitioners at Purdue University Libraries have devised a set of questions (displayed on a poster) that can be used by subject or liaison librarians to interview researchers and explore the suitability of a dataset for adding to the library or institutional collection. Witt and Carlson (2007) argue that the process of evaluating research datasets for selection as information assets and exploring the infrastructure and services needed for their preservation and access is similar to traditional collection development practices, although there are obviously differences in the formats of the material being considered and also its status that make the process more complicated, hence their suggestion that an interview is an effective method for identifying and selecting potential additions to stock. These are the interview questions for data selection in collection development (Witt and Carlson, 2007), explained in more detail on their poster:

1. What is the story of the data?
2. What form and format are the data in?
3. What is the expected lifespan of the dataset?
4. How could the data be used, reused, and re-purposed?
5. How large is the dataset, and what is its rate of growth?
6. Who are the potential audiences for the data?
7. Who owns the data?

8. Does the dataset include any sensitive information?

9. What publications or discoveries have resulted from the data?

10. How should the data be made accessible?

These questions may lead on to more specific supplementary questions, notably on the potential uses and audiences for the data, which are identified as primary selection criteria for datasets to be added to a library collection (Witt and Carlson, 2007). The Purdue team has also provided comprehensive step-by-step guidance on conducting data interviews in an 'Interviewer's Manual' and an 'Interview Worksheet' (for completion by the interviewee) as part of their Data Curation Profiles Toolkit, which can be downloaded from the Data Curation Profiles Community website (Purdue University Libraries, 2010). The tools were developed as a result of a project investigating 'Which researchers are willing to share data, when, with whom, and under what conditions?' carried out by the Libraries with the Graduate School of Library and Information Science at the University of Illinois at Urbana-Champaign with funding from IMLS, which has also funded promotion and development of the toolkit through a national programme of training and evaluation for library and information professionals.

Professional education for data management

As research data become an increasingly important part of the information landscape and an essential dimension of the knowledge base supporting not only future research but also learning, teaching and evidence-based policy and practice, library and information professionals in all sectors must be prepared to facilitate access to various types of datasets, irrespective of the role played by their own library or other information organization in managing research data. Providers of professional education for library and information specialists have a key role to play here as part of their ongoing responsibility to ensure that the content of their programmes, courses and modules is continually reviewed and updated to anticipate change and reflect developments in the service environment. Education and training for data-related library activities needs to be provided for both new professionals and experienced practitioners to enable libraries to fulfil their potential and also to ensure that institutions do not assign responsibilities to others who have relevant subject expertise and/or technology know-how, but lack the informational, managerial and personal abilities that are essential to apply the desired specialist competencies successfully.

Many postgraduate LIS programmes include units on digital libraries and/or digital technologies as distinct elements of their curricula (Ray, 2009), but others have simply embedded digital developments into existing courses. Existing provision has been criticized for its rudimentary treatment of theoretical and practical aspects (Varalakshmi, 2009) and insufficient opportunities for hands-on practice (Dahlstrom and Doracic, 2009). Current coverage of data management and digital curation in postgraduate curricula is limited and uneven across the sector. Within the UK,

Loughborough University is the only information science department offering an elective course in digital curation as part of a postgraduate library programme, though there is more coverage of digital curation and preservation in other types of programmes, such as those in records management at the University of Dundee, information management at the University of Glasgow and the digital asset management at King's College, London (Pryor and Donnelly, 2009).

Provision in the USA is more extensive, where many grants from the IMLS over the past five years have enabled LIS schools to develop and launch new specialized postgraduate courses and concentrations (pathways) that can be taken as part of or an add-on to standard Masters' programmes (Hank and Davidson, 2009; Ray, 2009). These are some notable examples of initiatives funded by IMLS covering professional preparation and continuing education programmes:

- The University of North Carolina at Chapel Hill School of Information and Library Science *DigCCurr* project has developed an openly accessible graduate level curriculum to prepare master's students for work in digital curation and an international doctoral curriculum to prepare future faculty to teach and research in the field (Hank and Davidson, 2009). The objective was to 'build modules around topics, rather than construct entire courses, so that faculty can develop their own classes using the modules, and students can more easily develop courses of study around their own interests' (Ray, 2009, 364). The project also included the development and delivery of annual, multi-stage training institutes (five days followed by two days six months later) for professionals already working in the area, aiming to 'build an international community of digital curation practitioners', as well as developing their knowledge and skills. The 2010 Institute attracted 33 participants from academic libraries and archives, non-profit consortiums and corporations, government archives and public libraries (Costello and Brown, 2010).

- The University of Illinois at Urbana-Champaign Graduate School of Library and Information Science has developed a Data Curation Education Program (DCEP) as a four-course concentration (a designated pathway) within its existing MS in LIS. In addition to required courses on data curation, digital preservation and systems analysis, DCEP includes a period of field experience or internship, emphasizing the role of experiential learning (Ray, 2009). An initial focus on science data curation was later expanded to cover the humanities and the project also included delivery of a week-long summer in-service training institute in humanities data curation for 24 established professionals, which attracted an interesting mix of academic librarians that included subject or area specialists, cataloguing or metadata librarians, digital library or content specialists and data librarians. The Institute was over-subscribed and generated requests for additional in-service education adapted to specific roles and at different levels (Renear et al., 2010).

- The University of Michigan School of Information has established ten 360-hour summer internships at organizations with strong digital curation programmes for students taking a new preservation of information (PI) specialization within its MS in information. The PI specialization offers ten courses, in addition to the internship and a doctoral-level seminar on data curation (available to advanced master's students). The internship design was 'based on a cognitive apprenticeship model with the goal of strengthening each student's ability to think like a digital curator'. The funding also enabled the creation of a special internship course, practical engagement workshop in digital preservation, to provide instruction related to the students' projects, including organizational skills. Although the PI specialization originated as an alternative concentration to archives and records management (ARM), students may take it in addition to either the ARM or LIS specialization, which illustrates the growing convergence of interests among different professional groups (Yakel et al., 2011, 30).
- The University of Arizona School of Information Resources and Library Science has developed an online six-course graduate certificate in digital information management in partnership with the Arizona State Library, Archives and Public Records. DigIn aims to provide an interdisciplinary learning experience to prepare librarians, archivists, records managers, software developers, systems administrators and science data managers for 'boundary-spanning, technology-intensive roles as collection managers in their respective professional communities'. Although it has a 'strong hands-on element' that is intended to promote technical skills, its declared focus is not on specific technologies *per se*, but rather on 'technological and systems thinking' for 'technological fluency', with an emphasis on 'the learning skills needed to evaluate and work effectively with new technologies as they emerge'. The final course is a semester-long period of field experience working on a capstone project in an organization supervised by a practitioner (Fulton et al., 2011, 96–98).
- Syracuse University School of Information Studies has developed an e-science librarianship specialization within its MS in LIS in partnership with Cornell University Library to train students with a science or technical background as a new generation of 'eScience Librarians'. The digital curation curriculum for the eSLib project builds on work done in other projects, but emphasizes the management and preservation of science-related information. The required courses include scientific data management, cyberinfrastructure and scientific collaboration, database systems, metadata and data services (capstone). The eSLib Fellows are paired with library mentors and participate in special events and regular working group sessions at the Library. They are also involved in small scale research projects with Syracuse researchers and librarians, and in addition benefit from paid work experience, a paid summer internship and funded travel to various e-science-related conferences and events (Qin et al., 2010; Syracuse University, 2010).

Key issues in data management education

Despite the noticeable diversity in provision, some common themes emerge from published accounts of curriculum development for data management and curation. First, the importance of emphasizing digital lifecycle stages in the core curriculum is often mentioned as one of the key factors differentiating management and curation of digital data from stewardship of legacy library materials (Gregory and Guss, 2010). This is evident in the way that the DCC Curation Lifecycle Model (Higgins, 2008) has been used as a framework for instruction in courses and handbooks. For example, the DigIn programme team 'decided to offer one course that essentially covers the 'curate' half of the DCC's Curation Lifecycle Model, and a second course dedicated to the 'preserve' half of the model' (Botticelli et al., 2010, 4). Similarly, all the chapters in Parts 2 and 3 of Harvey's (2010) *Digital Curation: a how-to-do-it manual* are structured respectively around the full lifecycle and sequential actions of the DCC Model.

Second, the requirements for and role of technology in the digital curation curriculum are frequently mentioned. Commentators invariably highlight the need for a solid technological infrastructure, discussing problems and solutions for students and instructors (Fulton et al., 2011; Yakel et al., 2011), but they also stress that fundamentally their courses are not about developing advanced technical skills; their goals focus instead on learning skills. Thus at Arizona, 'our goal was to enable a broad range of information professionals to gain an essential level of fluency or literacy with the advanced technologies needed for curation, especially server-based repository applications and Web-based content management systems' (Fulton et al., 2011, 97) and at Michigan, 'Our goal is not to teach the tool, but to use the tools to enable students to learn how to learn new tools' (Yakel et al., 2011, 28).

Third, the value of practical field experience, typically internships with real projects to work on, is arguably the strongest and most consistent message from the cases examined (Hank and Davidson, 2009; Qin et al., 2010; Ray, 2009; Yakel et al., 2011). Practical placements are an established feature of postgraduate LIS programmes in the USA, though less common in the one-year UK master's degree, but clearly have particular value when students are being introduced to an emerging area of practice that lacks an established body of knowledge and supporting literature. When Stanton et al. (2011, 90) evaluated the experiences of five Syracuse library and information master's students placed in science research centres by analysing detailed logs of their activities and exit questionnaires rating changes in their capabilities, they concluded that a targeted internship of this type should be a 'critical part' of any programme for e-science professionals, identifying several key competencies that would be much harder to develop effectively in the classroom (e.g. 'Analyzing project or researcher needs'). Direct evidence from two graduates of the North Carolina DigCCurr project reinforces this view:

> Both fellows agreed that their practicum experiences and master's paper research projects were pivotal in reinforcing and enhancing topics covered in coursework. Whereas particular courses often touched on select functions, the master's papers and practical

> aggregated an entire spectrum of concepts and brought theoretical discussions into real
> life institutional contexts.
>
> Gregory and Guss, 2010, 9

The digital curation courses and programmes developed to date are aimed at students and practitioners intent on roles with a strong focus on digital curation. However, if research datasets really are to become mainstream resources for library and information professionals, they need to be covered explicitly in the core LIS curriculum, as well as being the subject of specialist courses, so that all new professionals gain at least a basic understanding of their value and use, which will also help them to make informed decisions on whether to take any relevant specialist courses offered. Good practice demands continual review and regular updating and development of all courses, lectures, activities, readings and assignments to ensure that teaching incorporates the latest thinking in the discipline and practice in the field. In the context of managing research data, educators must ensure that there is appropriate coverage of this emerging area of practice in courses covering topics such as collection development and management, reference and information services, information literacy and instruction, academic liaison and support, and library systems and technologies. If courses involve practitioners as guest lecturers, course leaders also need to check that they are prepared to discuss their involvement with research data.

Incremental curricular developments of this kind are rarely reported in the literature and are hard to track as they often do not require changes to course descriptions, but most professional educators are continually refreshing their modules. For example, at the University of Sheffield, our core unit on information resources and information literacy now includes primary research data among the resources discussed in the Week 2 lecture session on 'the information universe' as an example of emergent types of reference material. Similarly, the introductory lecture on 'the concept of the collection and collection management' in our core unit on libraries, information and society emphasizes that a library 'collection' may now encompass born-digital resources such as geo-spatial and numeric datasets along with the tools for their management and use (ARL, 2002), using the OCLC Collections Grid to show how research data created within an institution needs to be managed alongside externally sourced content (Dempsey, 2003). Our academic and research libraries elective extends this coverage to other types of data and introduces students to the DCC Curation Lifecycle Model (Higgins, 2008) in the context of e-research, involving a practitioner with experience in repository development for this session.

Specialist courses on new subjects also need continual review, particularly in emerging fields where practice is not well established. Borgman (2010) reports that as soon as a new course on data, data practices, and data curation at the University of California, Los Angeles (UCLA) had been delivered, the course team decided that a two-course sequence was needed for the subject.

The UCLA course provides a useful case study of the objectives and topics defined for 'masters and doctoral students in information studies and in data-intensive research fields' (UCLA, 2011). Significantly, Borgman (2010) notes that development of the course

Course objectives
1 Students will learn to distinguish between the many forms of data, how data vary by scholarly discipline, and how they are used throughout the scholarly lifecycle.
2 Students will learn some professional criteria for selecting and appraising data.
3 Students will learn to distinguish among different types of data collections, repositories, and services.
4 Students will learn the roles that data play in research collaborations.
5 Students will gain a basic knowledge of data curation practices in the library and archive fields.
6 Students will learn basic principles of public policies for data.

Figure 6.3 *Objectives of the UCLA course 'Data, Data Practices, and Data Curation' (UCLA, 2011)*

drew on curricula elsewhere, but mostly created new material, having found the scope of existing courses 'did not start early enough in the scholarly process'. Her key point here is that students need to understand the lifecycle for the whole research process in order to engage effectively as a partner in data management and curation, which confirms messages from the ARL Task Force that 'science librarians . . . need to understand not only the concepts of the domain, but also the methodologies and norms of scholarly exchange' – a requirement that goes well beyond the knowledge of the literature generally specified (Lougee et al., 2007, 5). Figure 6.3 displays the objectives for the UCLA course.

The two-course sequence runs over two ten-week periods. Part I 'lays the foundation for data practices and services across the disciplines' and Part II 'builds upon this background to provide practical experience in data curation' (UCLA, 2011). Part I is a prerequisite for Part II, but can also be taken on its own. Table 6.2 shows the topics covered in each part.

A recurring question, posed most recently by the European report, *Riding the Wave*

Table 6.2 *Topics for Parts I and II of the UCLA course 'Data, Data Practices, and Data Curation' (UCLA, 2011)*

	Part I	Part II
Week 1	Overview of data, data practice, and data curation	Course introduction
Week 2	Role of data in research	Selection and appraisal
Week 3	[Holiday – no class]	Data collections and repositories
Week 4	When are research results reproducible?	Data collections and repositories
Week 5	Data lifecycle and collaboration	Technologies for data curation
Week 6	Data archives and repositories	Persistent identifiers and identification
Week 7	Data sharing and public policy for research data	Collection management and policy
Week 8	[Holiday – no class]	Provenance and authenticity
Week 9	The role of libraries and archives in data management	Formal representations
Week 10	Class presentations	Student presentations

(HLG, 2010) is whether our goal here is to embed data-related competencies in existing professional disciplines and programmes or, alternatively, to establish data management and curation as a new professional field – which could be seen as either a sub-field within the information profession(s) or a hybrid, 'blended professional' (Corrall, 2010), located at the intersection of two or more professional disciplines (for example library and information science, information technology and computer science and/or archives and records management) or combining information-related expertise with an academic discipline. *Riding the Wave* asks 'How can we foster the training of more data scientists and data librarians, *as important professions in their own right?*' (HLG, 2010, 23, emphasis added), suggesting two new professions, as complementary career streams. However, members of the International Data curation Education Action (IDEA) Working Group have adopted a different position, expressing the opinion that 'we are training professionals to work in digital or data curation, rather than training digital or data curation professionals), while another perspective views data curation as an emergent specialist career *within the relevant scientific discipline*, as shown by the formation of the International Society for Biocuration in 2008 and the launch of a new specialist journal, *Database: The Journal of Biological Databases and Curation* (Howe et al., 2008).

Our discussion has concentrated on educating library and information professionals for roles in managing research data, but there is evidently scope for LIS to extend the inter-professional education that is already bringing practitioners from different information domains together (archivists, records managers, librarians, information technologists, and so on) and become involved in preparing other stakeholders for their roles in managing research data. Several i-schools already offer discipline-based information programmes (e.g. bioinformatics, chemoinformatics, health informatics), but there could be opportunities for many more institutions to offer postgraduate courses and certificates to master's and doctoral students in science, social science and humanities disciplines, which would significantly benefit library and information professionals, by enabling them to gain firsthand understanding of different disciplinary perspectives on data management and curation prior to entering the field. The needs of the different cohorts would vary, but there should be sufficient common ground for some shared courses, seminars or sessions to be feasible; giving students the chance to engage in inter-professional teamwork on problems and projects would be useful preparation for supporting multi-disciplinary research in practice.

Conclusion

Data-intensive e-research is having a visible impact on library thinking and practice around the world. Roles and responsibilities in the management of research data are not yet settled, but such fluidity has created a real opportunity for librarians to display leadership within their institutions and the research community. Many practitioners have already demonstrated what libraries can do to manage research data in collaboration with other stakeholders. Powerful synergies exist between the longstanding library commitment to open access and the philosophy of open science, between the principles underpinning library collection management and emerging protocols for curating digital data, between the track record of libraries in technology adoption and systems development and the complex demands for integrated infrastructure and novel workflows, and between the teaching mission of librarians and the educational agenda for e-research.

Libraries have taken impressive steps to establish their place in the research data space, advancing strategically, tactically and operationally, with exemplary practices evident in areas such as policy formulation, repository development, curriculum innovation, professional updating, undergraduate learning, postgraduate training, researcher advice, data advocacy, curation profiling and resource selection. New modules, courses, programmes, internships, institutes and fellowships have been designed and delivered for new professionals and experienced practitioners to prepare librarians and faculty for roles in data curation, digital humanities and e-science. Developments in the field have enriched our understanding of the need for domain knowledge and technical skills in data management and flagged particular areas of competency for library attention, notably disciplinary cultures, research methodologies, scientific workflows, lifecycle management, systems thinking, technological fluency, relationship building and institutional contexts.

The debate continues around the scale of change that libraries face entering the data arena. We have confirmed that librarians have relevant experience and expertise to contribute to the data challenge. Libraries that are already involved in digital library developments, secondary data services and specialized research support are well positioned to extend their activities incrementally into managing research data. Libraries and librarians with less experience will have more to learn but much visibility, credibility and authority to gain on campus. The whole research community is being challenged by data management and discontinuous change, but the challenge must be met and librarians can set the pace within their institution if sensibly prepared and fully committed.

Acknowledgements

I am indebted to Martin Lewis, Director of Library Services and University Librarian at the University of Sheffield, for discussion of the role of libraries and librarians in managing research data and for use of the research data management pyramid for libraries as a framework for the central part of the chapter. I am also very grateful to Christine Borgman, Professor and Presidential Chair in Information Studies, and to Jillian Wallis and Laura Wynholds, doctoral students in the Graduate School of Education and Information Studies, for their willingness to share the syllabus of the data course that they have developed at the University of California, Los Angeles.

References

ACRL (2000) *Information Literacy Competency Standards for Higher Education*, American Library Association, Association of College and Research Libraries, www.ala.org/ala/mgrps/divs/acrl/standards/informationliteracycompetency.cfm.

ANDS (2011) *Australian National Data Service: governance structure*, http://ands.org.au/governance.html.

ARL (2002) Collections and Access for the 21st-century Scholar: changing roles of research libraries, a report from the ARL Collections and Access Issues Task Force, *ARL Bimonthly Report*, **225**, Association of Research Libraries, www.arl.org/bm~doc/main.pdf.

Beagrie, N. (2006) Digital Curation for Science, Digital Libraries, and Individuals, *International Journal of Digital Curation*, **1** (1), 3–16, www.ijdc.net/index.php/ijdc/article/viewFile/6/2.

Berman, F. et al. (2002) The Grid: past, present, future. In Berman, F. et al. (eds) *Grid Computing: making the global infrastructure a reality*, John Wiley & Sons, 9–49.

Borgman, C. (2010) Why Data Matter to Librarians – and how to Educate The Next Generation. In Uhlir, P. F. and Levey, C. W. (eds) *The Changing Role of Libraries in Support of Research Data Activities: a public symposium, meeting recap*, The National Academies, Board on Research Data and Information, http://sites.nationalacademies.org/PGA/brdi/PGA_056901.

Botticelli, P. et al. (2010) Educating Digital Curators: challenges and opportunities, *6th International Digital Curation Conference, 6–8 December 2010, Chicago*.

Brophy, P. (2007) *The Library in the Twenty-First Century*, 2nd edn, Facet Publishing.

Carlson, J. et al. (2011) Determining Data Information Literacy Needs: a study of students and research faculty, *Portal: Libraries and the Academy*, **11** (2), 629–57.

Choudhury, G. S. (2008) Case Study in Data Curation at Johns Hopkins University, *Library Trends*, **57** (2), 211–20.

Corrado, E. M. (2005) The Importance of Open Access, Open Source, and Open Standards For Libraries, *Issues in Science and Technology Librarianship*, **42**, www.library.ucsb.edu/istl/05-spring/article2.html.

Corrall, S. (2010) Educating the Academic Librarian as a Blended Professional: a review and case study, *Library Management*, **31** (8/9), 567–93.

Costello, K. L. and Brown, M. E. (2010) Preliminary Report on the 2010–2011 DigCCurr Professional Institute: curation practices for the Digital Object Lifecycle, *D-Lib Magazine*, **16** (11/12), www.dlib.org/dlib/november10/costello/11costello.html.

Czarnocki, S. and Khouri, A. (2004) A Library Service Model for Digital Data Support, *IASSIST Quarterly*, **28** (2), 30–34, www.iassistdata.org/downloads/iqvol282_3khouri.pdf.

Dahlström, M. and Doracic, A. (2009) Digitization Education: courses taken and lessons learned, *D-Lib Magazine*, **15** (3/4), www.dlib.org/dlib/march09/dahlstrom/03dahlstrom.html.

DCC (2010) Digital Curation Centre, *Data Management Plans*, www.dcc.ac.uk/resources/data-management-plans.

Dempsey, L. (2003) The Recombinant Library: portals and people, *Journal of Library Administration*, **39** (4), 103–36.

Denniston, R., Herndon, J. and Mangiafico, P. (2011) *Research Data Planning at Duke: subject guide for data management plans*, Duke University Libraries, http://guides.library.duke.edu/dukedata.

Florance, P. (2006) GIS Collection Development within an Academic Library, *Library Trends*, **55** (2), 222–35.

Friedlander, A. and Adler, P. (2006) *To Stand the Test of Time: long-term stewardship of digital data sets in science and engineering*, a report to the National Science Foundation from the ARL Workshop on New Collaborative Relationships: The Role of Academic Libraries in the Digital Data Universe, www.arl.org/bm~doc/digdatarpt.pdf.

Fulton, B. et al. (2011) DigIn: a hands-on approach to a digital curation curriculum for professional development, *Journal of Education for Library and Information Science*, **52** (2), 95–109.

Gabridge, T. (2009) The Last Mile: liaison roles in curating science and engineering research data, *Research Libraries Issues*, **265**, 15–21, www.arl.org/bm~doc/rli-265-gabridge.pdf.

Genoni, P. (2004) Content in Institutional Repositories: a collection management issue, *Library Management*, **25** (6/7), 300–6.

Gorman, M. (2000) *Our Enduring Values: librarianship in the 21st century*, American Library Association.

Government of Canada (2011) *Research Data Strategy: working group members*, http://rds-sdr.cisti-icist.nrc-cnrc.gc.ca/eng/members.html.

Gray, T. (2011) *Scientific Data Repositories and Datasets*, Duke University Libraries, http://guides.library.duke.edu/sciencedata.

Green, A. et al. (2009) *Policy-making for Research Data in Repositories: a guide*, University of Edinburgh, Information Services Division, www.disc-uk.org/docs/guide.pdf.

Gregory, L. and Guss, S. (2010) Digital Curation Education in Practice: catching up with two former fellows, *6th International Digital Curation Conference, 6–8 December 2010, Chicago*.

Hank, C. and Davidson, J. (2009) International Data curation Education Action (IDEA) Working Group: a report from the second workshop of the IDEA, *D-Lib Magazine*, **15** (3/4), www.dlib.org/dlib/march09/hank/03hank.html.

Harper, R. and Corrall, S. (2011) Effects of the Economic Downturn on Academic Libraries in the UK: positions and projections in mid-2009, *New Review of Academic Librarianship*, **17** (1), 96–128.

Harvey, R. (2010) *Digital Curation: a how-to-do-it manual*, Facet Publishing.

Hey, T. and Hey J. (2006) E-science and its Implications for the Library Community, *Library Hi Tech*, **24** (4), 515–28.

Higgins, S. (2008) The DCC Curation Lifecycle Model, *International Journal of Digital Curation*, **3** (1), 134–40, www.ijdc.net/index.php/ijdc/article/view/69.

HLG (2010) *Riding the Wave: how Europe can gain from the rising tide of scientific data*, High Level Expert Group on Scientific Data, European Commission, http://cordis.europa.eu/fp7/ict/e-infrastructure/docs/hlg-sdi-report.pdf.

Howe, D. et al. (2008) The Future of Biocuration, *Nature*, **455** (4 September), 47–50.

Hswe, P. and Holt, A. (2010) *Guide for Research Libraries: the NSF data sharing policy*, Association of Research Libraries, www.arl.org/rtl/eresearch/escien/nsf/index.shtml.

Hswe, P. and Holt, A. (2011) Joining in the Enterprise of Response in the Wake of the NSF Data Management Planning Requirement, *Research Library Issues*, **274**, 11–17, http://publications.arl.org/17gcns.pdf.

Humphrey, C. and Hamilton, E. (2004) Is It Working? Assessing the value of the Canadian Data Liberation Initiative, *The Bottom Line: Managing Library Finances*, **17** (4), 137–45.

IFLA (2011) *IFLA Statement on Open access: clarifying IFLA's position and strategy*, International Federation of Library Associations and Institutions, www.ifla.org/files/hq/news/documents/ifla-statement-on-open-access.pdf.

Lee, H.-L. (2003) Information Spaces and Collections: implications for organization, *Library & Information Science Research*, **25** (4), 419–36.

Lewis, M. (2010) Libraries and the management of research data, in McKnight, S. (ed.), *Envisioning Future Academic Library Services: Initiatives, Ideas and Challenges*, 145–168, Facet Publishing.

Lougee, W. et al. (2007) *Agenda for Developing E-Science in Research Libraries*, prepared by the Joint Task Force on Library Support for E-Science, Association of Research Libraries, www.arl.org/bm~doc/ARL_EScience_final.pdf.

Luce, R. (2008) A New Value Equation Challenge: the emergence of eResearch and roles for research libraries, in Council on Library and Information Resources, *No Brief Candle: Reconceiving Research Libraries for the 21st Century*, 42–50, Council on Library and Information Resources, www.clir.org/pubs/reports/pub142/pub142.pdf.

Lynch, C. (2003) Institutional Repositories: essential infrastructure for scholarship in the digital age, *ARL Bimonthly Report*, **226**, 1–7, www.arl.org/bm~doc/br226ir.pdf.

Lyon, L. (2007) *Dealing with Data: roles, rights, responsibilities and relationships – Consultancy Report*, www.ukoln.ac.uk/ukoln/staff/e.j.lyon/reports/dealing_with_data_report-final.pdf.

Macdonald, S. and Martinez, L. (2005) Supporting Local Data Users in the UK Academic Community, *Ariadne*, **44**, www.ariadne.ac.uk/issue44/martinez.

MacDonald, S. and Uribe, L. M. (2008) Libraries in the Converging World of Open Data, E-research, and Web 2.0, *Online*, **32** (2), 36–40, http://ie-repository.jisc.ac.uk/227/1/Online_mar08.pdf.

MacMillan, D. (2010) Sequencing Genetics Information: integrating data into information literacy for undergraduate biology students, *Issues in Science and Technology Librarianship*, **61** (Spring), www.istl.org/10-spring/refereed3.html.

Martinez, L. (2007) *The e-Research Needs Analysis Survey Report*, CURL/SCONUL Joint Task Force on e-Research, www.rluk.ac.uk/files/E-ResearchNeedsAnalysisRevised.pdf.

Martinez-Uribe, L. (2007) Digital Repository Services for Managing Research Data: what do Oxford researchers need?, *IASSIST Quarterly*, **31** (3–4), 28–33, www.iassistdata.org/publications/iq/iq31/iqvol313martinez.pdf.

MIT (2011) Data Management Plans, Massachusetts Institute of Technology Libraries, http://libraries.mit.edu/guides/subjects/data-management/plans.html.

Newton, M. P. et al. (2010) Librarian Roles in Institutional Repository Data Set Collecting: outcomes of a research library task force, *Collection Management*, **36** (1), 53–67.

Nicholas, D. et al. (2010) The Impact of the Economic Downturn on Libraries: with special reference to university libraries, *Journal of Academic Librarianship*, **36** (5), 376–82.

NSB (2005) *Long-Lived Digital Data Collections: Enabling Research and Education in the 21st Century*, National Science Board, National Science Foundation, www.nsf.gov/pubs/2005/nsb0540.pdf.

NSF (2007) *Cyberinfrastructure Vision for 21st Century Discovery*, National Science Foundation Cyberinfrastructure Council, www.nsf.gov/pubs/2007/nsf0728/nsf0728.pdf.

Ogburn, J. L. (2010) The Imperative for Data Curation, *Portal: Libraries and the Academy*, **10** (2), 241–46.

Pryor, G. and Donnelly, M. (2009) Skilling Up to Do Data: whose role, whose responsibility, whose career?, *International Journal of Digital Curation*, **2** (4), 158–70, www.ijdc.net/index.php/ijdc/article/view/126.

Purdue University Libraries (2010) *Data Curation Profiles Toolkit*, Purdue University Libraries, www4.lib.purdue.edu/dcp/.

Purdue University Libraries (2011) Data Management Plan Self-Assessment Questionnaire, Purdue University Libraries and Office of the Vice President for Research, http://d2c2.lib.purdue.edu/documents/dmp_self_questionnaire.pdf.

Qin, J. et al. (2010) Educating eScience Librarians, poster, *6th International Digital Curation Conference, 6–8 December 2010, Chicago*, http://meganoakleaf.info/educatingsciencelibs.pdf.

Ray, J. (2009) Sharks, Digital Curation, and the Education of Information Professionals, *Museum Management and Curatorship*, **24** (94), 357–68.

Read, E. J. (2007) Data Services in Academic Libraries: assessing needs and promoting services, *Reference & User Services Quarterly*, **46** (3), 61–75.

Renear, A. H. et al. (2010) Extending an LIS Data Curation Curriculum to the Humanities: selected activities and observations, poster abstract, *iConference 2010 Proceedings, February 3–6, University of Illinois at Urbana Champaign*, www.ideals.illinois.edu/handle/2142/15061.

RIN (2008) *Mind the Skills Gap: information-handling training for researchers*, Research Information Network, www.rin.ac.uk/system/files/attachments/Mind-skills-gap-report.pdf.

Rice, R. (2009) *DISC-UK DataShare Project: Final Report*, Joint Information Systems Committee, http://ie-repository.jisc.ac.uk/336/1/DataSharefinalreport.pdf.

Rieh, S. Y. et al. (2007) Census of Institutional Repositories in the U.S.: a comparison across institutions at different stages of IR development, *D-Lib Magazine*, **13** (11/12), www.dlib.org/dlib/november07/rieh/11rieh.html.

Salo, D. (2010) Retooling Libraries for the Data Challenge, *Ariadne*, **64**, www.ariadne.ac.uk/issue64/salo.

SCONUL (2011) *The SCONUL Seven Pillars of Information Literacy: a research lens for higher education*, Society of College, National and University Libraries, Working Group on Information Literacy, www.sconul.ac.uk/groups/information_literacy/publications/researchlens.pdf.

Shearer, K. and Argáez, D. (2010) *Addressing the Research Data Gap: a review of novel services for libraries*, Canadian Association of Research Libraries, www.carl-abrc.ca/about/working_groups/pdf/library_roles-final.pdf.

Soehner, C. et al. (2010) *E-Science and Data Support Services: a study of ARL member institutions*, Association of Research Libraries, www.arl.org/bm~doc/escience_report2010.pdf.

Stanton, J. M. et al. (2011) Education for eScience professionals: job analysis, curriculum guidance, and program considerations, *Journal of Education for Library and Information Science*, **52** (2), 79–94.

Stephenson, E. and Caravello, P. S. (2007) Incorporating Data Literacy into Undergraduate Information Literacy Programs in the Social Sciences: a pilot project, *Reference Services Review*, **35** (4), 525–40.

Swan, A. and Brown, S. (2008) *The Skills, Role and Career Structure of Data Scientists and Curators: an assessment of current practice and future needs*, Key Perspectives, www.jisc.ac.uk/publications/documents/dataskillscareersfinalreport.aspx.

Syracuse University (2010) *Syracuse iSchool and Cornell University launch eScience Mentorship Program*, Syracuse University School of Information Studies, http://ischool.syr.edu/newsroom/?recid=980.

Szigeti, K. and Wheeler, K. (2011) Essential Readings in E-science, *Issues in Science and Technology Librarianship*, **64** (Winter), www.istl.org/11-winter/internet2.html.

Takeda, K. (2010) *Institutional Data Management Blueprint: initial findings report*, University of Southampton, www.southamptondata.org/1/post/2010/12/idmb-initial-findings-report.html.

UCLA (2011) *Data, Data Practices, and Data Curation, Parts I and II* [unpublished document], University of California Los Angeles.

University of Connecticut (2011) *Data Management Plans for Grant Funded Projects (NSF, NIH)*, University of Connecticut Libraries, www.lib.uconn.edu/scholarlycommunication/data.html.

University of Edinburgh (2011) *Policy for Management of Research Data*, www.docs.is.ed.ac.uk/docs/data-library/rdm-policy.pdf.

University of Massachusetts (2011) *eScience Portal for New England Librarians: a librarian's link to escience resources*, University of Massachusetts Medical School, http://esciencelibrary.umassmed.edu/index.

UW-Madison (2011a) *Research Data Services: About Us*, University of Wisconsin-Madison, http://researchdata.wisc.edu/get-help/about-us.

UW-Madison (2011b) *Research Data Services: our services*, University of Wisconsin-Madison, http://researchdata.wisc.edu/get-help/our-services.

Varalakshmi, R. S. R. (2009) Curriculum for Digital Libraries: an analytical study of Indian LIS curricula, *D-Lib Magazine*, **15** (9/10), www.dlib.org/dlib/september09/varalakshmi/09varalakshmi.html.

Vitae (2010) *Researcher Development Framework*, Vitae/Careers Research and Advisory Centre, www.vitae.ac.uk/rdf.

Walters, T. and Skinner, K. (2011) *New Roles for New Times: digital curation for preservation*, Association of Research Libraries, www.arl.org/bm~doc/nrnt_digital_curation17mar11.pdf.

Walters, T. O. (2009) Data Curation Program Development in U.S. Universities: the Georgia

Institute of Technology example, *International Journal of Digital Curation*, **3** (4), 83–92, www.ijdc.net/index.php/ijdc/article/viewFile/136/153].

Westra, B. (2010) Data Services for the Sciences: a needs assessment, *Ariadne*, **64**, www.ariadne.ac.uk/issue64/westra.

Westra, B. et al. (2010) Selected Internet Resources on Digital Research Data Curation, *Issues in Science and Technology Librarianship*, **63** (Fall), www.istl.org/10-fall/internet2.html.

Whyte, A. and Wilson, A. (2010) *How to Appraise and Select Research Data for Curation*, Digital Curation Centre and Australian National Data Service, www.dcc.ac.uk/node/9098#c9.

Willinsky, J. (2005) The Unacknowledged Convergence of Open Source, Open Access, and Open Science, *First Monday*, **10** (8), http://firstmonday.org/htbin/cgiwrap/bin/ojs/index.php/fm/article/view/1265.

Witt, M. (2008) Institutional Repositories and Research Data Curation in a Distributed Environment, *Library Trends*, **57** (2), 191–201.

Witt, M. and Carlson, J. R. (2007) Conducting a Data Interview, Poster/Libraries Research Publications, Purdue University Libraries, http://docs.lib.purdue.edu/lib_research/81.

Yakel, E. et al. (2011) Digital Curation for Digital Natives, *Journal of Education for Library and Information Science*, **52** (1), 23–31.

CHAPTER 7

Research data management: opportunities and challenges for HEIs

Rob Procter, Peter Halfpenny and Alex Voss

Introduction

We live in an information age characterized by a deluge of digital data (Hey and Trefethen, 2003a; Hey, Tansley and Tolle, 2009). The potential benefits to researchers are enormous, offering opportunities to mount multidisciplinary investigations into humankind's major social and scientific challenges on a hitherto unrealizable scale by marshalling artificially produced and naturally occurring data of multiple kinds from multiple sources. However, this newfound wealth of research data will be without value unless it can be managed in ways that will ensure that it is discoverable, accessible and (re)usable.

Over the past ten years, the efforts of national e-research programmes to innovate research methods, tools and infrastructure – as in the UK e-Science Programme (Hey and Trefethen, 2003b), the Australian e-Research Programme (Treloar, 2007) and the NSF Cyberinfrastructure Program (National Science Foundation, 2003, 2006) – have raised awareness among stakeholders that research data is a vital resource whose value needs to be preserved for future research by the data generators and by others. Achieving this requires that the data be systematically organized, securely stored, fully described, easily locatable, accessible on appropriate authority, shareable, archived and curated. Fulfilling all of these research data management tasks is a complex socio-technical challenge that all stakeholders, whether they are research funders, higher education institutions (HEIs), publishers, researchers or regulators, are currently ill prepared to meet. There are, as yet, no widely agreed, mature solutions. Moreover, given the combination of the data deluge and a world recession, the scale of the tasks is increasing while the financial and therefore human resources to undertake the tasks are shrinking.

In this chapter we review the drivers for research data management services, consider the challenges their provision poses for HEIs and explore how these might be met, including possible pathways to sustainability. To do this, we begin by drawing on the findings from several UK studies of researchers' everyday data management practices, which help us to understand the reasons why these practices exist and why they may not be easily changed. These studies include two projects undertaken at the University of Manchester: the MaDAM project, funded under the infrastructure strand of the Joint Information Systems Committee (JISC) Managing Research Data programme, with the objective of developing a pilot data management infrastructure for university biomedical researchers (Collins et al., 2010; Goff et al., 2010a; Goff et al., 2010b; Poschen et al., 2010); and the Storage, Archiving and Curation (SAC) project, led by Manchester Informatics (www.informatics.manchester.ac.uk), which is charged with developing and implementing a research data management strategy across all four faculties of the University. To broaden our evidence base, we examine findings from UK reports that have looked at research data management practices within other discipline areas and we review the wider HEI policy landscape as set out by some of the principal stakeholders in this domain.

By synthesizing across these studies, we explore the opportunities and challenges faced by HEIs as the academic sector grapples with the implications of delivering the new and more complex research infrastructure – both their technical capability to deliver more powerful research tools and services, and the human capacity to support their effective use – that will be needed to deal with the data deluge. In particular, we will examine issues such as the diversity of current research data management practices; the challenges to HEI information and communications technology (ICT) and library services in understanding the needs of different research groups and disciplines for data management and adapting solutions to meet them; how HEIs might engineer a cultural change in researchers' attitudes towards data curation and preservation; and how this new research infrastructure can be made sustainable.

Current practices in research data management and sharing

In this section, we examine evidence from various studies of researchers' practices in data management and sharing in order to gauge perceptions of the added value of moving towards institutionally based research data management services.

Two surveys of UK researchers, one cross-disciplinary (RIN, 2010) and one focusing exclusively on the social sciences (Voss and Procter, 2010), confirm that research data utilization lags far behind the e-research vision of collaborative 'data-rich science' (Hey, Tansley and Tolle, 2009). In the first survey, 72% (N=1305) reported that they use a data repository based within their local research group; 37% (N=1279) reported that they share their research data with selected collaborators, whereas only 20% reported that they share their data openly with other members of their research community. The second survey revealed that 86% of respondents reported that research data they themselves collected was their essential or important source of data (N=1062). Only just over half said that data shared by a colleague in their own institution (51%) or in another institution (53%) was an essential or important source of data. Less than a third identified data acquired from national (30%) or international data repositories (26%) as essential or important to their research.

While the often highly discipline-dependent nature of data management and sharing practices make generalizations difficult, these findings collectively suggest that – at least at the local research group level – the use of data repositories is commonplace. However, when we look more closely at how, for example, social science researchers actually manage their data, we find that we cannot assume that this implies the widespread adoption of systematic data management practices: 85% of respondents in the second survey report store their data on a personal hard-drive during the course of a project, 65% on a USB stick and 27% on CDs or DVDs. In contrast, only 33% use an institutionally managed repository. The large majority of respondents (80%) reported that they or a team member were responsible for storing and caring for the data after the project was completed, with only 21% using an institutional repository and 17% a national data repository, despite the Economic and Social Research Council (ESRC) promoting the UK Data Archive as the national repository for social science data. These findings are broadly in line with findings reported by Takeda (2011, 21–22) from a smaller scale survey conducted across different academic departments at Southampton University.

A number of complementary case-studies paint a similar picture. Life science researchers, for example, use only a limited range of data management services and are more reliant on colleagues for informal advice about appropriate services than they are on institutional support: 'Life science research encompasses a huge, indeed "Baroque", array of diverse formal and informal information discovery, collection, processing and dissemination activities' (RIN, 2009, 4). The report also suggested 'there is a significant gap between how researchers behave and the policies and strategies of funders and service providers' (2009, 5). In the humanities, a similar picture prevails (RIN, 2011). There is 'only limited uptake of even simple, freely-available tools for data management and sharing. Rather, they manage and store information on their desktops and laptops, and share it with others via email' (RIN, 2011, 7).

For a more detailed picture of the realities of daily research data management practices we can turn to the findings of the MaDAM project. As part of the wider requirements gathering activity for the pilot research data management service, a detailed study was conducted of the working practices of University of Manchester research groups in two biomedical domains, the Life Sciences Group and the Neuropsychiatry Unit (Goff et al., 2010a; 2010b; Poschen et al., 2010).

Two main themes emerged from these investigations: first, patterns of individual and group reuse of data are contingent on a mixture of local and disciplinary factors:

> Microscopy researchers were keen to retain all data for potential reuse and reanalysis, even data without immediate obvious reuse value. For example, data from failed experiments may be kept in order to benefit from a 'lessons learned' process and to potentially uncover patterns in the future that might lead to new research questions and projects . . . It needs to be recognised, however, that in some fields of biomedical sciences this attitude to retention is overridden by the sheer impracticability of storing vast quantities of data . . . In certain fields it is easier and preferable to rerun an experiment . . . In short, researchers' attitudes

to managing data are grounded in the practical realities of their field and, in rapidly developing fields, where new instruments and computational techniques allow for greater throughput and acceleration of the research process, data is potentially more disposable.

Goff et al., 2010a, 1

Second, researchers within these groups have yet to work out a consistent policy on sharing data that balances to their satisfaction the risks and benefits: 'sharing by researchers takes place in the context of sharing with colleagues they know and trust and on whom they can rely to provide some reciprocal benefits that justify the risk and loss of control' (Goff et al., 2010a, 2) Such a thoroughly pragmatic attitude may be explained by individuals' desire for social capital: 'features of social life – networks, norms and trust – that enable participants to act together more effectively to pursue shared objectives' (Putnam, 1995a, 664), and whose accumulation is arguably more easily achieved – and value tested – through face-to-face interaction (Putnam, 1995b). Hence, and not surprisingly, researchers in the MaDAM study expressed concerns about the implications of the wider sharing of data following moves on the part of funders towards open access policies:

> Discussions about making research data available on open access initially elicited a unanimous 'no, we wouldn't want to share our data'. However, it was also evident that our researchers do deposit data in public repositories such as the Protein Data Bank. Further probing revealed a more nuanced attitude towards open access. These researchers do make their data open access; they just may not make all of their data open access.
>
> Putnam, 1995b, 2

The findings of the MaDAM project are consistent with those of other studies of the Life Sciences and with those of studies from other fields (Pryor, 2007; Whyte and Pryor, 2011). As a RIN report observes: 'Above all, data is generated through a considerable investment of time and effort by researchers and provides researchers with their "competitive advantage": "intellectual capital" which they will not wish to give up lightly' (2009, 5).

The picture of *ad hoc* practices for managing research data that emerges from these various studies may be explained as an understandable response on the part of researchers to the immediate pressures of work that push housekeeping tasks off the agenda, as well as academic citation and reward systems that give little incentive to manage data well. This being the case, it is a picture that is unlikely to be remedied simply by action on the part of individual HEIs to put in place a co-ordinated technical infrastructure for research data management or by making research data management practice the subject of institutional (or national) policy mandates. Such measures may be necessary but, as we argue below, they will not be sufficient. It is also notable, for example, that local solutions persist despite external requirements for research data management already being mandated by virtually all UK research funders (see Chapter 3 for a summary of funders' policies).

While it seems clear that HEIs are expected to take responsibility for the provision and support of data management infrastructure for their research communities, at the national level the UK research data management policy roadmap has yet to reach maturity. In January 2007, the Research Information Network (RIN) published a report on the 'Research funders' policies for the management of information outputs' (RIN, 2007), noting that there are significant differences in the extent to which funders see it as their responsibility to preserve and manage research data. Table 3.1 (pages 50–3) shows that only two funders (NERC and ESRC) are now funding data centres, although some also support the Atlas Petabyte Data Store (www.e-science.stfc. ac.uk/services/atlas-petabyte-storage/atlas.html). The difference between the approaches taken by funders is compounded by the various agencies undertaking research (for example, the JISC's Managing Research Data Programme), offering support (the Digital Curation Centre, www.dcc.ac.uk, and the UK Data Archive, www. data-archive.ac.uk/sharing) or proposing initiatives (UK Research Data Service, 2008).

The protection of personal information and sensitive data raises further issues that have, again, been addressed by a variety of agencies, each recommending a variety of practices. See for example, the ESRC's Secure Data Service and the UK Data Forum's National Data Strategy. Lyon (2007) seeks to provide some order to this plethora of recommendations in her summary of the various roles and responsibilities of researchers, institutions, data centres, reusers, funders, publishers and aggregators with respect to research data. Similarly, five principles are set out in the RIN's report *Stewardship of Digital Research Data* (RIN, 2008, 3):

I. The roles and responsibilities of researchers, research institutions and funders should be defined as clearly as possible, and they should collaboratively establish a framework of codes of practice to ensure that creators and users of research data are aware of and fulfil their responsibilities in accordance with these principles.

II. Digital research data should be created and collected in accordance with applicable international standards, and the processes for selecting those to be made available to others should include proper quality assurance.

III. Digital research data should be easy to find, and access should be provided in an environment which maximises ease of use; provides credit for and protects the rights of those who have gathered or created data; and protects the rights of those who have legitimate interests in how data are made accessible and used.

IV. The models and mechanisms for managing and providing access to digital research data must be both efficient and cost-effective in the use of public and other funds.

V. Digital research data of long term value arising from current and future research should be preserved and remain accessible for current and future generations.

The studies we have examined emphasize that one element essential for the successful adoption of HEI research data management policy is its close alignment with the everyday practices of researchers so that it fits seamlessly into the research data lifecycle.

The most widely recognized account of such an alignment is the lifecycle model designed by the Digital Curation Centre (Higgins, 2008). These studies clearly show that if this generic scheme is to be adopted successfully it needs to be tailored to the particular activities and cultures (local and disciplinary) of research groups.

Changes in researchers' attitudes to data sharing are unlikely to come about merely as a result of the practice being mandated by research funders. Instead, the way forward for HEIs is more likely to involve building the research data management infrastructure so that it facilitates the kinds of informal data sharing already in evidence. At the same time, stakeholders must work together to put in place incentives at the group, institution and community level that will encourage researchers to adopt the more open data sharing practices argued for in the e-research vision.

We now turn to considering the actions that HEIs might take to tackle the challenges outlined above. We argue that these actions are essential if systematic and sustainable solutions are to emerge which, while they respect the need for diversity, are able to deliver a research data management capability that is usable and fit for purpose in the 21st century.

ICT and library services

Inevitably, the ICT and library services deployed within HEIs have critical roles to play in ensuring the effective implementation of research data management services. Most important will be the manner in which they seek to engage with users, including how such engagement is co-ordinated and managed, how service requirements are initially established and subsequently tracked, and how well users perceive the engagement to be working. In this respect, we have emphasized the contribution that 'hybrids' or 'intermediaries' – people who by combining technical and domain-specific skills are able to bridge the divide between ICT specialists and end-users – can make to the strengthening of user engagement (Procter and Voss, 2009).

If HEIs are to deliver research data management services that are fit for purpose and usable, their ICT and library services will need to work closely with users, not only at the requirements gathering stage but also subsequently, as the research data management infrastructure goes into service. In other words, they must ensure that the development of the non-technical elements of research data management services provision receives equal priority with the creation of the technical infrastructure (Procter and Voss, 2009). Specifically, the latter needs to be embedded within a 'human infrastructure' (Lee, Dourish and Mark, 2006) consisting of the social and organizational arrangements that will enable the benefits provided by new technologies to be utilized to their fullest extent. What studies of e-infrastructure adoption, such as those conducted by the e-uptake (Procter and Voss, 2009; Voss et al., 2010) and AVROSS (Barjak et al., 2009, 2010) projects underline is that institutional capacity to deploy raw technical resources often outstrips the capacity to use them effectively. E-infrastructure adoption requires that technical and research (user) expertise be brought together in collaborative working arrangements over an extended period of time if the technical investment is to bear fruit.

The e-uptake project's findings emphasize the importance for successful e-infrastructure adoption of local research support services adopting new ways of engaging with their users; for example, supporting the building of deeper and more long-term relationships through the development and deployment of hybrids who work side by side with users (Procter and Voss, 2009). The importance of the contribution made by hybrids to research data management was underlined in the RIN report into data management in the life sciences:

> Whereas institutional information services have commenced strategies to engage with the research agenda, there is an implicit feeling across the groups we surveyed that only the researchers themselves – or hybrid specialists located within or close to the laboratory – can have the subject knowledge necessary to curate their own research data.
>
> Procter and Voss, 2009, 5

However, as the same report notes that

> the various new interdisciplinary roles that are emerging within life science research laboratories (e.g. 'hybrids' combining life science research and information and computation skills) may come up against research assessment systems and career development systems that are rooted in, and privilege, specific disciplines.
>
> Procter and Voss, 2009, 6

Success in encouraging the development of hybrids will depend in large measure on the capacity of ICT and library services to encourage the formation of higher-level institutional frameworks, policies and career structures (see Procter and Voss, 2009; BIS, 2010, 19). 'More explicit recognition and career rewards . . . would make humanities scholars more prepared to participate in building new resources, so that they are well designed for effective use' (RIN, 2011, 8). In turn, this will depend on HEI ICT and library services having influence in institutional strategy making circles. Unfortunately, the signs are not encouraging: in their report on the integration of technology into HEI strategy, Duke, Jordan and Powell (2008) observe that this representation is generally not in evidence.

Approaches to achieving stronger user engagement have variously been framed as 'co-realization' (Hartswood et al., 2008; Voss et al., 2009) and 'embedding'. What both terms refer to is the strategy of locating ICT expertise 'at the elbow' of users. They argue that this is the best way for ICT experts to understand user needs and for users to understand the potential of new technologies, and thus ensure the development of useful and usable ICT-based innovations.

The challenge of meeting researchers' needs for new and more complex infrastructure and services is occurring at a time when HEI ICT and library services are also under pressure to cut costs, the consequence of which, for some, leads to the centralization of ICT services (e.g. Hawtin, Davies and Hammond, 2010). While there is a plausible case that centralization will result in cost savings, the evidence from e-uptake and from previous studies (e.g. Fincham et al., 1994; Fichman, 2000; Gallivan, 2001) is that over-centralization of ICT services stifles innovation, because it leads to the expertise needed to make it successful becoming too remote from its potential users. Centralization inhibits 'agile' decision making and makes it more difficult for institutions to take advantage of 'bottom-up innovation' processes.

To accelerate progress and avoid making expensive mistakes, HEIs need to share their experiences of research data management service provision and how to work co-operatively, so as to establish and evolve 'best practice' across the sector. This is particularly important for smaller HEIs, which may not have the necessary breadth of knowledge in-house or sufficient dedicated research computing support, and therefore lack the structures to develop and support their own research data management strategy.

Implementation strategies

When deciding whether a research data management service is a strategic priority, HEIs will almost certainly face considerable reputational, financial and legal risks in the future if they do not opt to provide a fit-for-purpose research data management service. These risks are likely to increase as the open access movement expands and as external agencies increasingly monitor compliance. However, there are risks as well as benefits in being the 'early adopters' in any new field, so it is not surprising that not all HEIs are willing to move forward at the same pace. Indeed, at a national level, strategy for the adoption of research data management service has been formulated with this eventuality in mind. The strategy has made it possible for those HEIs that have not already taken their first steps to implement a research data management service to look to the outcomes of pilots funded under a variety of initiatives for demonstrators that they may adopt or adapt. These include the JISC Research Data Management Infrastructure programme (www.jisc.ac.uk/whatwedo/programmes/mrd/rdmi.aspx, available from mid-2011 onwards), the UK Research Data Service Pathfinders (www.ukrds.ac.uk/resources/download/id/47), and the JISC UMF Shared Services and the Cloud Programme (www.jisc.ac.uk/whatwedo/programmes/umf.aspx).

Similar considerations must surely apply when considering implementation strategy within individual HEIs. A 'big bang' approach where a fully fledged service is rolled out across an HEI on a given date is not feasible for several reasons. First, specifying all requirements across all research groups and disciplines would itself be a very time-consuming and complex undertaking, demanding a degree of consensus that might be impossible to reach. Second, research data management services is an evolving area and a once-and-for-all requirements survey would fail to capture unfolding developments. Finally, the one-off implementation cost would be too great in the constrained financial climate within which most HEIs are operating.

A more feasible approach is for individual HEIs to follow a phased and progressive roll-out, beginning with a pilot service and incrementally adding further research groups. This approach has seven key advantages:

- It enables continuous requirements gathering and system evaluation in a co-production process (Voss et al., 2009) that ensures user acceptance and system fitness for purpose.
- It enables progressively better estimates of resource requirements, based on unfolding experience.
- The rate of roll-out can be tailored to resources available.
- Earlier adopters provide demonstrators, and possibly training and support, for later adopters.
- It gives ICT services the time to evolve a generic research data management infrastructure that is capable of being customized to meet the needs of individual research groups and disciplines.
- It enables evolving developments in the field of research data management to be incorporated along the way.
- It enables the experiences and outputs of other major initiatives to be studied and incorporated as they become available – provided these are systematically monitored.

This phased approach has been implemented in the MaDAM project, which involves intensive requirements gathering within a small number of research groups, the close study of developers' responses to the requirements and rapid feedback of users' experiences of prototype systems; an iterative process of building a data management infrastructure that has the advantage of being embedded as part of the normal, everyday functioning of the research teams involved. In parallel, the project undertook an investigation of the viability of different financial models, a benefits realization strategy and a cost-benefit analysis of different financial models that could be designed to sustain the system in the long run.

In a highly constrained funding environment, instead of struggling to finance a 'big bang' implementation that starts by assembling a developer team to produce a generic infrastructure and then imposes it on researchers, a bottom-up, phased roll-out, with researchers buying into an infrastructure that evolves over time and within broad guidelines, is far more likely to prove to be financially feasible. A phased approach could also provide the incentive for researchers to sign up to systematic research data management, as research groups realize first the short-term gains of improved access to their own, systematically stored data and then begin to gain longer-term benefits, such as increased citation of their work by linking research data and publications in institutional repositories (see Piwowar, Day and Fridsma, 2007).

Service management and governance

The long-term preservation of research data involves active management; decisions need to be reviewed regularly, especially given that the cost of preserving all archived data for all time is impossible financially. Although the views of research grant holders and their teams should play a part in preservation decisions, it is important to counter their instinct to hoard data, which is effectively a consequence of their failure to make active preservation decisions. It may therefore be advisable that preservation decisions be the responsibility of a data custodian group, bringing to bear rigorous selection criteria for the continued preservation of archived data.

These criteria should include, *inter alia*, the data's academic and financial value, the extent of its use, its uniqueness (is it possible to re-create the data by rerunning the protocol that generated it or does the nature of it make the protocol unrepeatable?) and the affordability of its preservation (and curation), which, in turn, will be partly determined by the size of the data files. Selection of data for preservation is notoriously difficult given, on the one hand, the scale of the data deluge and, on the other, the unpredictability of the future value of research data. Although eased by the falling price of storage media, the overall cost of preservation rises inexorably given the necessity that preserved data must be curated, as we shall comment later. In some cases, the costs might be reduced by transferring the preservation and curation of research data to external repositories and data services; indeed, this is already a requirement by some research funders (described in the following chapter), as well as by some publishers.

A second key area for research data management governance lies in the realm of publication policies. As HEIs move towards implementing the linking of data with publications, the evidence of the MaDAM study and of others is that researchers will wish to retain some control over who has access:

> Our studies found that researchers in the life sciences want to know who is going to use the information or data they could be required to deposit and for what purpose. They also indicate that whilst the deposit of publications may be promoted as an opportunity to improve the dissemination of research results, without threatening any loss of control over the data from which they were derived, the development of institutional data repositories will require significantly greater safeguards than are provided for publications . . . it will be essential not only to demonstrate that mechanisms for embargoing or providing restricted or closed access to data collections can be reliably achieved, but that the researchers' strong desire to be consulted about the reuse of their data will be met. Here, active engagement between data producers and institutional data custodians is necessary for the agreement of workable processes, checks and balances.

RIN, 2009, 42

Developing the business case and modelling for sustainability

The final challenge to HEIs as they deliberate on whether, when and how much they should invest in developing research data management services is to weigh up the costs and benefits. Here, it would appear that the business case for investing is becoming clearer if not yet irrefutable. The RIN report *Stewardship of Digital Data* (2008) admitted,

> Neither costs nor benefits have been clearly identified at present, and so it is difficult to construct a clear business case for investment in the infrastructure of services necessary to ensure that research data are properly managed. It is important that assessments of costs and of the evidence of value are built into pilot and early implementation projects.
>
> RIN, 2008, 7

Two years later, the study *Keeping Research Data Safe 2* developed a cost model for preserving research data and provided in-depth case studies, which demonstrated that there are considerable cost-benefits to current researchers in the short term as well as long-term benefits (Beagrie, Lavoie and Woollard, 2010). The costs it identified include:

- potential cost of non-compliance – financial, legal and reputational
- cost of implementing and maintaining the service – hardware, software, network, training, support
- cost of research inefficiencies and lost data through poor data management.

Benefits for HEIs identified by the study include:

- compliance with internal and external policy mandates
- increased reputation for research
- easier and more efficient data discovery, access and reuse, especially in the long term
- increased opportunities for collaboration through data sharing
- ability to cost data management transparently and include it in full economic costing research funding bids
- possible data licensing opportunities and revenue generation
- new opportunities for staff career development based on recognition and rewards for research data creation, linking and management
- better management of risks associated with data (in)security or loss
- reduction in recurrent costs as local, *ad hoc* storage arrangements are replaced by energy-efficient centralized facilities.

At the University of Manchester, the MaDAM project and SAC have gone further in investigating how sustainable ongoing financial support of the research data management infrastructure can be achieved. Funding models investigated include direct cost recovery and free at the point of use models.

The direct cost recovery model recovers costs directly from research awards under full economic costing guidelines. Investigators would include the cost of research data management infrastructure in proposals as estimated by the extent and type of anticipated storage capacity and any tailoring of the infrastructure needed to meet special requirements (such as particular curation needs and compliance standards). This model can deliver an excellent customer-driven service provided accurate and transparent accounting systems assure customers that they are receiving what they have paid for.

The free at the point of use model provides research data management infrastructure free at the point of use, paid for either by the indirect costs included in research proposals, costed under full economic costing, or through block or quality-related research funding from the funding councils. It is probably easier to ensure accountability by adopting the full economic costing route, which provides a transparent costing of HEI research infrastructure, though it could be resisted by research councils already troubled by wide differences in HEIs' indirect costs. Similarly, the funding council or quality-related research route could reopen past debates about dual funding that neither party is keen to address. In both cases, HEIs' strategic goals and obligations to external compliance will have to be balanced against competing demands on funds.

Despite evidence of progress towards putting decisions on research data management service investment on a sounder footing, it remains doubtful whether HEIs are yet in a position to proceed in total confidence. Many of the cost-benefits remain unquantified or underquantified and how researchers (or, indeed, funders) might respond to different charging models is yet untested. Added to this are the challenges arising from operating in a time of rapid technical change and the inevitable uncertainties this creates for deciding on storage infrastructure implementation strategy. For example, should HEIs choose to build their own, local storage infrastructure, or elect to outsource the infrastructure via a 'cloud' service provider (cf. Badger et al., 2011)? The cost-benefits of each of these options need to be carefully reviewed. Unfortunately, the way forward is again hindered by the absence of clear evidence. As Hammond et al. (2010, i–ii) note in relation to cloud computing: 'Unless an organization has fully identified the costs of local provision, and understood how those costs would be changed by adoption of cloud systems, it is not possible to judge which approach is less expensive overall.'

Conclusion

We have seen how the adoption of new research data management services presents both opportunities and challenges to HEIs. Those that are successful in implementing services that are sustainable and fit for purpose should find their reputation for research enhanced as their researchers reap the benefits: more efficient data discovery, access and reuse, and increased opportunities for collaboration. The challenges, however, are formidable: changing the incentive structure for researchers; creating a new career structure for hybrids; and achieving sustainability in an uncertain financial environment when neither the costs nor benefits can be precisely measured.

To meet these challenges, HEIs need to consider the ways in which academic recognition and reward structures are locked in to traditional modes of validation and dissemination, which act as a disincentive to innovation. New information sharing practices are emerging (Procter et al., 2010) and institutional structures need to give due cognizance to these processes. At the very least, they must avoid inhibiting them; preferably, they will recognize and motivate the early and wide circulation of research findings. Broadly similar issues arise around attempts to promote data curation and reuse.

The growing attention to the 'third stream mission' of HEIs to promote knowledge transfer into the wider economy and society (HEFCE, 2009) and to the 'impact' of research on non-academic stakeholders, measurement of which is proposed under the UK's Research Excellence Framework, ought to encourage HEIs to revise management practices and cultures that have traditionally preferred scholarly publications at the expense of new forms of output, particularly where the latter are linked to open access and the publishing of research data. Evidence that linking research data to publications leads to increased citations is likely to serve as a strong incentive to individuals to adopt new practices for research data management. However, this will need to be balanced against the equally strong desire on the part of HEIs to protect valuable intellectual property and it is imperative that HEIs act to develop intellectual property policies and provide researchers with clear guidelines appropriate to exploiting new forms of scholarly communications.

If research data management services that are sustainable and fit for purpose are to be implemented, and if data management practices within the research community are to be transformed, then co-ordinated action is required from a range of stakeholders. In particular, it is important that funders also recognize and incentivize new forms of dissemination and research outputs. Given that dissemination, knowledge transfer and impact have never been higher on funders' agendas, it would seem timely for funders to encourage new practices. Impact measurements, such as those included in the Research Excellence Framework, might also acknowledge a wider variety of research outputs and scholarly contributions, including curated datasets and research data management activities, respectively. Such an approach will surely encourage researchers to adopt more systematic and comprehensive research data management practice, as well as the development of staff with the hybrid skills that will be essential to support them.

Finally, planning for sustainability in the longer term will need to take on board the prospect of research becoming more collaborative and research teams being more widely distributed, as signalled in the e-research vision of researchers worldwide addressing key challenges in new ways. The implications for data management services are summarized in a report from the Department for Business, Innovation and Skills (BIS), which concluded, 'A federated infrastructure will be essential to exploit existing and future investments effectively' (BIS, 2010, 9). If such a federated infrastructure is to be achievable, establishing effective inter-institutional service models will take on increasing importance. HEIs will need to develop strategies and infrastructure solutions that enable the federation of individual data repositories and the virtualization of data services. This will add a further layer of sustainability issues, the opportunities, costs and benefits of such collaborations will need to be carefully examined, and HEIs (large and small) will need to develop competencies in managing services that span administrative and funding boundaries.

References

Badger, L. et al. (2011) DRAFT Cloud Computing Synopsis and Recommendations, National Institute of Standards and Technology, U.S. Department of Commerce, Special publication 800-146.

Barjak, F. et al. (2009) Case Studies of e-Infrastructure Adoption. In Halfpenny, P. and Procter, R. (eds) Special Issue on e-Social Science, Social Science Computing Review Journal.

Barjak, F. et al. (2010) E-Infrastructure Adoption in the Social Sciences and Humanities: cross-national evidence, Information, Communication & Society, 13 (5).

Beagrie, N., Lavoie, B. and Woollard, M. (2010) Keeping Research Data Safe 2, www.jisc.ac.uk/media/documents/publications/reports/2010/keepingresearchdatasafe2.pdf.

BIS (2010) Delivering the UK's e-Infrastructure for Research, Department for Business, Innovation and Skills, www.rcuk.ac.uk/escience/einfrastructure.htm.

Collins, S. et al. (2010) Towards a Generic Research Data Management Infrastructure, UK e-Science All Hands Meeting, September 2010.

Duke, J., Jordan, A. and Powell, B. (2008) A Study for the JISC into the Integration of Technology into Institutional Strategies, www.jisc.ac.uk/whatwedo/programmes/programme_jos/project_lfhe.aspx.

Fichman, R. (2000) The Diffusion and Assimilation of Information Technology Innovations. In Zmud, R. W. (ed.), Framing the Domains of IT Management: projecting the future through the past, Pinnaflex Press, 105–28.

Fincham, R. et al. (1994) Innovation and the Management of Expertise: case studies from the financial services sector, Oxford University Press.

Gallivan, M. (2001) Organizational Adoption and Assimilation of Complex Technological Innovations: development and application of a new framework, ACM SIGMIS Database, special issue on adoption, diffusion, and infusion of IT, 32 (3).

Goff, M. et al. (2010a) The Implications of Disciplinary Practices for Emerging Modes of Data Sharing: a case study of biomedical researchers, UK e-Science All Hands Meeting, September 2010, www.escholar.manchester.ac.uk/item/?pid=uk-ac-man-scw:117514.

Goff, M. et al. (2010b) Understanding Research Practice and Enhancing Digital Curation in the Biomedical Domain: requirements for the participatory development of a pilot data management infrastructure, International Digital Curation Conference, December.

Hammond, M. et al. (2010) *Cloud Computing for Research*, report for JISC by Curtis+Cartwright Consulting Ltd,
www.jisc.ac.uk/whatwedo/programmes/researchinfrastructure/usingcloudcomp.asp.

Hartswood, M. et al. (2008) Co-realisation: evolving IT artefacts by design. In Ackerman, M., Halverson, C., Erickson, T. and Kellogg, W. (eds) *Resources, Co-Evolution and Artifacts*, Springer.

Hawtin, R., Davies, C. and Hammond, M. (2010) *Review of Models of Advanced ICT Support for Researchers*, report for JISC by Curtis+Cartwright Consulting Ltd,
www.jisc.ac.uk/whatwedo/programmes/researchcommunities/modelsofsupport.aspx.

HEFCE (2009) *Evaluation of the Effectiveness and Role of HEFCE/OSI Third Stream Funding*, report to HEFCE by PACEC and the Centre for Business Research, University of Cambridge, www.hefce.ac.uk/pubs/hefce/2009/09_15.

Hey, T. and Trefethen, A. (2003a) The Data Deluge: an e-science perspective, *Grid Computing: making the global infrastructure a reality*, 809–24.

Hey, T. and Trefethen, A. (2003b) E-science and its Implications, *Philosophical Transactions of the Royal Society of London A*, 15 August, **361**, 1809–25.

Hey, T., Tansley, S. and Tolle, K. (2009) *The Fourth Paradigm: data-intensive scientific discovery*, Microsoft Research.

Higgins, S. (2008) The DCC Curation Lifecycle Model, *International Journal of Digital Curation*, **1** (3), www.dcc.ac.uk/resources/curation-lifecycle-model.

Lee, C., Dourish, P. and Mark, G. (2006) The Human Infrastructure of Cyberinfrastructure, *Proceedings of the ACM Conference on Computer Supported Cooperative Work, Banff, Alberta, Canada, November*, 483–92.

Lyon, E. (2007) *Dealing with Relationships with Data: roles, rights and responsibilities*, UK Office for Library and Information Networking,
www.jisc.ac.uk/media/documents/programmes/digitalrepositories/dealing_with_data_re
port.final.pdf.

National Science Foundation (2003) *Report of the National Science Foundation Blue-Ribbon Advisory Panel on Cyberinfrastructure*, www.nsf.gov/od/oci/reports/toc.jsp.

National Science Foundation (2006) *NSF's Cyberinfrastructure Vision for 21st Century Discovery*, www.nsf.gov/od/oci/ci_v5.pdf.

Piwowar, H. A., Day, R. S. and Fridsma, D. B. (2007) Sharing Detailed Research Data is Associated with Increased Citation Rate, *PLoS ONE*, **2** (3), e308.

Poschen, M. et al. (2010) User-Driven Development of a Pilot Data Management Infrastructure for Biomedical Researchers, *UK e-Science All Hands Meeting, September 2010*.

Procter, R. and Voss, A. (2009) *eUptake Project Deliverable 1.4 Community Engagement Recommendations*, www.engage.ac.uk/e-uptake/e-uptake-deliverables.

Procter, R. et al. (2010) Adoption and Use of Web 2.0 in Scholarly Communications, *Philosophical Transactions of the Royal Society, A special issue on e-Science*, **368,** 4039-56.

Pryor, G. (2007) Project StORe: making the connections for research, *OCLC Systems & Services*, **23** (1), 70–78.

Putnam, R. (1995a) Tuning In, Tuning Out: the strange disappearance of social capital,

America, Political Science and Politics, **28** (4), 664–83.

Putnam, R. D. (1995b) Bowling alone: America's declining social capital, *Journal of Democracy,* **6** (1), 65–78.

RIN (2007) *Research Funders' Policies for the Management of Information Outputs,* Research Information Network, www.rin.ac.uk/our-work/research-funding-policy-and-guidance/research-funders-policies-management-information-outpu.

RIN (2008) *Stewardship of Digital Research Data: a framework of principles and guidelines,* Research Information Network, www.rin.ac.uk/our-work/data-management-and-curation/stewardship-digital-research-data-principles-and-guidelines.

RIN (2009) *Patterns of Information Use and Exchange: case studies of researchers in the life sciences,* Research Information Network, www.rin.ac.uk/our-work/using-and-accessing-information-resources/patterns-information-use-and-exchange-case-studies.

RIN (2010) *If You Build It, Will They Come? How researchers perceive and use web 2.0,* Research Information Network, www.rin.ac.uk/our-work/communicating-and-disseminating-research/use-and-relevance-web-20-researchers.

RIN (2011) *Reinventing Research? Information practices in the humanities,* Research Information Network, www.rin.ac.uk/news/events/reinventing-research-information-practices-humanities.

Takeda, K. (2011) *Institutional Data Management Blueprint Project Initial Findings Report,* University of Southampton, www.southamptondata.org/uploads/7/3/0/0/730051/idmbinitialfindingsreportv4.pdf.

Treloar, A. (2007) The Data Acquisition, Accessibility, Annotation and e-Research Technologies (DART) Project: supporting the complete e-research lifecycle, *UK e-Science All Hands Meeting, September 2007.*

UK Research Data Service (2008) *The UK Research Data Service Feasibility Study: report and recommendations to HEFCE,* www.ukrds.ac.uk/resources/download/id/16.

Voss, A. and Procter, R. (2010) Patterns of Adoption of Digital Research Tools in the Social Sciences, *UK e-Science All Hands Meeting, September 2010.*

Voss, A. et al. (eds) (2009) *Configuring User-designer Relations: interdisciplinary perspectives,* Springer.

Voss, A. et al. (2010) Adoption of e Infrastructure Services: configurations of practice, *Philosophical Transactions of the Royal Society A,* **368** (1926), 4161–76.

Whyte, A. and Pryor, G. (2011) Open Science in Practice: researcher perspectives and participation, *International Journal of Digital Curation,* **6** (1).

CHAPTER 8

The national data centres

Ellen Collins

Introduction
....

In recent years, interest in research data as a primary output of academic work has grown substantially. So, too, have questions about the best way to ensure that such data is curated and made available in a way that allows easy reuse. This chapter examines one response to such questions: the research data centre.

Research data centres feature as a significant component of the research infrastructure in the UK, and the data centres discussed in this chapter are all national resources that bring together datasets or databases from a variety of sources in order to provide ready, usually online, access by researchers to usable data. Beyond this, the exact nature of what they do varies considerably, reflecting the centre's holdings and the purpose for which it was established. In particular, there is a distinction between data centres that exist to collect, curate and store original research data, and those that focus on providing access to data services from a range of external sources. For this reason, it is difficult to characterize research data centres as a group; each one is a response to the specific needs of the discipline or disciplines that it serves, as well as the types of data that it supplies.

The data centres
....

Within the UK, data centres have a comparatively well established presence in the research ecosystem, with the first incarnation of the social sciences' UK Data Archive (UKDA) emerging as early as 1967. As Table 8.1 shows, data centres support a wide range of disciplines, although coverage is by no means universal.

Most data centres are supported by funding from one or more of the UK's research councils, seven publicly funded agencies responsible for co-ordinating and funding particular areas of research, and/or the Joint Information Systems Committee (JISC). There is considerable diversity in how such support is offered and maintained, even within the remit of a single research council. For example, the Natural Environment Research Council (NERC) has six designated data centres, marked with an asterisk in Table 8.1, which are responsible for collecting and managing data and for the

Table 8.1 *UK data centres (Compiled from data centre websites, April 2011)*

Name	Acronym	Host institution	Field
Archaeology Data Service	ADS	University of York	Archaeology
British Atmospheric Data Centre*	BADC	STFC Rutherford Appleton Laboratory	Atmospheric science
British Oceanographic Data Centre*	BODC	National Oceanography Centre	Marine science
Chemical Database Service	CDS	STFC Daresbury Laboratory	Chemistry
EDINA		University of Edinburgh	Various but with a focus on geo-data
Environmental Information Data Centre*	EIDC	Centre for Ecology and Hydrology	Terrestrial and freshwater science
European Bioinformatics Institute	EBI	Wellcome Trust Genome Campus	Bioinformatics
Mimas		University of Manchester	Various, as a source of data ranging from census records to the biosciences
Natural Geoscience Data Centre*	NGDC	British Geological Survey	Earth sciences
NERC Earth Observation Data Centre*	NEODC	STFC Rutherford Appleton Laboratory	Earth observation
Polar Data Centre*	PDC	British Antarctic Survey	Polar science
UK Data Archive	UKDA	University of Essex	Social science
UK Solar System Data Centre	UKSSDC	STFC Rutherford Appleton Laboratory	Solar science
*NERC-designated data centres.			

implementation of NERC data policies. Science-based archaeology is not covered by any of these centres but, rather than establish a new unit to support this field, the NERC provides funding to the Archaeology Data Service (ADS), an organization that falls primarily under the aegis of the Arts and Humanities Research Council (AHRC). This provides maximum efficiency for the funders and ensures that data from different but related disciplines is held in one place.

The NERC directly funds more data centres than any other research council, although financial support from other research councils may be provided in the form of contributions to established services rather than by independent provision. Hence, while the Engineering and Physical Sciences Research Council (EPSRC) has not established designated centres in the same way as the NERC, it does support the European Bioinformatics Institute (EBI) and funds the Chemical Database Service (CDS) on a three-year cycle. Similarly, the UK Solar System Data Centre (UKSSDC) is part of the international World Data Center network, established in the 1950s, which is funded on behalf of the UK by the NERC and the Science and Technology Facilities Council (STFC).

Many data centres have a portfolio of funders that extends beyond the research councils. These may be other prominent charitable organizations, such as the Wellcome Trust, which provides significant funding to the EBI, or they may be government departments like the Department for Environment, Food and Rural Affairs (DEFRA), which has supported the British Atmospheric Data Centre (BADC) through its Climate Impacts Project.

Commercial services for external clients can also be a valuable source of income: the ADS, for example, curates data from English Heritage and Historic Scotland for a fee, and the EBI has schemes for big businesses, small and medium enterprises and pre-competitive research. In these instances, the desire to generate income for the data centre is balanced with a desire to ensure the services remain fully accessible, typified perhaps by the EBI service for small and medium enterprises, which aims to provide the necessary support at a minimal cost (EMBL-EBI, 2010). In other instances, the data centres cover some of their costs by charging for collation and the provision of complex datasets, while maintaining a basic service free of charge.

Funding tends to follow the recognition by a research council that their ambition to encourage data sharing within a specific field requires support. The CDS, for example, was established after an EPSRC committee in 1992 recognized the advantages of having a central system for chemical database provision for UK academics. Development of the UKDA also followed a recommendation from a research council committee, which had been established specifically to look at the problems of data archiving and reuse in the social sciences. Its concern had been prompted by the knowledge that much data was either being unnecessarily re-created or, even worse, sold abroad to the USA and consequently 'lost' to British researchers (UKDA, 2007).

Research council support for data centres is not limited to funding. Through their policies and mandates, funders seek to ensure that centres are populated with the data that makes them useful to researchers. Four of the seven research councils (AHRC, ESRC, NERC and BBSRC) either mandate or recommend researchers to offer data for deposit within a specific data centre. A further two (MRC and EPSRC) specify the conditions under which data is to be retained by the originating institution, and only the STFC does not have a specific data policy – something which the UKSSDC has actually highlighted as a problem (UKSSDC, 2009). That said, the rate at which researchers actually deposit data suggests that compliance with these mandates is not particularly high (RIN and JISC, 2011), although they do provide an impetus for the increased sharing of data and over time may help to change the norms of practice in research fields.

In general, data centres are hosted by established academic institutions such as universities, national research centres or laboratories. In some cases, an institution will have been offering the service for a considerable time before being recognized as hosting a national data centre. The CDS, for example, had operated at the Daresbury

Laboratory before being selected by the EPSRC in 1992 to provide a national service; EDINA, which won its JISC contract in 1995, grew out of the Edinburgh University Data Library, which had been established in 1983. In other instances of institutional provision the service did not exist until the institution won a bid to provide it – as was the case with the UKDA's inception at the University of Essex.

Data centre services

Most data centres were created or funded in direct response to researchers' data-related needs. Researchers may consider their requirements to be relatively straightforward: they simply want to be able to find, share and reuse data as easily as possible. However, in order to meet these expectations, a number of processes need to take place that researchers may not be aware of when they submit, find or access datasets (Wilson et al., 2010). These subsidiary processes, which routinely exercise the data centres, converge around two main areas: the data itself and the facilities that enable access to this data. The role of data centres in undertaking such processes varies, depending on their relationship with the data they supply.

Some centres, such as the NERC's designated data centres, the ADS or the UKDA, are the designated repositories for their discipline: they have been made responsible for the collection, curation and long-term preservation and provision of datasets produced from research funded by 'their' research council. They are responsible for storing the data, ensuring that data is held in a format that allows reuse and which is protected against technical obsolescence. They are the closest analogue to what computer scientists mean when they talk about a 'data centre' – a physical facility for storing large amounts of data – although, as we shall see, they do a lot more than that, including providing access to datasets held elsewhere.

At the other end of the scale are centres such as the CDS, which does not hold any original data. Rather, it has been established to provide UK academic staff with ready access to existing chemical databases, managed by external suppliers. It does not need to worry about the technicalities of data storage, although it does take an interest in these issues. Its focus is much more on creating applications that make it easier for users to access the information they need and on training them in how to optimize their use of those applications. Most data-holding centres also provide these services but they are most critical to centres whose sole focus is access.

Somewhere in the middle are services such as those delivered by Mimas and EDINA. These JISC-funded data centres provide data storage but they are not the mandated repositories for specific disciplines. Therefore, their work with data tends to be project based (although such projects can be very long term) and it is often undertaken in alliance with other stakeholders – as with the JSTOR archive, a digital collection of core scholarly journals. Each project is usually devolved to a specific team with its own identity and website, as with Mimas's Archive Hub (http://archiveshub.ac.uk). Many of these projects focus on the provision of overlay services that make it easier to access data that are held elsewhere; such services are more numerous and often more discrete than those delivered by, for example, the CDS.

Services are thus determined to an extent by how much responsibility a data centre has for the original datasets that it is providing to end users. As the following sections will show, the services that collect and store data have a particular interest in issues like metadata standards, selection and appraisal, although most centres express some level of interest in these fundamental areas. All data centres provide services that enable users to access and download the data that they make available, although some are more complex and highly developed than others. As we shall see, most data centres also offer additional ancillary services designed to ensure that data continue to be collected and provided in a way that optimizes potential discovery and use, producing benefits for current and future generations of researchers.

Dealing with the idiosyncrasies of data

Raw data created by researchers is rarely presented in the kind of shape that permits easy sharing or reuse (RIN, 2008). For the most part, data is the idiosyncratic and somewhat messy product of a particular research process. Metadata, the term used to describe the content and context of data, is therefore absolutely crucial, as it enables new users to understand the process by which the data was collected and thus whether it is suitable for a particular type of reuse. Ideally, metadata should be generated alongside the original research data (Baker and Yarmey, 2009); however, it also needs to conform to a generic structure which cuts across individual experiments, thereby allowing search and comparison on an aggregating platform (Schopf and Newhouse, 2007). Significantly, researchers often need support in the creation of data in such a format (Donnelly and North, 2011; Pryor and Donnelly, 2009).

The creation of useful metadata is a priority for data centres with large onsite holdings and it is relatively common for them to set and maintain standards for research data within a discipline. The Polar Data Centre (PDC) considers 'setting standards for data collection, format and documentation' to be one of its key responsibilities and most data centres provide written guidance for researchers, explaining the importance of metadata and the necessity of documenting their research process so that metadata is created alongside the data being generated (BADC, 2007; BAS, 2007). Data centres that do not hold original datasets are less likely to offer hands-on, practical guidance, but they will still take an interest in the development of metadata standards and related issues. Mimas, for example, does not provide any direct guidance to researchers, but its developers work with core Mimas projects to investigate and innovate in areas such as semantic search and automated metadata generation (Mimas, n.d. (b)).

Many data centres actively help researchers to create data that are ready for curation and reuse, which is a step beyond ensuring they comply with the relevant metadata standards and includes dealing with collection methods and format. Here, the ADS provides online guides to 'best practice' for researchers in a range of sub-disciplines, which includes information on how to address version control, dealing with mixed formats (e.g. both digital and paper records) and documentation (ADS, 2009b). The British Oceanographic Data Centre (BODC) takes a more interactive 'end-to-end' approach, where data centre staff work alongside marine scientists from the beginning of projects to ensure that data is managed well and are finalized in a format that is ready for storage and reuse (BODC, 2011a).

The long-term usefulness of datasets is also a principal consideration for data centre managers. Beagrie, Beagrie and Rowlands (2009) found that researchers were most interested in the medium- and long-term preservation and curation of data, as opposed to short-term storage for periods lasting less than 12 months. But with a combination of finite resources for storage and the rapid increase in research data volumes, difficult decisions must be taken about the priorities for long-term preservation. (This fundamental need for the critical appraisal and selection of the most significant data, and consequently the rejection of other datasets, is recognized within the DCC Curation Lifecycle Model, as discussed in Chapter 2.) Changes in technology also represent a threat to the long-term viability of datasets, which will become unreadable as the systems used to create them reach a state of obsolescence. Data centres therefore need to 'future-proof' the data accepted into their custody, to take account of changes in software and hardware that may occur during their useful lifetime (Waller and Sharpe, 2006).

Hence we find that data centres play an absolutely crucial role in the process of selection and appraisal. In some instances this can be seen as a reactive undertaking, often in direct response to the mandate of a research council or other funder. The AHRC, for example, requires all funded projects in the field of archaeology to offer their research outputs to the ADS; the onus is then on the data centre to decide whether it will accept them or not (AHRC, 2011). The ADS makes such decisions based on a range of criteria, including whether the data is likely to be reused, whether data may viably be managed, preserved and distributed to secondary users, and whether there is any other suitable archival home for the materials that are offered (ADS, 2007). In other cases, the process is much more proactive, with centres actively seeking out important datasets for preservation and presentation to the research community, even when these are not covered by funding council mandates for deposition. This is the case for most of the NERC data centres, which are also tasked with the regular review and purging of data in their subject area to ensure their collections remain current and relevant (BGS, 2011).

Centres that hold research data consider future-proofing against technological change to be central to their mission. The STFC (n.d.) describes the UKSSDC as 'ensuring the long-term viability and usability' of the data that it holds; the BADC (2010a) talks about the 'long-term integrity' of its holdings and the BODC (2011b) approach specifically mentions looking after data 'so they are unaffected by changes in technology and will be available into the future'. Where alterations are made to the data after submission, centres usually adopt best practice by providing metadata to describe such changes; the

UKDA, for example, provides information so that researchers can see how original datasets have been transformed so as to be sustainable in the long term (UKDA, 2010).

The dynamics of data discovery and access management

Imaginary researchers can expect to be given an assurance of the provenance of data to be found in a regulated data centre and then, with confidence, proceed in the knowledge that the most useful datasets have been selected and protected against the obsolescence that might result from technological change. However, until they can actually access the data, their expressed headline need remains unmet.

Locating the data they require is but the first in a series of hurdles and researchers can struggle to find data online, even when they know what they are seeking (Lambert et al., 2007). It becomes more of a challenge when they are not looking for a specific, known dataset since, while most researchers do share their data, many rely on informal, *ad hoc* routes to sharing, which can limit the opportunity for colleagues who are browsing large data collections to find useful material (Beagrie, Beagrie and Rowlands, 2009, RIN, 2010a); and once researchers have identified the data they need, there is still no guarantee that it will be available in the format that they require, a particular consideration when they are planning to use or integrate it with their own original research. The application of standards would not necessarily solve this problem, as there are valid reasons for enabling creation and access to data using a wide range of formats (Lambert et al., 2007).

The selection and appraisal procedures undertaken by data-holding centres go some way towards ensuring that useful datasets do not become lost or obsolete. Because of their curatorial reputation, research data centres are known to researchers as trusted central repositories of those datasets considered to be of importance to a discipline and they therefore feature as a first port of call for their user community (RIN and JISC, 2011). All centres have an online facility that allows researchers to browse their holdings or the external databases to which they provide access. In some cases this is enhanced by a search facility that supports searching across databases or datasets, such as the EB-eye search engine created by the EBI (EMBL-EBI, 2010) or the CDS programme that allows researchers to search by chemical structures (McMeeking and Fletcher, 2004).

Data centres also work hard to publicize the access to data that they offer; this is often a key part of their funding agreement with research councils. NERC's data centres are responsible for 'promoting the use of data in their subject area by devising and promulgating catalogues, directories, leaflets and brochures' (BGS, 2011). To this we might now add social media as a way of keeping users up to date on what is available, with several data centres using Twitter feeds or blogs as a communication tool. For many data centres, such engagement is best done via human contact as well as printed and online materials. The CDS, for example, has received feedback from the academic community that, while online materials have their place, they cannot be the sole means of communication. As a result, the Service is increasing the number of off-site training visits that it offers, to ensure that researchers receive the support they need (McMeeking and Fletcher, 2004, 63). Most other centres also offer user training programmes that enable researchers to understand and get the most out of resources and services, either at the centre itself, or offsite at the users' own facilities, as with the EBI Bioinformatics Roadshow (EMBL-EBI, 2010).

To counteract the data format issues that can hinder data reuse, a number of data centres develop overlay programmes and technologies that allow researchers to define the way in which they view the data. Such a facility is offered by several of the data-holding centres. The NERC's BADC and Earth Observation Data Centre (NEODC) have, for example, worked with the Centre for Environmental Data Archival (CEDA) to create a portal that allows users to visualize a range of datasets layered on a user-defined map, with the option to download the data that underlie the image they create in a variety of predefined formats (CEDA, n.d. (b)).

These portals form the core of the service offered by data centres with the principal role of providing access to external datasets. Although Mimas hosts some information assets, it may more correctly be observed that its main expertise is vested in 'building applications that enable a wide range of users to make the most of this rich [data] resource' (Mimas, n.d. (a)). Under this service-orientated mantle data centres will develop and deliver utilities and products such as those offered by the Census Dissemination Unit, which helps researchers to interrogate a number of recent Census-related datasets and generate outputs tailored to their research projects (CDU, n.d.). EDINA has a similar mission, having developed a particular expertise in geospatially enhanced data (EDINA, 2010).

Access to data is of course subject to a spectrum of legislative and regulatory regimes. The exact nature of the relationship between publicly funded research data and freedom of information legislation is still being tested, but as demonstrated in 2009 by the University of East Anglia (UEA) climate change controversy, commonly known as 'Climategate', it is important to understand that requests can be made under these regulations. In this instance, the Climatic Research Unit at the UEA received an unusually large number of freedom of information requests as part of an organized campaign, after it failed to comply with earlier requests. The UEA researchers' unwillingness to release the requested datasets, because they believed the requests were vexatious and aimed at undermining their research, were documented in a series of leaked emails. This leak led to a review, which incorporated an examination of the researchers' obligations under the Freedom of Information Act. The review found that part of the problem stemmed from a lack of clarity about the kind of data that are covered by freedom of information legislation. While data, metadata, code and algorithms relating to a specific publication are covered, the position is less clear in relation to long-term datasets that may have been held for a number of years (Russell et al., 2010). Clarification of this issue is particularly important for data centres, many of which hold exactly this kind of resource.

The reuse of data is also governed by academic convention and will reflect the importance of citation and acknowledgement to those pursuing a career within higher education. Here, the OECD's pioneering declaration on open access to research data recognizes the importance of protecting intellectual property through the formal recognition of different copyright regimes and a less formal but equally important system of acknowledgement to be applied in the reuse of research data, thereby ensuring that credit accrues to the researcher who originally generated the datasets being reused (OECD, 2004).

Researchers are also concerned about protecting the confidentiality of their subjects, which is particularly important for research in social science or biomedical fields (Lievesley and Jones, 1998). Social science research data often contain highly personal information about the subjects; the same is true for biomedical data, which may also be considered proprietary information, as research is often funded by pharmaceutical and biomedical businesses seeking possible commercial applications (RIN, 2010b). In many cases, researchers also need to offer varying levels of access to different groups of people at different stages of their project (Schopf and Newhouse, 2007).

These are all priority concerns for the managers of data centres, whose function would be invalidated were there any serious loss of faith in their reputation as professional custodians. All data centres must acknowledge the critical importance of protecting the information assets entrusted to them and will, as in the case of the Natural Geoscience Data Centre (NGDC), explicitly state as one of their aims the protection of intellectual property rights for the data funders, researchers and other relevant stakeholders. Similarly, the ADS recognizes that concern about copyright may prevent some researchers from depositing their data, offering user-specific guidance about the protection that online data enjoy (ADS, 2008b). In other cases, data centres must comply with specific legislation beyond the generic provisions of copyright. This is the case for the PDC, which is subject to the Antarctic Treaty and relevant resolutions of the Antarctic Treaty Consultative Meetings (BAS, 2007). In the spirit of the OECD's Declaration, data centres also offer advice and guidance on conventions for data citation to ensure that when data is reused both the original source researchers and the data service host (where appropriate) are given the appropriate credit (BADC, 2010c).

It is also crucial that data centres recognize the complexity of managing the different levels of access that researchers may require. In some instances this relates to the ethical agreements between the original data collectors and their research subjects. The UKDA, which deals with social science datasets derived from the study of individual human subjects, specifically requires that deposits be 'free from any legal or ethical issues that may limit the sharing of data' (UKDA, 2011). To help researchers meet this criterion, the UKDA provides extensive guidance on how to obtain the appropriate permissions from research participants. In a completely different subject domain the EBI, which holds biological data about individuals, also recognizes the challenge of balancing accessibility with the need to protect the confidentiality of human subjects (EMBL-EBI, 2010). There is a positive side to these constraints, since having an awareness of the issues means that the data centres must work closely with their depositors to ensure that as much data as possible are made available, while at the same time still protecting the rights of individual research participants. Such an approach inevitably contributes to the integrity and quality of the service they provide.

This active involvement with their research communities in managing access and dissemination is not uncommon, to the extent that one can find data centres providing assistance to researchers who need to share their data as a work in progress, rather than as the final output of a research project. The BADC, for example, offers File Transfer Protocol (FTP) workspaces for researchers who need to create an offsite, shareable version of their data for a restricted audience during the lifetime of a project. In this case the BADC provides the disk space and manages access for users who have been given permission by the data originators, but it has no further interaction with the data (BADC, 2006). The BADC also creates licences for data generated within certain NERC funding programmes, which give the original researchers exclusive access to their datasets for a year after deposit. This minimizes the risk of 'scooping', which can be a major deterrent to data sharing, while ensuring that the data is safely preserved at the end of a project when, importantly, it is a matter that is still fresh in researchers' minds (BADC, 2010b).

Additional attributes

As well as gathering, curating, preserving and providing access to research data for external audiences, many data centres undertake research in their own right. As one might expect, this is often anchored in the specific field in which they are already operating. The EBI, for example, has a community of researchers based at its facilities near Cambridge who are working on new approaches to interpreting biological data (EMBL-EBI, 2010). Other data centres focus less on their discipline and more on the generic challenges facing suppliers of digital information. One such instance is Mimas, which is involved in research that supports its aim of experimenting and pushing the boundaries of technological knowledge around issues including the automatic assignment of metadata, linked data and semantic searching (Mimas, n.d. (b)).

Data centres apply and export their expertise in national and international fora. For some, this can remain discipline-focused, as with the NERC data centres, which are all required to represent their discipline on the NERC Data Management Advisory Group (BGS, 2011). Others are valued for their expertise on a specific technological issue. EDINA, for example, has brought its corporate geospatial knowledge to a wide range of UK and international projects (EDINA, 2010). As a welcome spin-off, the international connections made by the centres can be leveraged to help UK researchers access collections that are held abroad (RIN and JISC, 2011).

Data centres may also act as a hub for the distribution of other kinds of scholarly information that may otherwise be difficult to discover online. The ADS, for example, has an extensive collection of grey literature, a resource of particular importance within archaeology where much research is carried out by public or commercial sector researchers who do not necessarily publish their findings as a matter of course (RIN and JISC, 2011). The BADC offers the endearingly named 'Poster Heaven' – an afterlife for conference posters – which are stored in the CEDA repository (BADC, 2009; CEDA, n.d. (a)). Many researchers struggle to access conference papers – often because they are never formally published – so other data centres in other domains may also wish to consider offering a central facility for data that underlie the posters, and perhaps even the posters themselves, as part of their aim to improve access to research information (RIN, 2011).

Measuring the impact of data centres

The previous section outlined some of the main ways in which research data centres attempt to meet researchers' needs and how, more generally, they support the development of data services. This and subsequent sections will explore the impact that their activities have had, offset by some consideration of those areas where they may have been less successful. To round off this discussion, some observation of the arts and humanities domain will be used to provide an example of what happens in disciplines where data centres are not sustained.

Although data centres undertake some research into user needs and behaviours, as well as receiving *ad hoc* feedback from their users, relatively little of this information has been made publicly available. For this reason, the Research Information Network (RIN) and the JISC commissioned a study of the users of five UK data centres (RIN and JISC, 2011). Owing to the small sample sizes taken and the idiosyncratic nature of each UK data centre, the findings of this research cannot be taken as being representative of all UK data centre users. However, from a user perspective they do provide some useful context, highlighting areas of strength and weakness, and can be combined with the information that is openly available information from the data centres themselves to develop a broader insight.

To understand impact it is necessary first to establish exactly who uses the data centres. Academic, public sector and commercial researchers all have a legitimate interest in accessing research data but in many instances they will experience different levels of access, each determined by the licence agreements in place with the original suppliers of the data. Where the licence terms for datasets within their holdings vary, data centres provide details of the different conditions of access and use that apply, either through a page on their website, as does the BADC, or by including such information with the metadata for each dataset, as is the practice of the Environmental Information Data Centre (EIDC) and the UKDA.

Data centres that supply external data do so primarily to support the UK academic community, the key constituency for most data centre funders. Licence agreements between data centres and data holders reflect this priority, meaning that many datasets and services are not available to anyone outside academia. The CDS, which only supplies third-party data, puts this particularly bluntly, stating that 'a key point is that no commercial use is made of the Service' (CDS, 2009). Similarly, the BADC, while relatively open with its own datasets, can offer Met Office and European Centre for Medium-range Weather Forecast data only to UK academic researchers (BADC, 2010 b). However, the definition of 'UK academics' can be loose and may include technicians, librarians, information officers and even visiting academics from non-UK institutions. The CDS has adopted Shibboleth, a single sign-on authentication system for higher education funded by the JISC, as a means of ascertaining whether intending users have the right to access data that are restricted to UK academics.

Commercial and public sector users have a more mixed experience when seeking to access data that is held by the data centres primarily for use by academic researchers, where the range of terms and conditions applied by the data centres often reflect the priorities of the research funders. This condition need not necessarily prove restrictive. Data created through NERC grants, for example, is considered a public good and must be made available without any restrictions on reuse (NERC, 2011). This is reflected in the policies of the BADC, which does not even require registration for access to much of its data, and the BODC, which mentions a specific interest in supplying data to industry and the wider public (BADC, 2010b; BODC, 2011c). But other centres take a more didactic approach to commercial reuse, the ADS permitting access to data for use in commercially sponsored research as long as the results are placed in the public domain and made freely available to others, 'according to the normal principles of professional and academic practice' (ADS, 2008a). In other instances, specific services may be universally available thanks to targeted funding. Since September 2010, for example, JISC funding has made data from the Mimas Hairdressing Training service (http://hairdressing.ac.uk) open to all users, rather than limiting it to the original target audience of further education lecturers and students.

User numbers from the RIN and JISC study are given in Table 8.2 and confirm that most data centre users come from the academic sector. They represent the majority of users for four of the five national data centres; the anomalous numbers for the NGDC are explained by the fact that almost all of the survey respondents worked for the British Geological Survey. The strict eligibility criteria applied by the CDS are reflected in the fact that 99% of its users come from academia or public research organizations – the only sectors licensed to access the Service's databases. The BADC and ADS have more mixed user groups. Their offer to provide data to any user, without the need for preregistration or proof of eligibility, is probably responsible for this outcome. However, they also have the potential for a more diverse audience than other centres; the ADS, for example, will attract local authority planners, private businesses such as builders and independent archaeological consultants as well as academic researchers.

Table 8.2 *Origin of data centre users (Source: RIN and JISC, 2011)*					
Sector	Data centre				
	ADS	BADC	CDS	ESDS	NGDC
Academic	51%	67%	95%	78%	4%
Public research organisation	0%	21%	4%	4%	86%
Private research organisation	8%	2%	1%	4%	0%
Private or independent researcher	8%	2%	1%	2%	2%
Central or local government	10%	5%	0%	7%	2%
Business	5%	1%	0%	1%	0%
Community or charity organization	11%	1%	0%	2%	0%
Other	8%	3%	1%	3%	6%
N=	83	759	200	292	51
Because of rounding errors, totals may not sum to 100%					

Data centres, their strengths and weaknesses

The most common benefit to be derived from using data centres, as highlighted by respondents to the RIN and JISC survey, was improvements in research efficiency, which for most meant that the data centre saved them time within their projects (RIN and JISC, 2011). This perception is echoed by the users of some of EDINA's services, whose experiences were surveyed in late 2010. In that earlier analysis, 81% of respondents to the Digimap Ordnance Survey questionnaire agreed that their work would take longer if the collection were not available (EDINA, 2011a). But efficiency can also relate to financial savings, another popular response within the RIN survey and among users of some of the EDINA services. One user of EDINA's Unlock tool estimated that the service had saved him around £25,000 annually in subscription fees (EDINA, 2011c).

Data centres can also claim to enhance the value for money that research funders enjoy from their investment in research and research output, as well as from increases in efficiency. By encouraging the reuse of data, national centres aim for the maximum possible value to be extracted from data deposited with them. Acting as the executive arm of their research council or sponsoring trust, they contribute directly to the strategic goals of the major funders by encouraging and enabling good practice in the management of data throughout the research lifecycle and, in more recent times, facilitating the growth of data-based research in fields that extend beyond the scope of the projects originally funded by a specific research council (Pepler, 2010). This function as authoritative host and hub has a positive flip-side too, since data centres can also help ensure that new money is not spent on the duplication of research that has already been undertaken: witness 68% of CDS users who said that the data centre had helped to prevent the unnecessary re-creation of data (RIN and JISC, 2011).

One can argue that data centres have taken great strides in helping to make data discoverable, not least by becoming the first port of call for a corpus of researchers seeking information – those who 'wouldn't think to look anywhere else for it' (RIN and

JISC, 2011). The reason that they have become so dominant is hinted at in the responses to an EDINA survey of users of SUNCAT, a free tool for locating serials held in the UK. Many survey respondents mentioned the importance of SUNCAT's single front-end and straightforward interface, which allowed them to navigate a fairly complex and distributed dataset with ease (EDINA, 2011b). There is also a suggestion that data centres have encouraged data sharing within a research discipline, thereby further increasing the number of datasets available to researchers, as indicated in Table 8.3.

Table 8.3 *Impact of data centres on improving the culture of data sharing within disciplines (Source: RIN and JISC, 2011)*

Level of impact on data sharing culture	Data centre				
	ADS	BADC	CDS	ESDS	NGDC
To a large extent	84%	69%	72%	54%	68%
To a small extent	16%	29%	27%	40%	30%
Not at all	0%	2%	1%	7%	3%
Numbers of responses	*61*	*601*	*164*	*244*	*37*
Because of rounding errors, totals may not sum to 100%					

It is important to note, however, that user surveys by definition tend only to capture the views of people who have, at some point, benefited from the services being examined. There is no absolute way of knowing whether non-users do not require data centres, or whether they simply do not know about them. One would hope, given the number of training schemes and awareness days run by data centres, that it is a lack of need rather than a lack of awareness that explains the lack of engagement by some potential users. User surveys by EDINA and the BADC indicate that researchers from a wide range of disciplines are using their quite discipline-specific services, which suggests that their reach is relatively good (Pepler, 2010). But until empirical evidence about non-users becomes available, claims of extensive and successful data discoverability must remain cautious.

The explicit curatorial activity of data centres is a further characteristic that is rated highly by researchers. Respondents to the RIN and JISC, and EDINA surveys identified the high quality of curated data as a benefit to their research, referring especially to the work of the centres in ensuring that data is presented in a standardized format. They also mentioned the importance of creating high quality collections of data, as opposed to assuring the quality of individual datasets, which is of particular importance in the context of unique observational data that cannot be re-created, where the data centres' active collecting strategies help to prevent the loss of irreplaceable datasets that will have long-term value (RIN and JISC, 2011).

There is some evidence from the RIN and JISC research that data centres are showing progress in ensuring that data is created in a format that makes them ready for deposit and reuse, and that they are achieving success in encouraging better metadata quality by setting standards for researchers to follow. However, other sources suggest that this is an area where data centres, as national bodies, cannot drive the kind of change that is needed, since support for creating curation-ready data is best provided at a very local level. Whyte's 2008 case study of a psychiatric research group found a disconnect between the national standards for neuroimaging metadata laid out by research funders and councils, and the more semi-structured formats used by researchers on the ground, showing that national initiatives may not always have an effect at the institutional level. Whyte suggests that funders need to 'think global, act local' if they are to improve metadata standards, and also recommends that curation lifecycle management training should be provided to master's and doctoral level students – which is about as local as support can get (Whyte, 2008).

Research projects are highly idiosyncratic and academics generally prefer to do things their own way, according to their own preferences and culture (Donnelly and North, 2011), so it is important to have expert advice and support provided from the very beginning of the research process, at a level that can reflect and accommodate the specific needs of the project and the researcher. But it is very difficult to parachute this in from some remote centre (Pryor and Donnelly, 2009). The BODC 'end-to-end' approach is something of an exception among data centres, many of which limit their support to best practice guides provided online or to sporadic contact with researchers. In any case, there would undoubtedly be capacity issues for data centres if they were to try and support every researcher within their discipline in person.

In other areas researcher training is proving to be more effective. Many respondents to the RIN and JISC survey identified the importance of data centre resources as a means of helping new graduate students engage with the datasets that will be crucial to their future careers (RIN and JISC, 2011). This aspect of data centre service was also identified by users of EDINA's Geology Digimap survey; most of the users of this service are undergraduates and they rated Digimap highly in its teaching and learning value (EDINA, 2011a). Similarly, informal comments received by the ADS frequently refer to the value of the service for teaching new students (ADS, 2009a).

Life without data centres

As Table 8.1 showed, not all disciplines enjoy access to a research data centre. The arts and humanities are one such example, although until 2008 they were served by the Arts and Humanities Data Service (AHDS), which had been funded by the AHRC and the JISC since 1996. Looking at what has happened within this discipline since the demise of the AHDS, and examining the kinds of data-related problems that exist in this subject area, helps to reaffirm the value and importance of data centres as has already been described.

The defining originality and value of research datasets in the humanities tends to lie in the way they have been curated as a collection, rather than in the fact that they are newly generated by researchers. In support of this interpretation, many of the AHDS holdings were digitized versions of existing physical objects, manuscripts or artworks for example, or collections of material such as linguistics corpora that had been produced as the by-products of a research process. In such a context it is significant that the AHDS referred to its 'resources' rather than 'datasets', unlike most other data centres (AHDS, 2008).

AHDS support was particularly important for research outputs generated through the AHRC Resource Enhancement Funding Programme, which 'provides support for projects aiming to improve access to and use of research resources and materials' (AHRC, 2005). Most projects produced some kind of application or tool, usually either an online catalogue or a searchable resource, and a main role of the AHDS was to assure the long-term security of the data underlying these applications, as well as advising on the sustainability of the applications themselves (Robey, 2007a, 2007b).

When the AHRC withdrew funding from the AHDS it did so on three grounds. First, it claimed that researchers (and the HEIs in which they work) had developed the technical knowledge and expertise to undertake their own data curation and storage. Second, it expressed the view that long-term storage and sustainability is best handled by active engagement with HEIs, rather than through a central service. And third, given the two previous points, the AHDS had become an unnecessary expense, and one that was only likely to increase (Ball et al., 2007). There is no doubt that all three of these arguments contain an element of truth but reactions from within the discipline, at the time of closure and subsequently, endorse a widespread view that the AHDS had been providing a very useful service, well beyond what was available from any individual institution.

The first ground for closure, that individuals and institutions had become sufficiently expert in technical fields, appeared to be true in some HEIs but by no means in all. Denbo, Haskins and Robey (2008) undertook a survey of principal investigators who had created resources through the Resource Enhancement Funding Programme, finding around half of their respondents believing their institution's support for their digital project to be 'good' or 'excellent'; but around a fifth considered it to be 'minimal' or to have 'none' at all. One respondent commented that it was '"infuriating" to read that part of the AHRC's rationale for defunding the AHDS was that the necessary expertise now exists in HE institutions. This has simply not been my experience' (Denbo, Haskins and Robey, 2008, 11).

It is perhaps not surprising to find that researchers' confidence in their institution's ability to undertake long-term storage and sustainability is also somewhat mixed. The Denbo, Haskins and Robey survey discovered that researchers have the most confidence in university libraries and external specialist centres when it comes to the long-term sustainability of their work, but are less confident about resources deposited in other parts of the university. In some cases, this is simply because 'tasks are being left to academics which they are not fully qualified, and/or do not have the time, to carry out' (Denbo, Haskins and Robey, 2008, 10).

Of course, storage and sustainability are not the only responsibilities of a dedicated data centre; many other benefits flow from a centralized resource (Robey, 2007b). In the case of the AHDS we find a national centre that had begun to play an important role in supporting individual researchers throughout their project, and in advising on the standards for data creation (Dunning, 2006). While single institutions may be able to help in implementing such standards, it is much harder for them to drive developments and improvements at a national level.

Another important issue is discoverability, as argued by Ball et al. (2007), which might be considered to be a further facet of sustainability. But it is important to note that the AHDS may not have been universally successful in this respect, since Warwick et al. (2006) found that around 30–35% of digital arts and humanities resources were unused. That said, the Service did provide a single, visible gateway to a wide range of resources and, in the wake of its demise, researchers still want to publicize their work but 'with a limited budget, we are more likely to prioritize updating and correcting over advertising' (Denbo, Haskins and Robey, 2008, 10).

The final point made by the AHRC, that the AHDS was unjustifiably expensive, is also problematic. Defunding the Service simply meant that these costs, instead of being centralized, have become devolved to individual projects and institutions, which in general cannot afford adequately to cover them. Data storage is a particular problem: one researcher has suggested that since the AHRC encourages projects that need large infrastructures such as data storage but will not cover the cost of these infrastructures, 'an unknown number of project proposals can never even be submitted' (Denbo, Haskins and Robey, 2008, 11). Ensuring that research outputs remain compatible with changing technologies is also an expensive business, particularly when the products are complex resources and often custom-built. This is an aspect of data curation that can require ongoing support from a dedicated computer technician, a facility that is rarely available within individual institutions. Often, one finds instead that updates are undertaken by principal investigators *pro bono*, or by recourse to funds that they have diverted from subsequent grant applications (Denbo, Haskins and Robey, 2008).

Conclusion

The UK experience of data centres has largely been positive. The complex ecology of UK research is reflected in the interwoven network of data centre provision. It is difficult to define a data centre *per se*, since their characteristics and services are determined by the types of data they hold and the kinds of community they serve. At their core, however, they all focus on working with researchers to support data reuse, both to individuals and by providing generic guidance.

It can be demonstrated that this work coalesces around four main functions. First, the creation and storage of data that is ready to reuse, which is more of a priority for centres designated as repositories for particular disciplines or funders. Here, data centres work alongside researchers to ensure that data is supplied in a format that is ready for reuse. This may involve promoting standards within a discipline and supporting researchers to meet those standards, or it may require data centre staff to take responsibility for cleaning and annotating data themselves.

Second, data centres create and curate collections of data that will provide fruitful raw material for new research projects. This is true for centres that hold their own data and those that primarily provide access to data held elsewhere. By working with researchers, funders and other experts within their discipline, they can fulfil their responsibility to maintain collections which stimulate and encourage reuse of datasets.

Third, data centres provide access to data, ensuring that the manner in which it is offered meets the needs of researchers as both users and suppliers of data. Guarantees of legal and ethical compliance are particularly important for this latter function, as is the stipulation by most data centres that users must acknowledge the original data creators when reusing their work.

Finally, data centres help to raise the profile of data within a discipline. They achieve this by ensuring that researchers are aware of the services that they offer and the needs of data users are acknowledged within funding and policy bodies, in the UK and beyond.

Data centres have been demonstrably successful in most of these areas. When asked, data centre users will comment typically on the efficiency that data centres bring to the research process. They save researchers time by providing an alternative to repeating experiments and observations; and they simplify the process of finding and accessing data that otherwise might necessitate journeys of discovery across a myriad of routes, including making contact with the original researchers. They can also contribute to cost efficiencies by ensuring that the maximum value is extracted from data generated by publicly funded research, a benefit with political as well as pecuniary kudos.

Allied to research efficiency, data centres also appear to increase discoverability. As a centralized, relatively high-profile resource within a research domain they generally become a point of first contact for researchers seeking data. The experience of researchers following the closure of the AHDS suggests that data centres are able to provide publicity and promotion on a scale that is not viable for an individual researcher with a dataset to share. There is also some evidence that data centres encourage data sharing, thereby increasing the number of datasets available for reuse. But the fact that the extent of data centre usage and their reach within a discipline remains unknown, places an important caveat on these benefits.

In other areas, data centres are more effective when working alongside institutions and other stakeholders in the field of research data management. While data centres are important in helping to set standards for data creation and metadata, they cannot provide the individual, tailored support that individual researchers need as they work on their individual projects. In this respect they are, as Macdonald and Martinez (2005) argue, part of a network of data service provision, and should aim to work alongside institutional services to support researchers. In this context, Baker and Yarmey (2009) introduce the concept of repositories that exist on a scale from 'local' to 'remote', using these terms to mean the socio-technical, rather than physical, distance from the data originator. Against this measure, data centres may be considered more as 'remote' repositories, working to create, sustain and publicize data collections, rather than supporting researchers at a 'local' level in the creation of curation-ready data and metadata. However, as they emphasize, a remote repository has an important role to play in setting standards that will apply across disparate local services, ensuring that the data created meet the needs not just of local research projects but also of the wider discipline.

Notwithstanding these caveats, the UK data centres represent an important and valued asset within the research infrastructure. Not only do they support researchers in the creation, discovery and reuse of data assets, they are also conspicuous in their engagement with other actors who have an interest in data creation, whether in research institutions, national and international centres of excellence or funding and policy bodies. Perhaps most tellingly, the RIN and JISC survey prompted a number of responses from researchers based outside the UK who envy the UK's data centres and the services that they provide, expressing their wish that their own countries would support a similar level of provision (RIN and JISC, 2011). As former users of the AHDS might be able to tell us, the value of research data centres is perhaps brought into its clearest focus when the services that they offer are no longer available.

References

ADS (2007) *Collections Policy*, 4th edn, Archaelogy Data Service,
     http://ads.ahds.ac.uk/project/collpol.html#evaluating.
ADS (2008a) *Common Access Agreement*, Archaelogy Data Service,
     http://ads.ahds.ac.uk/cap.html.
ADS (2008b) *Frequently Asked Questions*, Archaelogy Data Service,
     http://ads.ahds.ac.uk/project/faq.html#copy.
ADS (2009a) *Annual Report: 1 August 2008 to 31 July 2009*, Archaelogy Data Service,
     http://archaeologydataservice.ac.uk/about/annualReport2008.
ADS (2009b) *Guides to Good Practice*, Archaelogy Data Service,
     http://ads.ahds.ac.uk/project/goodguides/g2gp.html.
AHDS (2008) *About AHDS Collections*, Arts and Humanities Data Service,
     www.ahds.ac.uk/collections/about.htm.
AHRC (2005) *Resource Enhancement Scheme*, Arts and Humanties Research Council,
     www.ahrc.ac.uk/FundedResearch/Pages/ResourceEnhancementSchemeReview.aspx.
AHRC (2011) *AHRC Research Funding Guide*, Arts and Humanties Research Council.
BADC (2006) *BADC Project Spaces*, British Atmospheric Data Centre,
     http://badc.nerc.ac.uk/community/project_spaces.html.
BADC (2007) *Metadata*, British Atmospheric Data Centre,
     http://badc.nerc.ac.uk/help/metadata/.
BADC (2009) *Retired Services*, British Atmospheric Data Centre,
     http://badc.nerc.ac.uk/community/retired.html.
BADC (2010a) *About the BADC*, British Atmospheric Data Centre,

http://badc.nerc.ac.uk/home/about.html.

BADC (2010b) *Access Rules*, British Atmospheric Data Centre,
http://badc.nerc.ac.uk/data/rules.html [Accessed 20 April 2011].

BADC (2010c) *How to Acknowledge Data*, British Atmospheric Data Centre,
http://badc.nerc.ac.uk/help/acknowledgement.html.

Baker, K. and Yarmey, L. (2009) Data Stewardship: environmental data curation and a web-of-responsibilities, *International Journal of Digital Curation*, **4** (2), 12–27.

Ball, S., Comer, S., Fowler, W., Knight, J., Knott, P., Lambert, N., Reynolds, L., Smith, B. and White, I. (2007) *Open Letter: to the Arts and Humanities Research Council*,
http://futurehistories.wordpress.com/category/ahds.

BAS (2007) *Role of the Polar Data Centre*, British Antarctic Survey,
www.antarctica.ac.uk/about_bas/our_organisation/eid/pdc/index.php.

Beagrie, N., Beagrie, R. and Rowlands, I. (2009) Research Data Preservation and Access: the views of researchers, *Ariadne*, **60**, www.ariadne.ac.uk/issue60/beagrie-et-al.

BGS (2011) *About the National Geoscience Data Centre (NGDC)*, British Geological Survey,
www.bgs.ac.uk/services/ngdc/about.html.

BODC (2011a) *Data Management*, British Oceanographic Data Centre,
www.bodc.ac.uk/projects/data_management.

BODC (2011b) *What is BODC?*, British Oceanographic Data Centre,
www.bodc.ac.uk/about/what_is_bodc.

BODC (2011c) *Where to Find Data*, British Oceanographic Data Centre,
https://www.bodc.ac.uk/data/where_to_find_data.

CDS (2009) *About the CDS*, Chemical Database Service,
http://cds.dl.ac.uk/cds/service_info/about.html.

CDU (n.d.) *Census Dissemination Unit*, Census Dissemination Unit,
http://cdu.mimas.ac.uk/index.htm.

CEDA (n.d. (a)) *About the Repository*, Centre for Environmental Data Archival,
http://cedadocs.badc.rl.ac.uk/information.html.

CEDA (n.d. (b)) *Data Visualisation*, Centre for Environmental Data Archival,
http://ceda.ac.uk/data-viz/index.php/data-visualisation.

Denbo, S., Haskins, H. and Robey, D. (2008) *Sustainability of Digital Outputs from AHRC Resource Enhancement Projects*, AHRC, www.ahrcict.rdg.ac.uk/activities/review/sustainability.htm.

Donnelly, M. and North, R. (2011) The Milieu and the MESSAGE: talking to researchers about data curation issues in a large and diverse e-science project, *International Journal of Digital Curation*, **6** (1), 32–44.

Dunning, A. (2006) The Tasks of the AHDS: ten years on, *Ariadne*, **48**,
www.ariadne.ac.uk/issue48/dunning.

EDINA (2010) *EDINA Annual Review 2009–2010*,
http://edina.ac.uk/about/annual_review2010.

EDINA (2011a) *Benefits and Impact Achievements – Digimaps Ordnance Survey Collection*,
http://edina.ac.uk/impact/docs/os_digimap_Benefits_and_Impact_Achievements_Feb2011.pdf.

EDINA (2011b) *Benefits and Impact Achievements – SUNCAT*,
    http://edina.ac.uk/impact/docs/SUNCAT_Benefits_and_Impact_Achievements_Feb201
    1.pdf.

EDINA (2011c) *Benefits and Impact Achievements – Unlock Service*,
    http://edina.ac.uk/impact/docs/unlock.pdf.

EMBL-EBI (2010) *EMBL European Bioinformatics Institute in a Nutshell*, European Molecular
    Biology Laboratory-European Bioinformatics Institute,
    www.embl.de/aboutus/communication_outreach/publications/brochures/EBI_brochure
    .pdf.

Lambert, P., Gayle, V., Tan, L., Turner, K., Sinnott, R. and Prandy, K. (2007) Data Curation
    Standards and Social Science Occupational Information Resources, *International Journal of
    Digital Curation* 2 (1), 73–91.

Lievesley, D. and Jones, S. (1998) *An Investigation into the Digital Preservation Needs of Universities
    and Research Funders*, UKOLN,
    www.ukoln.ac.uk/services/papers/bl/blri109/datrep.html#Heading1.

Macdonald, S. and Martinez, L. (2005) Supporting Local Data Users in the UK Academic
    Community, *Ariadne*, **44**, www.ariadne.ac.uk/issue44/martinez.

McMeeking, B., and Fletcher, D. (2004) The United Kingdom Chemical Database Service,
    Cheminformatics, **1**, 37–64.

Mimas (n.d. (a)) *About Mimas*, http://mimas.ac.uk/about.

Mimas (n.d. (b)) *What We Stand For*, http://mimas.ac.uk/about/what-we-stand-for.

NERC (2011) *NERC Data Policy Statement*, Natural Environment Research Council,
    www.nerc.ac.uk/research/sites/data/policy2011.asp.

OECD (2004) *Declaration on Access to Research Data from Public Funding*, Organisation for
    Economic Co-operation and Development.

Pepler, S. (2010) The Economics of Applying and Sustaining Digital Curation: why should
    NERC pay for BADC? In *Research Data Management Forum 5, Economics of Applying and
    Sustaining Digital Curation held on 27–28 October 2010, at Chancellors Hotel and Conference Centre,
    Manchester*.

Pryor, G., and Donnelly, M. (2009) Skilling Up to Do Data: whose role, whose responsibility,
    whose career?, *International Journal of Digital Curation*, **4** (2), 158–70.

RIN (2008) *To Share or not to Share: publication and quality assurance of research data outputs*,
    Research Information Network.

RIN (2010a) *If You Build It, Will They Come? How researchers perceive and use Web 2.0*, Research
    Information Network.

RIN (2010b) *Open to All? Case studies of openness in research*, Research Information Network.

RIN (2011) *Gaps and Barriers to Access to Research Information*, Research Information Network.

RIN and JISC (2011) *Benefits and Impact of Research Data Centres*, Research Information Network
    and Joint Information Systems Committee.

Robey, D. (2007a) *Consequences of the Withdrawal of AHDS Funding*, Arts and Humanities
    Research Council,
    www.ahrcict.rdg.ac.uk/activities/review/consequences%20of%20the%20withdrawl%20of

%20ahds%20funding.pdf.

Robey, D. (2007b) *Sustainability of AHRC-funded Digital Resources*, Arts and Humanties Research Council, www.ahrcict.rdg.ac.uk/activities/review/sustainability.htm.

Russell, M., Boulton, G., Clarke, P., Eyton, D. and Norton, J. (2010) *The Independent Climate Change Emails Review Final Report*, The Independent Climate Change Emails Review.

Schopf, J. and Newhouse, S. (2007) User Priorities for Data: results from SUPER, *International Journal of Digital Curation*, **2** (1), 149–55.

STFC (n.d.) *UKSSDC*, Science and Technology Facilities Council, https://www.stfc.ac.uk/roadmap/rmProject.aspx?q=107.

UKDA (2007) *Across the Decades: 40 years of data archiving*, UK Data Archive.

UKDA (2010) *UK Data Archive Preservation Policy*, UK Data Archive, www.data-archive.ac.uk/media/54776/ukda062-dps-preservationpolicy.pdf.

UKDA (2011) *Deposit Data: how to deposit*, UK Data Archive, www.data-archive.ac.uk/deposit/how.

UKSSDC (2009) *Status of UK Solar System Data Centre Funding from STFC Programmatic Review*, UK Solar System Data Centre, www.ukssdc.ac.uk/wdcc1/news/ukssdc_funding.html.

Waller, M. and Sharpe, R. (2006) *Mind the Gap: assessing digital preservation needs in the UK*, Digital Preservation Coalition.

Warwick, C., Terras, M., Huntington, P., Pappa, N. and Galina, I. (2006) *The LARIAH Report: log analysis of digital resources in the arts and humanities final report to the Arts and Humanities Research Council*, University College London.

Whyte, A. (2008) *Curating Brain Images in a Psychiatric Research Group: infrastructure and preservation issues*, SCARP Case Study 1, Digital Curation Centre, www.dcc.ac.uk/sites/default/files/documents/publications/case-studies/SCARP_B4821_NeuroCase_v1_1.pdf.

Wilson, J., Fraser, M., Martinez-Uribe, L., Jeffreys, P., Patrick, M., Akram, A. and Mansoori, T. (2010) Developing Infrastructure for Research Data Management at the University of Oxford, *Ariadne*, **65**, www.ariadne.ac.uk/issue65/wilson-et-al.

CHAPTER 9

Contrasting national research data strategies: Australia and the USA

Andrew Treloar, G. Sayeed Choudhury and William Michener

This chapter looks at two national approaches to research data infrastructure, responding to very different government and research sector environments: Australia and the USA.

Australia: a national research data service

The Australian National Data Service (ANDS) is working to enable the transformation of research data that are unmanaged, disconnected, invisible and single-use into structured collections that are managed, connected, findable and reusable. This will form a nationally significant resource so that Australian researchers can easily publish, discover, access and use Australian research data.

The beginnings of ANDS can be traced back to one of the most significant investments made by Australia in research infrastructure: the National Collaborative Research Infrastructure Strategy (NCRIS). This was an A$542 million, seven year strategy originally spanning from 2004/05 to 2010/11 but with some investments extended to 2012/13 (the Australian financial year, referred to here, runs from 1 July to 30 June). NCRIS provides and supports major research infrastructure, allowing Australia to conduct world-class research. In November 2006, 12 priority areas (capabilities) were announced and projects have since been funded in each of these areas. NCRIS has adopted a strategic and collaborative approach to providing research infrastructure, which can be accessed by researchers across Australia. This type of collaboration is proving effective in delivering wider access to better infrastructure.

A key enabler of research collaboration is the high performance computing, data management and electronic communication tools provided by the new information and communication technologies (ICT). The Australian Government continues to support the deployment of these ICT tools so researchers can readily share access to research data and collaborate in analysing the data. The NCRIS investment in this area was collectively called Platforms for Collaboration (PfC) and the Australian National Data Service is one of its major components. Its current status can best be understood through its four sequential stages: establishment, initial funding, additional funding and time extension.

Establishment of ANDS

During the course of the PfC facilitation process, a number of workshops were held to determine the activities that might be included in the investment plan to assist research data management. Following the approval of the overall PfC investment plan by NCRIS, an implementation workshop with wide representation was held to confirm the proposal to establish an Australian National Data Service. This workshop took place on 29 May 2007. It endorsed the ANDS concept and proposed that a technical working group (the ANDS TWG) should be formed to draft a more detailed statement on the purpose and goals for ANDS, moving beyond the conceptual definition provided in the PfC investment plan. This working group drew on relevant Australian expertise from the e-research, institutional repository, public sector data and data-intensive research sectors. Meeting physically and virtually over the course of 2007, by October of that year it had produced *Towards the Australian Data Commons: A proposal for an Australian National Data Service* (Australian Government, 2007). The idea of the Australian Data Commons (later renamed the Australian Research Data Commons) was meant to evoke a shared resource with benefits for all.

In late 2007, the then Department of Education, Science and Training (DEST) asked Monash University (Australia's largest university, based in Melbourne) to act as the lead agency to work with the Australian National University (ANU) and the Commonwealth Scientific and Industrial Research Organisation (CSIRO) to take on the project to establish the ANDS. Monash was selected because of its lead role in a number of previous e-research projects (ARROW, DART and ARCHER) and because of its early commitment to institutional data management activity, growing out of its whole-of-institution information management strategy. This ANDS establishment project concluded in December 2008, with ANDS commencing officially on 1 January 2009; by 1 March ANDS had 16 staff and a defined series of programs. These included:

- *Developing Frameworks* – aimed to influence and simplify the overall policy framework within which the ANDS goal is to be achieved, and to define how activities by researchers (in order to comply with their grant conditions) and institutions (in order to comply with funding requirements) could contribute to a national research data commons
- *Providing Utilities* – aimed to provide fundamental utility services for a cohesive network of data collections and provide discovery, access and other value-add services across the resulting data commons
- *Seeding the Commons* – aimed to seed the Australian Research Data Commons by seeking to make more content available through it, first through a general

content recruitment program, and then moving on to much more highly focused assistance for institutions

* *Building Capabilities* – aimed to build research data capability across the research and scholarly communications lifecycle in organizations, systems, services and people.

At this stage of its existence, the closest UK analogue to ANDS was the Digital Curation Centre (DCC). The funding was mostly directed towards consultancy and advice activity, with some allocated to national infrastructure.

Additional funding

In its May 2009 budget, the Commonwealth Government announced a series of initiatives collectively labelled 'Super Science'. Super Science was funded not by NCRIS, but by the Education Investment Fund (EIF), which had been set up to finance the 'creation and development' of conventional physical infrastructure. The decision to use it for funding Super Science imposed a number of restrictions on what could be undertaken. In general terms, EIF funding can only be applied to the 'creation and development' of infrastructure. In particular, EIF funds may not be used for recurrent costs, such as the maintenance of infrastructure or operating costs.

One facet of the Super Science initiative was the funding of the Australian Research Data Commons (ARDC) Project, which was tasked with making the ARDC a reality. The implications of using EIF money for this activity were that ANDS could fund specification development for software, software development at enterprise level, installation, configuration and testing of software, and the documentation of that software. ANDS was not permitted to use EIF funding for a range of other things that were requested, such as:

* purchase of software licences
* purchase or leasing of IT hardware for storage or any other purpose
* digitization of any kind
* travel
* training courses for project members in task-related skills, website development or portal infrastructure, which were to be provided instead by host institutions as an in-kind contribution
* research activities, excluding research or investigation into the provision and management of data (see discussion of NCRIS below)
* staffing for operational activities
* 'proof of concept' software development
* funding of work by parties based outside Australia
* scoping exercises or studies in the amount of research data available at an institution

- manual creation of metadata, beyond that required for software specification and testing.

The consequence of these constraints was that ANDS was essentially required to fund large amounts of outsourced software development, mostly inside existing institutions.

The ANDS 2009/10 business plan was submitted in March 2009 (before the Super Science announcement) and accepted in July 2009 (after this announcement). The substance and execution of this plan was therefore substantially affected by the ARDC project. Consequently, considerable effort was expended on creating a project plan for the ARDC that was complementary to the NCRIS-funded activities. There were three significant challenges in doing this. The first was the constraints on what could be funded, described above. The second was the amount of money provided under Super Science. The original NCRIS budget for ANDS was around A$24 million. The additional funding from Super Science was another A$48 million. In other words, the total ANDS budget had tripled. The third challenge was that despite this budget increase, there was no extra time provided.

The ANDS Steering Committee decided in mid 2009 to recommend to the Department of Innovation, Industry, Science and Research (DIISR) that ANDS manage the NCRIS-funded and EIF-funded activities as an integrated project. The Steering Committee also decided to reshape the portfolio of ANDS programs to better reflect the implications of, and constraints on, the added funding. As a consequence, the existing separate Frameworks and Capabilities programs were merged, and the Utilities Program was moved from NCRIS-funded to EIF-funded and renamed ARDC Core. Four new EIF-funded programs were instated: Data Capture, Metadata Stores, Public Sector Data and Applications. In the period from July 2009 to March 2010, ANDS consulted widely on these changed plans, and after some fine-tuning to respond to consultation feedback commenced executing against them.

The final result of all these changes were seven programs established to meet the aims of ANDS and to create the infrastructure needed for the ARDC:

- *Frameworks and capabilities* – an ANDS driven program ensuring that institutions have the capability and the research system has the structures in place to enable researchers to manage, publish, share and reuse research data (NCRIS funded)
- *Seeding the Commons* – an institutionally based program to ensure that well managed data is made available through the ARDC with a focus on data that cannot be automatically captured (NCRIS funded)
- *Data capture* – an institutionally based program to automate the capture of data and metadata from instruments in data intensive research (EIF funded)
- *Public sector data* – an outsourced program of making more public data collections visible and available through the ARDC (EIF funded)
- *Metadata stores* – an institutionally based program that enables metadata to be stored coherently across an institution that supports data management,

publishing, sharing and reuse (EIF funded)
- *ARDC core infrastructure* – an ANDS driven program that puts in place the national services that enable research data to be published and discovered (EIF funded)
- *ARDC applications* – a program that develops tools and services to support demonstrations of the value of exploiting data in the ARDC (EIF funded).

One of the requirements of the ARDC project was that ANDS would provide to DIISR an initial specification for the ARDC that would detail A$10 million of early expenditure to support the creation of the ARDC. This required commitment of funds by 30 September 2009. This initial commitment was described in the preliminary specifications report as 'early activity' expenditure, but has come to be known as 'fast start'. Consequently ANDS produced a description of engagements based on discussions already under way and relationships that had already been established, with two goals:

- to start expending the allocated funds, thus smoothing somewhat the expenditure curve
- to quickly undertake a range of activities from which ANDS could learn and thereby fine-tune the process of expending the remainder of the Super Science funding.

The reason for emphasis on urgency was that by late 2009, the entire ANDS budget had to be expended by mid 2011. As a result, ANDS needed to turn itself into a funding organization and spend most of the money with partners outside ANDS (a mini-JISC, in UK terms).

Program extension

In April 2010, DIISR advised that there was an opportunity to extend the time allocation for ANDS by another two years to harmonize with other NCRIS and EIF investments, but without any additional funding being provided. ANDS staff and the Steering Committee managed to identify shifts of funding and timing across reasonably permeable boundaries that still delivered a viable ANDS, one able to continue to deliver on behalf of the Australian research community through to June 2013. This extension of time required a reallocation of funds between programs, as well as a change to the funding profile within programs. It also required the funding of the project office over a much longer period. Consequently an additional A$0.5 million was provided by DIISR under NCRIS funding to support the operation of ANDS over a longer period. A three-year high-level project plan was developed, so that ANDS:

- honoured all existing commitments

- continued with existing partnerships, continuing to actively engage with the research institutions
- had the capacity to work with data champions
- maintained an ongoing capability of engaging with the sector.

The resulting project plan showed an uneven level of expenditure, as ANDS had already made substantial commitments, but it balanced the need to engage with the sector over a longer period of time, and to demonstrate value from an early stage.

Stakeholders, data and financial dimensions

Table 9.1 shows the intended size and focus of each of the programs over the whole ANDS funding period. It takes into account interest earned as well as project funding.

Table 9.1 ANDS programs and funding				
Programs	EIF (A$m)	NCRIS (A$m)	%	Focus
Frameworks and capabilities		4.40	6.0	ANDS
Metadata stores	6.54		9.0	Institutions
Data capture	18.47		25.4	Institutions
Seeding the Commons		13.10	18.0	Institutions
Public sector data	6.85		9.4	Contractors
ARDC core infrastructure	7.8		10.7	ANDS
ARDC applications	9.87		13.5	Contractors
EIF project management	1.83		2.5	ANDS
Project office		4.00	5.5	ANDS
Total (A$72.85m)	51.35	21.50	100	

Another way of visualizing this information is its budget expenditure by program over the life of ANDS. Figure 9.1 shows this allocation as of the middle of 2011. The large peak for the first half of 2011 reflects the decision to push out funds quickly before

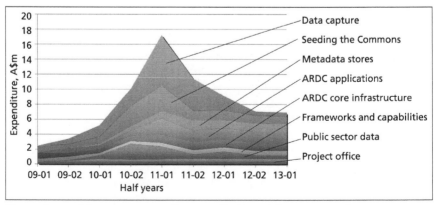

Figure 9.1 ANDS program expenditure profile (Copyright ANDS, 2011)

the granting of a time extension. The expenditure profile would look quite different if the Super Science announcement had come with the extra two years of time that were later granted.

ANDS principles

In responding to the new objectives and program requirements, ANDS continues to follow those principles agreed during the establishment project:

- *Commons framework* – ANDS has started in a way that anticipates the need to scale up and adapt over time via an extensible framework of data stores, federations and services that enable better data creation, capture, management and sharing.
- *Focus* – ANDS will continue to identify and work with those who are ready, willing and able to contribute significantly to the ARDC vision, and who provide the most strategic return to the ARDC for the effort expended. However, ANDS will endeavour to directly support all of the larger research institutions directly, in order to rapidly achieve critical mass.
- *Content* – ANDS is initially focusing on content recruitment into stores and federation across stores so as to achieve a wide coverage of data quickly at an agreed level of quality; in later years the emphasis will shift towards quality improvement.
- *Service provision* – ANDS is focused on service provision and infrastructure development, not research and exploration; its programs will develop, integrate, and continually improve production-level systems in support of well understood services.
- *Strategic partners* – ANDS recognizes the need to be open to, and engage appropriately with, innovations and external institutions relevant to the ARDC, including the Australian Access Federation (AAF), the Australian Research Collaboration Service (ARCS), the National Computational Facility (NCI), and the establishing activities in National eResearch Collaboration Tools and Resources (NeCTAR) and Research Data Stores Initiative (RDSI).
- *Stores* – ANDS assumes an environment where storage and long-term curation occur in nationally or institutionally supported stores, either existing or brought into being over the life of ANDS. These stores will preferably hold objects described by various discipline-specific and documented metadata schemas. ANDS will work with whatever repositories exist, national, institutional or disciplinary.
- *Sustainability* – Research data management requires a long-term commitment. ANDS has developed its plans on the assumption that this does not represent a one-off investment in data. The enduring changes forecast in this document within each program are also intended to be sustainable beyond the end of the ANDS planning period.

- *Constituency* – ANDS works with a variety of publicly funded institutions that produce, manage or consume research inputs and outputs to achieve its aims. The scope includes all higher education providers in Australia, all research organizations that are publicly funded, including CSIRO, GeoScience Australia (GA), Bureau of Meteorology, Australian Bureau of Statistics (ABS), Australian Institute of Marine Science (AIMS), the Australian Antarctic Division, the Department of Primary Industry, and members of the cultural collections sector (galleries, libraries, archives and museums).
- *Platforms for Collaboration* – As a component of Platforms for Collaboration, ANDS is funded to work with all research disciplines in Australia, not just the NCRIS capabilities. This means that the specific concerns of the humanities and social sciences will need to be taken into account.
- *ANDS community* – The ANDS community consists of providers of research data and ANDS services, consumers of research data and those services, and managers of research inputs and outputs. This includes key stakeholder aggregations such as CAUDIT and CAUL. The ANDS community includes the general public only to the extent that they will be able to use some ANDS services to discover and access publicly available data.
- *Data* – ANDS is concerned with the digital data that is produced by researchers as well as data used by and made accessible to them. Data is the information that researchers study, that is transformed by researchers and produced by researchers. Research publications are not included within the scope of ANDS but files, images, tables, databases, models, computer outputs and similar digital representations are included. ANDS will support the ability to create links between data, publications, software code and visualizations, where these may appear as either research inputs or research outputs.

Key features of the ANDS approach

As indicated at the start of this chapter, ANDS is working to enable four significant transformations of data into structured collections: from unmanaged to managed, from disconnected to connected, from invisible to visible, and from single-use to reusable. The result will form a nationally significant resource so Australian researchers can easily publish, discover, access and use Australian research data. A key differentiator for ANDS is the description of data at collection level, not item level. This is because we believe this to be an appropriate level of granularity for cross-discipline discovery and eventual reuse.

ANDS is driving these four transformations in part by creating the ARDC, the focus of the Super Science project. The ARDC is a combination of the set of shareable Australian research collections, the descriptions of those collections including the information required to support their reuse, the relationships between the various elements involved (the data, the researchers who produced it, the instruments that

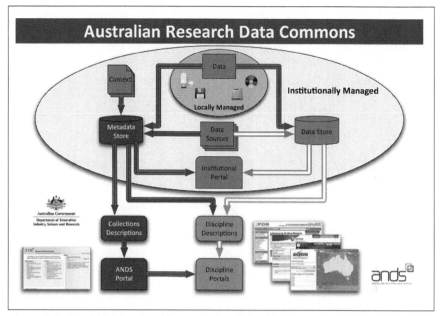

Figure 9.2 *ARDC high level architecture (Copyright Elliot Metsger, 2011)*

collected it and the institutions where they work), and the infrastructure needed to enable, populate and support the commons. It is important to stress that ANDS does not hold the actual data, but points to the location where the data can be accessed. The ARDC that ANDS envisages is depicted in Figure 9.2, where ANDS is contributing to the activities shown as dark coloured pipes and boxes.

ANDS is thus creating a combination of national services and coherent institutional research data infrastructure, combined with the ability to exploit that infrastructure with tools, policy and capability.

So, given these overriding principles, constraints and its general approach, what are the seven ANDS programs of activity being undertaken through to the middle of 2013? The NCRIS and EIF process requires an annual business planning cycle and the descriptions of the programs given here are adapted from those in the 2011/12 business plan. But the main changes from year to year will from now on be in the detail of what is done, rather than the higher level aims and objectives.

Frameworks and capabilities (NCRIS-funded)
Program aims
The Framework activities within the program aim to support new approaches to data-intensive research by strengthening the overall policy context for, and facilitating the emergence of, the ARDC. The Capabilities activities aim to improve the level of

capability for data management, data-intensive research and associated technologies across Australia by partnering with willing institutions and NCRIS facilities to improve core data competencies. This program aims to directly support the ANDS IT services provided through ARDC Core as well as the institutional infrastructure projects managed through the Access to Public Sector Data, Data Capture, and Seeding the Commons programs.

Program overview

The Frameworks and Capabilities Program addresses two of the systemic obstacles to the emergence of the ARDC: policy irregularity or absence and the constraints inherent in human capability.

The common approach to addressing both of these generic issues is to partner with collaborators around specific solutions. The Frameworks and Capabilities Program produces materials that address some of the fundamental shared issues in data intensive research. The key collaborators for the Capabilities activities within the program are e-research support groups and the key collaborators for the Frameworks activities are research leaders and funding agencies. A central concern of the program as a whole is the desire for research organizations and research groups to have effective policies around the full lifecycle of data management.

The Frameworks activities are focused primarily on the research community and the institutions in which they work (as well as the collaborators described below). The activities are working towards harmonizing and streamlining the overall policy framework within which a data commons can operate. The result will be a shared vision of the opportunities, benefits and responsibilities of a data commons. It is important to acknowledge that the Frameworks activities work through facilitating the goal of an effective research data commons rather than prescribing the specific policies required to achieve that end.

The Frameworks activities are bridging between researchers, research institutions, research funders, and data creators and curators. In addition, the program is engaging with current and emerging initiatives such as the Government 2.0 Taskforce report (in collaboration with the Public Sector Data Program) and the National Committee for Data for Science. Primary collaborators of ANDS include:

- institutional data holders (CSIRO, NCRIS Capabilities, National Library of Australia, National Archives of Australia, the Department of Primary Industry, GeoScience Australia, the Australian Bureau of Statistics, and so on)
- national initiatives such as the National Committee for Data for Science
- cross-governmental groups such as Australian Government Information Management Office (AGIMO), Open Spatial Data Mapping (OSDM) and the Australian Spatial Consortium
- research funding departments such as DIISR and the Department of

Employment, Education and Workplace Resources (DEEWR)
- research funding schemes such as the Australian Research Commission (ARC), National Health and Medical Research Council (NHMRC), and Research Infrastructure Block Grants (RIBG)
- discipline leaders within institutions
- research office staff at institutions.

As cohesive networks of research data is increasingly regarded as an important and enduring part of the collaborative research infrastructure, the Capabilities activities focus in particular on building the capability of researchers and support staff to contribute to and better exploit national data infrastructure. The various activities are working with the sector to identify and document the fundamentals of working with research data and the specifics of discipline-based data-intensive research. They are also working with research communities and local e-research support services to improve particular data-related competencies, as well as enhancing and adding national focus to institutionally based support, materials development and training initiatives.

The Capabilities activities are leading to services such as consultancy, informal knowledge transfer, workshops, documentation, and training materials directly and by re-enforcing local services. Staff from this program are working within an integrated engagement activity with staff from all other ANDS programs. ANDS is identifying and engaging the community of researchers and e-research support services. These groups themselves are engaged in capability building, within their own institutions and with their own staff.

Seeding the commons (NCRIS-funded)
Program aims
The aims of this program are to improve the fabric for data management in a way that will increase the amount of content in the data commons; and to improve the state of data capture and management across the research sector, with a focus on the tertiary education sector, CSIRO and the NCRIS Capabilities. The visual metaphor is sowing seed to turn the commons from bare dirt into verdant pasture.

Program overview
An analysis of research intensity for the major Australian research-producing institutions was undertaken in late 2009 based on the most recent publicly available data, and A\$4.55 million of Seeding the Commons funds were allocated in bands of A\$250,000, A\$125,000 or A\$75,000. Institutions were sent an invitation to take part in an expression of interest process in late 2009. This offer was accepted by all of the institutions with the exception of Charles Sturt University. In addition, the Australian Nuclear Science and Technology organization (ANSTO) was allocated A\$125,000 in

funding to undertake similar work. During 2010 ANDS devoted considerable resources to helping institutions define and describe work that can be undertaken in these areas. Those universities that did not receive funding as part of this program have been offered further support and advice by program staff.

ANDS has a significant existing set of commitments for this program. Its major activities are:

* 34 research institutions developing local capability for managing research data and making collections visible in the ARDC through funded projects (this is largely through ANDS-funded local staff working within the institutions)
* regional local support through funded positions
* national advice and direct support, focused on growing the Commons, supporting partners, and providing national advice.

This last activity complements the written guides and training provided in the Frameworks and Capability Program. Specific contributions to growing the data commons are providing:

* advice on metadata standards and requirements to ensure that metadata is prepared in a manner consistent with ANDS' needs
* advice on ANDS service requirements to ensure that metadata is available in ARDC
* advice and support on requirements to enable the creation and sustainability of research data infrastructure
* funding of staff at partner projects and institutions to provide support for ANDS' goals
* identification of as much content as possible and making it discoverable.

Activities that involve working more closely with partners over the remainder of the ANDS Development Program are providing:

* review and assessment of partner projects to ensure they are completed on time and as specified
* advice to these projects and other ANDS programs
* advice and assistance on data management and related policy and procedures
* advice and assistance in the use and deployment of ANDS produced or funded services, applications and material
* identification of and partnering with exemplar institutions to maximize data management
* analysis, reuse and redeployment assistance of the outputs of the projects funded by ANDS or drawn from the ANDS catalogue of tools.

ANDS is creating a community of data managers through:

- continuing to support the several state based or related groups of data managers established during 2010/11, with effective communication channels between them
- training provided to community members as required (in conjunction with Frameworks and Capabilities Program)
- expanding the ANDS knowledge bank, for use by the community
- capturing information about successes for dissemination within the community and beyond
- developing relationships with equivalent activities overseas to share approaches to data management systems that can inform ANDS.

Data capture (EIF-funded)

Program aims

The aims of this program are to simplify the process of researchers routinely capturing data and rich metadata as close as possible to the point of creation, and depositing these data and metadata into well managed stores. Metadata will need to be held at collection and object level in order to support reuse.

Program overview

The Data Capture Program is achieving this aim by augmenting and adapting existing data creation and capture infrastructure commonly used by Australian researchers and research institutions. This is done to ensure that the data creation and data capture phases of research are fully integrated so as to enable effective ingestion into the research data and metadata stores at the institution or elsewhere. This integration will make it easier for researchers to contribute data to the ARDC directly from the lab, instrument, fieldwork site and so on. It will also ensure that higher quality metadata (critical for reuse and discovery) is produced through automated and semi-automated systems. The approach taken is to partner with leading research groups and Super Science initiatives to augment or adapt data creation and capture systems.

The resulting infrastructure components include software to integrate tightly with the experimental environment of the researcher to take the data that is being captured or created, and augment this with metadata that describes the setting within which the data is being captured or created, as well as other relevant details (where available) about the research project, researcher, experiment, sample, analysis and instrument calibration. ANDS is also adopt, adapt and develop software to facilitate automatic or semi-automatic deposit from instruments into data stores and repositories.

The Data Capture Program was originally allocated A$12 million in the EIF ARDC Draft Project Plan. Following the process of public consultation around this draft project plan, this amount was increased to A$18.47 million. The consultation process also validated the decision to take an institutional approach in allocating the bulk of the available funds. An analysis of research intensity for the major Australian research-producing institutions was undertaken in late 2009 based on the most recent publicly available data on research productivity (the same allocation process as for Seeding the Commons), and A$11.6 million of Data Capture funds was allocated in bands of A$1 million, A$500,000, or A$200,000. In late 2009 institutions were each sent an individual invitation to take part in an expression of interest process. Since then, ANDS staff have been working with the institutions to identify projects that help the institutions to meet their research data ambitions, and assist ANDS to build the ARDC. As of the middle of 2011, nearly 100 of these projects had been agreed and commenced.

Metadata stores (EIF)

Program aims

The aims of this program are to assist institutions and disciplines to better manage the collection and object level metadata associated with research data outputs and associated entities.

Program overview

Information that can be held about data (often called metadata) can be grouped into four categories:

- information for discovery, which is primarily held at the level of a collection, consisting of the range of pieces of information that will assist in the discovery of the collection
- information for determination of value (also primarily at collection level), including information such as the name of the researcher, institution or funding program that might help a potential user to decide whether they want to access the data
- information for access that might be a direct link to the data objects (stored elsewhere, such as on national and institutional data stores), at collection and possibly object level, or contact details for where to source the data
- information for reuse, including things like reading scales, field names, variables and calibration settings that are needed in order to reuse the data effectively; this is mostly at object level.

In practice, the distinction between data and metadata can be somewhat arbitrary and depends on the system being used to manage the data. If this system is file-orientated, the metadata will almost always be separately managed in some sort of associated system. If the data management system is database-orientated, much of the metadata will either be attributes of rows and columns for the database tables.

ANDS is concerned with information about data collections and data objects, but importantly also with information about associated entities. These include parties (people and organizations), activities (that produce the data) and services (associated with the capture of, and access to, the data). These associated entities serve as part of the rich context for the data collections, and also contribute to the information for discovery and information for determination of value. This rich context will come from existing institutional systems via software infrastructure that might be thought of as pipes along which the contextual information flows. There are also pipes between metadata stores and data stores, and between metadata stores and the ARDC core infrastructure.

So, software that is being developed or deployed by the Metadata Stores Program needs to support a range of functions for different kinds of objects. The first is the creation and management of these kinds of information, or their harvesting from other sources (research management systems, human resources systems, finance systems). In addition, the software needs to manage the relationships between the information about data collections and objects and the data collections and objects themselves. The software may need to support queries over the data by users within the institution. Finally, the software needs to be harvestable by ANDS services, as well as by other organizations. This program is therefore developing, configuring and making available this metadata infrastructure at research producing institutions.

The required functions can be provided in a wide variety of ways, and via different configurations of software components. In practice, a small number of design patterns are appearing, in part because of the ways in which ANDS has been funding activity at institutions. The current environment contains four kinds of extant stores:

- *combined stores* – manage collections and object metadata for a single institution across a range of disciplines
- *collection stores* – manage the information about data collections within an institution; may also accept feeds from enterprise systems (some of which ANDS has funded), and also feed the ANDS Data Collections Registry
- *instrument stores* – tightly coupled to particular instruments or clusters of instruments; a significant number of these have been developed, not with metadata stores funding, but with data capture funding; these solutions feed the ANDS collections registry either directly (the commonest pattern), or via an institutional collections store (much less common)
- *discipline store solutions in some disciplines* – well established international practices for managing data and metadata, as well as associated software, which might be deployed within institutions or at national or international data centres; ANDS might fund some pipes from instances of these to institutional collection stores.

In addition to these, ANDS sees the need for an object store. This would hold metadata crucial to enable reuse of the data. It would meet the needs of an institution to manage object-level metadata for researchers whose needs are not met either by a discipline store or instrument store. This solution (and the pipes connecting it to data stores and the institutional collection store) is not currently part of the ANDS offering (nor deployed in any institutions) and will need to be adapted from existing software offerings. The final solution will need to manage metadata that is common to a range of disciplines and specific metadata from particular disciplines.

As well as these different kinds of metadata stores, the data itself needs to be stored somewhere. This might be a local data store (either just associated with an instrument or institutionally supported), one of the offerings that might be made available through RDSI, or an international disciplined-focused data store, such as the PDB (Protein Data Bank) or European Molecular Biology Laboratory-European Bioinformatics Institute (EMBL-EBI).

Based on our existing engagements with ANDS partners, the most common implementation pattern at an institutional level is a collection store to support Seeding the Commons funded projects, combined with one or more instrument stores associated with data-capture-funded projects. In this pattern, the collection description for the data capture data is usually fed directly to ANDS rather than via the collection store.

Public sector data (EIF-funded)

Program aims

The aims of this program are to develop the infrastructure necessary to ensure the establishment of automated feeds of rich collection level information from federal, state and territory government and non-government agencies into the ARDC and thus the Research Data Australia, as well as to engage with government agencies and provide them with funding or assistance to ensure that key data holdings are identified and the automation of data feeds into the ARDC are established.

Program overview

Many areas of research are heavily dependent on government data – from cadastral data to economic data to government-organized surveys – or could increase their use of such data if it were more widely discoverable and accessible. The responsibilities inherent in data custody are a shared challenge and include the need to address preservation, access and description. There is thus a very close potential relationship between ANDS' concerns and those government agencies that are custodians of data or that are influential in data policy.

The Public Sector Data Program is providing the infrastructure necessary to ensure that feeds of data collection descriptions are made available from a range of public sector agencies. Identified agencies include producers of research data, such as the Bureau of Meteorology (BOM), the Australian Bureau of Statistics (ABS), GeoScience

Australia (GA), the Australian Antarctic Division (AAD), CSIRO and the Department of Primary Industry (DPI). Owners of data gathering activities and collections that might be possible inputs to other research activities, such as the museum and library sectors, are also in scope. ANDS also needs to maintain and develop stronger relationships with other organizations with significant data holdings or interest in these areas such as the National Archives Australia (NAA) and the Australian Government Information Management Office (AGIMO), for example. Finally, ANDS is exploring ways to incorporate public data collected by citizens, through exemplar projects.

The key deliverable from this program is to make existing public sector data resources more discoverable to the research community and to work with federal, state and territory government agencies to improve access to data. Activities vary across agencies according to their existing infrastructure and the types of data being made available. In all cases there is a strong preference to have data services exposed using relevant international standards.

The Public Sector Data Program was originally allocated an A$10 million budget in the ARDC Draft Project Plan. During the review phases for ANDS mid 2010 this budget was reduced to A$6.45 million. This was as a result of discussions with key government agencies in the first quarter of 2010 where staff identified that their desire was for capability assisted infrastructure development from ANDS in preference to the provision of funding to undertake the infrastructure development themselves.

ARDC core infrastructure (EIF-funded)
Program aims
The aims of this program are to ensure necessary technical and 24x7 operational services are established so that the content in repositories can be findable, reusable and linkable, thus underpinning the development of the Australian Research Data Commons; to ensure that services develop and evolve to meet changing data reuse requirements; and to catalyze the emergence of core data commons infrastructure operated by government agencies and research organizations.

Program overview
The ARDC Core Infrastructure Program provides fundamental services for a cohesive network of data collections and enables discovery, access and other value-add services across the resulting data commons. A technical consultancy is also available to assist integrating distributed data commons infrastructure at research and government instrumentality repositories with core ANDS utilities. The program has three areas of activity:

- To establish a range of utility data services at a sector-wide level (such as cross-discipline discovery services, national collections registry, persistent identifier service, and so on). As appropriate these utility services either aggregate information nationally or provide component services across several NCRIS domain areas, Super Science facilities, and other research organizations and communities. This ANDS program also improves existing services and establishes new data commons utility services. Robust infrastructure is being established together with a service delivery framework that defines the roles and responsibilities of those providing, supporting and participating in the services.

• To commission the establishment of a distributed set of data commons infrastructure typically run and operated by government agencies and research organizations. This information infrastructure allows elements of the research data commons to be connected in an information mesh of interconnected references to the people, organizations, projects, fields of research, and locations related to research data.

• To offer specialist technical advice and consultancy services around establishing data federation utility services. This advice and assistance applies to government agencies and research organizations establishing their own data commons infrastructure and others seeking to make use of and integrate with ANDS core infrastructure.

The most publicly visible of the ANDS service offerings can be seen at the ANDS Online Services page (http://services.ands.org.au/home/orca/search.php) and the main discovery mechanism, Research Data Australia (http://services.ands.org.au).

ARDC applications (EIF-funded)

Program aims

This program aims to develop a range of compelling demonstrations of the overall value of the ARDC by bringing together a range of data sources combined with new integration and synthesis tools to enable new research or generate new policy.

Program overview

ANDS has been funded to bring about an Australian Research Data Commons. This has required a set of co-ordinated programs of activity that are described elsewhere in this chapter. The resulting infrastructure supports data discovery and access. Once accessed the data can be reused as is, but bringing together different datasets can enable new kinds of research. Before this can occur the data may need to be transformed or recoded. Once combined special analysis techniques may be needed to provide the right starting point for further research. There are many possibilities here across a whole range of research problems, and so ANDS is selecting a subset to demonstrate what is possible.

The goal of the Applications Program is to produce compelling demonstrations of the value of having data available for reuse. These demonstrations of value should:

- result in data being transformed or integrated across multiple sources to produce new forms of information that enable innovative, high-quality research outcomes
- have broad rather than narrow applicability
- engage with national research capabilities.

These demonstrations of value will be in a range of sizes, depending on the opportunities that become available. Some of the demonstrations of value will consist of discrete activities that are aggregated together to meet the needs of an overall program of work. The sum of all the activity across this program will be designed to build a balanced portfolio of activity.

The Applications Program is the last of the ANDS programs to commence. Therefore it is best placed to leverage the outputs from the other ANDS programs. Data capture ensures that data and associated rich metadata is captured as close as possible to a range of instruments. Seeding the Commons is making a selection of existing data and associated metadata available from the bulk of Australia's research-producing universities to complement the new data coming from data capture. Metadata stores ensure that this rich reuse metadata for data is managed and accessible to support the requirements of applications. Not all of the data that might be needed for particular problems comes from research institutions, and so the work of public sector data in making data and associated metadata available from government departments will be critical. ARDC Core provides the pieces of underpinning infrastructure to support discovery and citation of datasets for recombination and analysis. The Frameworks and Capabilities Program underpins the Applications Program by putting in place the overall policy and practice frameworks to support better data management and reuse.

ANDS is, over time, funding an evolving and balanced portfolio of activities under the Applications Program. The nature of the portfolio and the kinds of activities that will be of interest are the subject of a gradually expanding engagement between ANDS and institutions. The criteria for elements of this expanding engagement can be described as portfolio criteria and institutional criteria. These criteria are not mandatory, but ANDS intends to maximize as many of them as possible. For the overall portfolio they should contain activities that:

- deliver early demonstrations of value
- align with the national research priorities
- are based on, and contribute to, research of recognized excellence
- address a range of NCRIS capabilities
- lead to data being available in a form which was not previously possible, through; transformation and/or integration across multiple sources
- exploit data that is already in place
- enable the answering of new questions (previously not possible) and support innovative high-quality research outcomes.

The criteria for institutions are that they:

- have demonstrated the ability to deliver early demonstrations of value
- are already engaged with ANDS through a combination of data capture and Seeding the Commons projects
- are producing excellent research in the required areas, as indicated by objective research measures
- have a demonstrated understanding of, and enthusiasm for, the project at researcher, management and leadership levels within the institution.

Status of the ANDS initiative in 2011/12

ANDS has been operating since January 2009 and in that time has worked towards building a consensus on the importance of research data and research data infrastructure. In 2010/11, ANDS created a number of national research data services and engaged with a large number of organizations to start the realization of the Australian Research Data Commons.

In 2011/12, the outcome of ANDS activity will be that for the first time ever, Australian researchers will be able:

- systematically, reliably and authoritatively to connect their research data to project, institutional and disciplinary descriptions
- simultaneously to publish citable research data collections through institutional, disciplinary and national services.

This will ensure that Australia has a mature, globally leading capability in research data, making it a key locus for data intensive research.

It will be possible to do this as a result of ANDS and its partners developing a wide-ranging set of coherent outputs that support the Australian Research Data Commons.

By July 2012, ANDS will have in place the following additional and enhanced national services:

- a national gazetteer service
- a data citation service
- a researcher identification service
- a research project identification service
- an enhanced Research Data Australia.

By July 2012 additional coherent institutional research data infrastructure will be available, comprising:

- 60 tools that will have been deployed to automatically capture rich metadata

along with the data for a wide range of instruments
- six institutions operating metadata stores
- 40 institutions providing collections description feeds to ANDS, both research institutions and public sector data holders
- at least 10,000 collections available for discovery through Research Data Australia
- five discipline-orientated portals cross connected to Research Data Australia.

By July 2012 the following tools, frameworks and capability will be in place to exploit the ARDC:

- further institutional guidance for internal institutional data management
- institution-wide research data management planning frameworks at ten research institutions, and all institutions ANDS partners will have improved research data management
- increased institutional capability for research data management with 150 more staff trained with research data management capability
- 20 new tools that enable more effective reuse of research data.

The USA: the NSF DataNet Program
The role of libraries in data management

Research libraries have been an important foundation of the US research enterprise for decades. Winston Tabb, Dean of Libraries at Johns Hopkins, has stated that libraries comprise collections, services and infrastructure. The rise of data-intensive scholarship presents a paradigm shift on all these dimensions. The principles that have guided libraries may still apply but the practices clearly need to change. While much of the emphasis focuses on infrastructure, the 'data deluge' also has important implications for collection and service development. Choudhury and Stinson (2007) have asserted that data represent the new special collections. Aesthetic differences aside, data share characteristics of being primary research materials, fragile and reflective of current societal concerns. From a collection development perspective, data offer a compelling opportunity and challenge for US research libraries and universities.

Research libraries have a well established track record in the provision of information services; however, there are important differences with data that relate to scale and complexity. Unlike print documents, data is inherently produced by and interpreted by machines. For this reason, it is essential that libraries create next-generation infrastructure (organizational, human and technical) that incorporate new archiving and computational capabilities. The US National Science Foundation (NSF) DataNet Program provides an important opportunity for research libraries to develop such capabilities in partnership with various communities both within and without the USA.

Science and engineering are becoming increasingly data-intensive (Hey, Tansley and

Tolle, 2009) and a massive volume of data is generated annually via remote and embedded sensing systems. The DataNet Program at the NSF was created with the objective of advancing science and engineering by developing new methods, technologies and approaches for managing current and future large, diverse and complex data streams. In particular, funded DataNet awardees were expected to support all aspects of the data lifecycle including discovery and access, digital preservation, integration, and analysis and visualization, as well as to engage in scientific research critical to supporting DataNet functions. Furthermore, it was recognized that new types of organizations encompassing the library, information, computer and physical and natural sciences would be required not only to develop the new technical capacity but also to educate relevant stakeholders and to engage the broad community in all phases of DataNet development.

In the remainder of this section, we describe the first two DataNet projects supported in the USA: the Data Conservancy and the Data Observation Network for Earth (DataONE). For each project, we present the context for the effort and present project objectives, an overview of the project architecture, community engagement and education activities, and anticipated impacts and outcomes.

Data Conservancy

Objectives

Data Conservancy is a multi-disciplinary, diverse group of individuals, institutions and partners that are well suited to accomplish the vision and meet the goals outlined in the DataNet solicitation. The project is supported by the NSF ($4 million/year for the first five year period). The project comprises 60 individuals from ten partner institutions within the USA and engages additional individuals within Europe and Australia. Data Conservancy includes four objective teams, science working groups, a visiting committee, technical advisory group and a partners' council. Data Conservancy embraces a shared vision: scientific data curation is a means to collect, organize, validate and preserve data so that scientists can find new ways to address the grand research challenges that face society. Data Conservancy's unique approach reflects this overarching vision through four major components: diversity of domain sciences, data preservation, educational programs and library-led organizational framework. Data Conservancy is committed to research, design, implement, deploy and sustain data curation infrastructure for cross-disciplinary discovery with an emphasis on observational data. The project will highlight astronomy, earth sciences, life sciences and social sciences.

Description of architecture and added value to community

Data Conservancy embraces the concept of principles of navigation rather than a rigid road map for infrastructure development. These principles have been realized through an initial prototyping effort by providing web-enabled APIs for search, access and ingest functionality; a services layer that may be orchestrated to provide higher-order, rules-based functionality; and an archival storage layer that abstracts the use of archival systems and storage technology. This platform enables interoperability with scientific domain services, teaching and learning environments and publication systems.

Data Conservancy's underlying design and architecture reflect the need for flexibility, openness, modularity, access and an ability to evolve, as prescribed in the DataNet solicitation. For these reasons, Data Conservancy design has been motivated by these three major concepts in particular: the Open Archival Information System (OAIS) reference model for curation and preservation systems; a service-orientated architecture approach to the development of features and services, which provide an adaptive capability; and an initial data model (derived from the conceptual model developed by the PLANETS project) that addresses the heterogeneity of Data Conservancy.

Figure 9.3 depicts a mapping between the OAIS reference architecture (on the left) and the Data Conservancy service-orientated architecture (on the right). The colour coding identifies the specific mapping of OAIS components to the current Data Conservancy service-orientated architecture framework. This emphasis on preservation represents a foundational element for Data Conservancy. It is important to note that preservation is not considered for its own purpose but rather as the pathway for data sharing and reuse. Ruth Duerr of National Snow and Ice Data Center (NSIDC) has defined preservation as 'providing enough representation information, context, metadata, fixity, and so on such that someone other than the original data producer can use and interpret the data' (personal communication, 3 December 2010). This appropriate definition reflects the notion that preservation and reuse are mutually reinforcing. Actions taken to prepare content and design systems for data preservation represent natural opportunities to develop corresponding capabilities for data reuse.

Within its first 18 months, Data Conservancy ingested astronomy, igneous petrology and coastal bays data and demonstrated interoperability through several proofs of concepts, pilots and operational services including:

- Antarctic glacier photos from Data Conservancy and the existing NSIDC glacier photo service (http://nsidc.org/data/glacier_photo/index.html)
- connection of data and publications through arXiv.org
- access to Data Conservancy data through the Sakai collaboration and learning environment
- integration of Data Conservancy data with an existing science research framework through the International Virtual Observatory Alliance
- visualization and access to Dry Valleys and Coastal Bays data via a Google Earth interface
- a proof of concept focused on ice road development in Alaska that demonstrates data synthesis and integration from distributed sources.

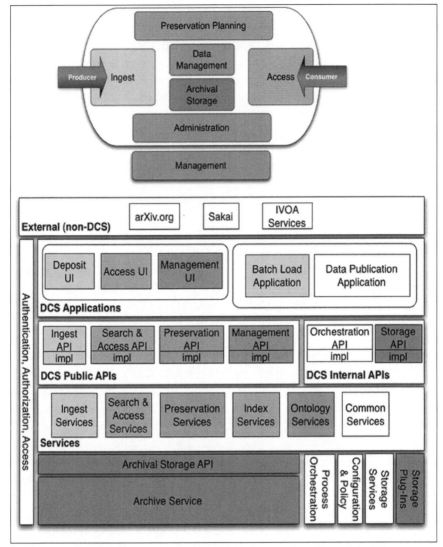

Figure 9.3 *OAIS and Data Conservancy architecture mappings (Copyright Elliot Metsger, 2011)*

Community engagement activities

Data Conservancy's community engagement strategy has emphasized depth by targeting individuals and organizations for particular objectives. Data Conservancy has engaged domain and information scientists, librarians, educators, students and data scientists as well as universities, national laboratories and private organizations. Data Conservancy has tapped into its internal network of experts, its science working groups, professional societies and library organizations.

Data Conservancy's domain scientists are leaders within their respective fields. They have developed use cases, shared insights regarding data practices and provided invaluable feedback on the technical architecture and infrastructure. Their contributions across the range of Data Conservancy scientists have revealed a diverse set of requirements, data types, workflows and curation profiles. Across Data Conservancy teams, workshops, observations, interviews and ethnographic techniques are continually engaging scientists in research and development and building awareness.

Data Conservancy features an extensive program of educational and outreach activities. Data Conservancy believes that important aspects of sustainability are capacity building, diversity and workforce development. Highlights of formal education efforts include:

- summer institutes for professional development
- a research data workforce summit during the 6th International Digital Curation Conference, in 2010
- data curation fellowships
- internships
- new courses within library and information science programs at the University of California at Los Angeles and University of Illinois.

One of the key aspects of Data Conservancy's sustainability relates to raising awareness and capacity within the research library community. In addition to being led by the Sheridan Libraries at Johns Hopkins University, Data Conservancy includes individuals who are leaders in the library field. Data Conservancy offers a pathway for sustained support of community-wide data curation infrastructure by embedding both technical and human infrastructure within a research library and university context. Data Conservancy has engaged the US Association of Research Libraries (ARL), which plans to organize three e-science institutes for over 60 research libraries which have already committed funding. These institutes will focus on strategic planning and implementation of data curation activities. Additionally, Data Conservancy is working closely with the US Council on Library and Information Resources and Digital Library Federation for capacity building related to data curation.

Impacts and outcomes

Data Conservancy represents a robust data curation infrastructure, which is embedded within a research institution context for supporting a range of data types and associated services. Fundamentally, Data Conservancy is a model for libraries and universities that could be emulated or even replicated verbatim to create a distributed network of human and technical infrastructure. One of Data Conservancy's taglines is 'A Blueprint for Research Libraries'. At the most basic level, Data Conservancy provides a mechanism for supporting the NSF data management plans, which were discussed in Chapter 5, through consultation for developing plans and implementation for depositing, preserving and sharing data. On a broader and long-term scale, Data Conservancy represents the first set of steps toward establishing reliable, sustainable national-scale data curation infrastructure. With such infrastructure in place, scientists can reliably deposit, manage and share data such that they can focus on science rather than data management.

DataONE

Objectives

It is predicted that numerous environmental challenges will affect humankind over the next several decades including climate change, water scarcity, land-use changes and the loss of ecosystem services — all of which will require unprecedented access to data that encompass an array of scientific, spatial and temporal domains. Key data challenges lie in discovering relevant data, dealing with extreme data heterogeneity, converting the massive amounts of data to more tractable information and, subsequently, to knowledge. Addressing these challenges requires new approaches for managing, preserving, analysing and sharing data, which are equally challenging from technical and socio-cultural perspectives.

DataONE is a federated data network that enables new science and knowledge creation by improving access to data about life on Earth and the environment that sustains it. Further, it aims to provide scientists and librarians with the tools needed to support all aspects of the data lifecycle, from data acquisition and discovery, through processing and quality assurance and quality control, analysis, visualization, decision making and preservation.

Description of architecture

The overall design is based on several precepts:

- It is recognized that data is best managed at the data repositories that already support particular communities of users. Thus, DataONE supports distributed management at existing repositories (DataONE Member Nodes) and enables replication and caching across these repositories for preservation and performance.
- The DataONE software must provide benefits for scientists today, yet be able to adapt to software and standards evolution.
- DataONE software and hardware infrastructure development activities should support and adapt existing community software efforts, emphasizing free and open source software.

The DataONE architecture represented in Figure 9.4 comprises three major components: member nodes which are existing or new data repositories that support the DataONE Member Node Application Program Interfaces (APIs); co-ordinating nodes that are responsible for cataloguing content, managing replication of content and providing search and discovery mechanisms; and an investigator toolkit, which is a modular set of software and plug-ins that enables interaction with DataONE infrastructure through commonly used analysis and data management tools. Each of the three components is described in more detail below.

Figure 9.4 illustrates the co-ordinating nodes (triangles) and member nodes (dots) distributed across the globe as well as the investigator toolkit, which provides scientists with the tools they need for managing all aspects of the data lifecycle.

Data is principally acquired and maintained by member nodes that are located throughout the world. Member nodes include a wide variety of institutions including data centres or repositories associated with Earth observing institutions, research projects and networks, libraries, universities, and governmental and non-governmental organizations. Each member node supports a specific constituency through its own implementation and often provides specific value-added support services (e.g. user help desk, quality assurance and quality control peer-review). DataONE has been designed

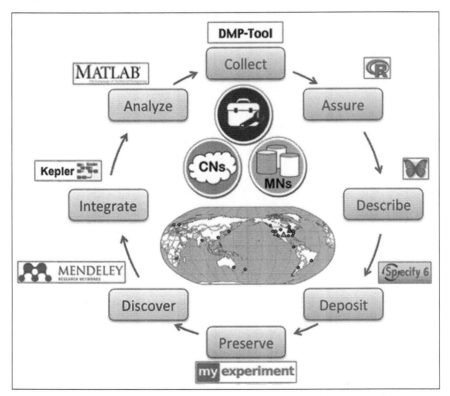

Figure 9.4 *Conceptual overview of DataONE (Copyright Bill Michener, 2011)*

so that it can ultimately accommodate hundreds of highly geographically distributed and diverse member node implementations that support different software platforms, services, metadata standards, levels of curation, and data submission approaches.

Co-ordinating nodes are designed to be tightly co-ordinated, stable platforms that provide network-wide services to member nodes, including the network-wide indexing of digital objects, data replication services across member nodes and mirrored content of science metadata present at member nodes. The three initial co-ordinating nodes were located in the USA at Oak Ridge Campus (a consortium comprised of Oak Ridge National Laboratory and the University of Tennessee), the University of California Santa Barbara Library and the University of New Mexico. The DataONE plan also allowed for a small number of co-ordinating nodes to be added on other continents to enhance the global network.

DataONE provides a suite of software tools for researchers, called the investigator toolkit, which is fully integrated with the infrastructure through the APIs, and enables easy discovery of and access to relevant data. Communication between a tool and DataONE resources (data and metadata at the various Member Nodes) is supported via software (service interfaces) that enable low-level data access and higher-level business logic (e.g. packaging metadata and data, relationships between content). The overall objective is to support both general purpose (e.g. R, MATLAB) and domain-specific tools (e.g. GARP, Phylocom). DataONE emphasizes free and open source tools, but also supports commercial products like Microsoft Excel and various statistical and modelling software programs like MATLAB. A library of tools supports all components of the scientific data lifecycle including data management and preservation, data query and access, data analysis and visualization, process management and preservation. The toolkit is well documented and includes examples for developers that illustrate how to interact with the infrastructure to enable support for new tools. The investigator toolkit also includes client libraries implemented in two widely used languages (Java and Python), and includes a proof-of-concept 'DataONE drive', which enables users to mount the entire DataONE cloud infrastructure as a file system. The DataONE drive was designed so as to enable scientists and data librarians to easily create and manage collections of data, much like librarians preserve and manage collections of documents.

Community engagement

Implementing the global infrastructure, expanding digital content, and promoting socio-cultural change in science practice requires that DataONE bring communities together in new ways. This is achieved via three approaches. First, a DataONE users' group represents the diversity of stakeholders and guides DataONE development in evolution of policies and procedures, prioritization of software supported in the investigator toolkit, promotion of education and outreach, and other activities.

Second, cyberinfrastructure and community engagement working groups actively involve diverse groups of graduate students, educators, government and industry representatives, and leading computer, information and library scientists. Working groups focus their efforts on performing computer science, informatics and social science research related to all stages of the data lifecycle; development and usability-testing of DataONE interfaces and prototypes; identifying interoperability standards; creating value-added technologies (e.g. semantic mediation, scientific workflow and visualization) that facilitate data integration, analysis and understanding; addressing socio-cultural barriers to sustainable data preservation and data sharing; and promoting the adoption of best practices for managing the full data lifecycle.

Third, DataONE supports communication with its stakeholders and the broader community via several modalities including newsletters, e-mail, FaceBook, Twitter, the DataONE.org web portal, Wikipedia and annual face-to-face meetings of the DataONE Users Group.

Impacts and outcomes

DataONE provides a critically needed foundation for innovative environmental research that addresses questions of relevance to science and society. Three key impacts and outcomes are envisioned:

- DataONE enables and promotes discovery, sharing and access to multi-scale, multi-discipline and multi-national data through a single location.
- DataONE provides access to and assists with the development of transformational tools that shape our understanding of Earth and biological processes from local to global scales.
- Via its community and education resources, DataONE provides essential skills (e.g. data management training, best practices, tool discovery) to enhance scientific enquiry, and supports the integration of expertise and resources across diverse communities to collectively educate, advocate and support the trustworthy stewardship of scientific data.

Conclusion
Australian perspectives – a uniquely national approach

Among organizations around the world seeking to assist with research data, the Australian National Data Service is unique in its combination of approaches. The national approach to data services that has been taken is seen as an enabler for tackling larger problems with more efficiency and greater synergy. A coherent institutional approach to engagement is leading to increased buy-in from this important stakeholder and greater research efficiency. The Australian Research Data Commons provides a collection-focused means of discovering and sharing research data. And the creation of national and institutional capability to exploit tools, policy and skills improves the efficiency and effectiveness of data management. The very significant investment that Australia is making in data management is fundamentally changing the Australian data management landscape.

Sociocultural change among libraries and scientists in the USA

In the USA, the NSF report *Understanding Infrastructure* (Edwards et al., 2007) reinforced the notion that infrastructure development is a sociotechnical enterprise. Issues such as trust, reliability and sustainability are equally important to the technical dimensions of infrastructure. Both Data Conservancy and DataONE comprise an attempt to move data sharing from its historically idiosyncratic methods to a more systematic, seamless approach. Rather than rely on individual researchers e-mailing data or posting them to websites, both DataNet projects envisage a world with a peer-to-peer model for data sharing. If researchers truly believe that data can be deposited reliably, preserved, shared and reused in a seamless manner, it will become possible for researchers not only to focus on science but also to ask new questions or construct new lines of inquiry. The 2010 community-wide effort for sharing data related to Alzheimer's disease has demonstrated the benefits of this type of approach.

The best partnerships arise from the alignment of enlightened self-interest. Effective data curation infrastructure will make it easier for researchers to identify such partnerships for team-based science.

Technological change

Libraries will continue to expand their offering of digital services to meet the needs of students, staff and faculty. In addition to potentially developing their own institutional data repositories or providing access to data-related tools and services (e.g. curation and preservation) associated with programs like DataNet and supported by projects such as the Data Conservancy and DataONE, many other technological changes are either envisioned or already underway for the library community. In particular, many libraries are reconfiguring their space by taking advantage of movable stacks and reducing their current and future physical holdings in order to create collaborative workspaces, support videoconferencing and distance education technologies, and add high-end computational, visualization, and immersive technologies. Such technological innovation requires an expansion of the bandwidth capacity at libraries. It also implies changes in staffing to include system administrators and a new breed of data librarians and data scientists with the necessary background in relevant technologies and domain sciences.

References

Websites

Alzheimer's Disease Initiative:
www.nytimes.com/2010/08/13/health/research/13alzheimer.html.

ANDS: http://ands.org.au.

ANDS Planning Documents: http://ands.org.au/resource/projectdocuments.html.

ARCHER: http://archer.edu.au.

ARROW: http://arrow.edu.au.

DART: http://dart.edu.au.

Data Conservancy: http://dataconservancy.org.

Data Observation Network for Earth: www.dataone.org.

DataONE: www.DataONE.org.

Education Investment Fund:
www.deewr.gov.au/HigherEducation/Programs/EIF/Pages/default.aspx.

Monash University Information Management Strategy:
www.monash.edu.au/staff/information-management/strategy.

National Collaborative Research Infrastructure Strategy (NCRIS):
www.innovation.gov.au/SCIENCE/RESEARCHINFRASTRUCTURE/Pages/
NCRIS.aspx.

PLANETS: www.planets-project.eu.

Platforms for Collaboration: www.pfc.org.au.

Super Science:
http://innovation.gov.au/Science/ResearchInfrastructure/Pages/SuperScience.aspx.

Citations

Australian Government (2007) *Towards the Australian Data Commons: a proposal for an Australian national data service*, Department of Education, Science and Training,
www.pfc.org.au/pub/Main/Data/TowardstheAustralianDataCommons.pdf.

Choudhury, S. and Stinson, T. L. (2007) *The Virtual Observatory and the Roman de la Rose: unexpected relationships and the collaborative imperative*,
www.academiccommons.org/commons/essay/VO-and-roman-de-la-rose-collaborative-imperative.

Edwards, P., Jackson, S., Bowker, G., and Knobel, C. (2007) *Understanding Infrastructure: dynamics, tension, and design*, final report of the workshop, History and Theory of Infrastructure: lessons for new scientific cyberinfrastructures,
http://deepblue.lib.umich.edu/handle/2027.42/49353.

Hey, T., Tansley, S. and Tolle, K. (2009) *The Fourth Paradigm: data-intensive scientific discovery*, Microsoft Research.

CHAPTER 10

Emerging infrastructure and services for research data management and curation in the UK and Europe

Angus Whyte

Introduction

Why try to predict the evolution of research data services and infrastructure? Enormous amounts have been invested in recent decades on programmes designed to strengthen the digital or 'e' aspects of research; the e-infrastructure for e-research or e-science. Emerging 'research data infrastructures' extend the reach of e-infrastructures, together with their agenda of transforming research knowledge production and use. What 'data infrastructures' bring to that agenda is the idea that research data itself can be provided as a utility, like computing or electricity grids. This idea envisages collaborative networks with a European and international span. Meanwhile, research funders and institutions are giving more attention to their own services for research data management and curation, in the effort to get more impact more efficiently from their investment in research.

The infrastructures and services they comprise can be thought of as supporting a common set of curation activities, at different levels of scale – institutional, national and international. Disciplinary domains and research questions cut across these, development resources are scarce, and the relationships between the actors involved in developing e-infrastructures are complex. So good conceptual tools are needed, whether to participate in these developments, evaluate their progress, guide researchers to make good use of the results, or critically engage with the very idea of data being usable 'any time, any place'.

This chapter aims to describe how research data infrastructures are currently conceived and surveys recent developments. The chapter has three main sections, which aim to do the following:

1 Review the context for developing 'research e-infrastructure' and the problems these are intended to address. The first section then considers concepts of infrastructure and how these apply to research data, identifying data management and curation services that would utilize and sustain these data infrastructures.

2 Summarize recent action to co-ordinate research data management and curation services and infrastructure. This second section considers action on the

international level by the European Union (EU) then, on the national level, by funding organizations in the UK, Netherlands and Germany. It then identifies initiatives at the level of educational institutions, focusing on the UK.

3 The final section of the chapter considers issues likely to affect the continued evolution of research data infrastructures.

In each case key policy, organizational and technical aspects are identified, including the geographical and disciplinary scope of current initiatives. Without claiming to be fully comprehensive the aim is to equip the reader with tools to understand 'the dynamics and the constraints surrounding these developments, for characterizing the problems and factors that underpin them, and identifying how these problems may be ameliorated' (Pollock and Williams, 2010).

Concepts of research data infrastructure and service
The nature of infrastructure and its importance for research

High ambitions are set for infrastructure development in research. Take for example the forward thinking to emerge from the review of the UK e-science programme in 2010. That review remarked that datasets are becoming 'the new instruments of science' (Atkins et al., 2010). These 'instruments' range from the globally accessible results of high-throughput gene sequencing to the datasets emanating from vast scientific facilities in the physics domain, such as colliders, synchrotrons and space telescopes. They are also notable for enabling collaborations across previously separate disciplines where, for example, digital datasets and methods are revolutionizing the cross-fertilization of linguistics with other fields; see the website for the Common Language Resources and Technology Infrastructure (CLARIN) at www.clarin.eu. Their use is the subject of 'data-intensive research', emerging from the federation and fusion of datasets and application of data exploration, mining and visualization techniques (Hey, Tansley and Tolle, 2009).

The same e-science review identified questions to guide a 'more transformative impact' for e-science:

- Might we aspire to create functionally complete virtual research environments (a.k.a. collaboratories) that provide science team's access through the Internet to all the colleagues, all the data, computational tools, and observatories required for the project? If so, could they seamlessly work together whether they are located in the same place or different places and interacting at the same or different times?
- How could we do this in agile ways; quickly setting up and taking down a virtual research environment (VRE) in response to new opportunities or threats?
- How could such capabilities increase the intellectual cross-section of ideas coming together to increase the probability of truly breakthrough discoveries?
- How could e-Science methods support more jointly beneficial research interactions with other countries?

- How can we deploy e-infrastructure and environments built upon it in ways that can serve multiple uses: research, education, citizen science, and more effective rapid response to natural or man-made disasters?
- How can services and knowledge from e-infrastructure and e-Science initiatives be applied to learning more generally, and especially to more socially based, experiential forms of learning?
- What does the emergence of e-science and e-humanities and arts say about the future of the university in the digital age?

> Atkins et al., 2010, 36

Scientific research that employs digital technologies in its lifecycle demands new supporting infrastructure. Advances in information and communications technologies (ICTs) are enabling researchers to organize their work across institutional and national borders. New organizational forms and social change are in turn driving novel technology developments, and in the midst of this cycle new forms of digital research data is emerging. These datasets are becoming part of a virtual environment for knowledge production and consumption. That is the message of *Riding the Wave*, a report from the European Commission's High Level Expert Group on Scientific Data (Wood et al., 2010), and curation is a key element of that message. According to Commission Vice President Neelie Kroes:

> with robust infrastructure for data transmission and data processing in place, we can now start to think about the next step: data itself. My vision is a scientific community that does not waste resources on recreating data that have already been produced, in particular if public money has helped to collect those data in the first place. Scientists should be able to concentrate on the best ways to make use of data. Data become an infrastructure that scientists can use on their way to new frontiers. Making this a reality is a more difficult task than it may seem. To *collect, curate, preserve and make available* ever-increasing amounts of scientific data, new types of infrastructures will be needed.
>
> Wood et al., 2010, 2, emphasis added

The argument for developing collaborative research infrastructures has various facets, which are discussed below.

Collaborative research is increasing in scope and impact

While researchers compete ever more intensively for research funding, there is a trend towards collaborative research projects that involve large scale inter-disciplinary partnerships; among researchers and research users, companies and communities with shared interests in the problems to be addressed. This trend has increased to the point that 35% of research articles are internationally co-authored (Wood et al., 2010).

Collaboration is an increasing trend across all disciplines, and leads to higher impact research, according to bibliometric analysis by Wuchty, Jones and Uzzi. The study concluded that 'teams typically produce more frequently cited research than individuals do, and this advantage has been increasing over time. Teams now also produce the exceptionally high-impact research, even where that distinction was once the domain of solo authors' (Wuchty, Jones and Uzzi, 2007, 1036).

Societal change is driving openness and broader participation

Paleontology is among the latest disciplines in which there has been a campaign for more open access to research data, data made available in more reusable formats, and with fewer licensing restrictions. *An Open Letter in Support of Paleontological Digital Data Archiving* highlights 'an unprecedented opportunity to disseminate palaeontological research data, in all its forms, far and wide, for better ease of accessibility, transparency, innovation, synthesis, and education and outreach' (Digital Data Archiving for Palaeontological Research, n.d.).

Interest in 'open' forms of research has broadened since the turn of the century. While in the early 1990s the open access movement focused on access to published research articles, a combination of factors has driven research policy and practice towards making a wider range of research materials accessible online. This includes data, and the aim of synthesizing and reusing for new research purposes provides an impetus for data mining researchers to demand that research follows open principles (Whyte and Pryor, 2011). This has coincided with greater demands from public policy makers for transparency in scientific knowledge production, and for investment in data gathering to be recouped through more reuse. The 'public good' view of research data articulated by the OECD in 2007 has been carried through to national funding body policy, including *Common Principles on Data Policy* by Research Councils UK (RCUK, 2011a).

An extra dimension to open research is brought by 'citizen science' methods that involve lay members of the public gathering and analysing data (Lyon, 2009). Building on amateur enthusiasm and voluntary effort, for example in the astronomy project Galaxy Zoo, the Citizen Science Alliance (www.citizensciencealliance.org) builds web services that promote 'learning by doing', and in return take advantage of volunteers' capabilities for observation and analysis.

Digital data sources are becoming pervasive

Technology is becoming embedded in social and domestic life in ways that generate enormous resources for economic and behavioural studies. Smart meters for electricity consumption, producing the equivalent of one CD-ROM of data for each household every year, are an example (Wood et al., 2010). Or consider the commercial research business generated by Twitter's publication of the 'firehose' of (at time of writing, summer 2011) 140 million tweets per day.

At the same time, miniaturized and networked instruments offer unprecedented sources of research data. Environmental and ecological research benefits from this; wirelessly networked sensors may be embedded across wide geographic areas, requiring innovation in data management to integrate and make sense of the flow of results (Donnelly and North, 2011). Similarly research on chronic health problems is benefiting from home-based health monitoring devices. These stream clinical data from patients' homes, potentially reducing their needs for hospitalization. Interpreting the data generated from 'telehealth' is challenging for clinicians, however, and curation issues include uncertain data ownership (Irshad and Ure, 2009).

Research data is escalating in volume and complexity

The paradigm case of 'big science data' is the Large Hadron Collider (LHC), expected to provide high energy physics experiments with around 15Pb (petabytes) annually, enough to fill more than 1.7 million DVDs (CERN, 2011). Similarly, in astronomy, the Large Synoptic Survey Telescope (www.lsst.org/lsst) is predicted to generate 100Pb of data over ten years.

The challenges of managing data and making it accessible from these very large scale facilities will be instructive for other domains. Yet it would be unwise to focus on the ever-higher stacks of imaginary DVDs rather than the conceptual, social and legal complexities involved. Equally important are datasets distributed across many smaller scale facilities. For example in health care, where data may fulfil the dual purpose of clinical care and research, an estimated 2.5Pb is held in mammograms gathered in the USA alone (Hey and Trefethen, 2003). According to a survey of researchers carried out in the PARSE Insight project (www.parse-insight.eu), only 16% of researchers estimated their research project would store more than 1 terabyte (Tb) of data over the next two years; the most common data type reported was 'office docs', and only 25% of researchers made their data openly available.

The data management challenges associated with large data is therefore not about their volume in any single location. They are about integrating datasets conceived and gathered for different purposes, moving them around, and making them accessible and reusable to the varying requirements of a distributed user community. In most cases of data-intensive research these will be complex requirements. According to Atkinson et al. (2010) 'data-intensive' research develops as a collaborative response to scale and complexity in the phenomena being studied. It is best understood by looking at three factors:

- typical activities of the researchers and data curators
- structural and organizational models employed
- the nature of the phenomena that are being studied.

In their view 'data-intensive' research emerges when a community perceives from these factors a need for extensive collaboration and consequently develops agreed goals, standards and practices to enable sharing and inter-working. Once the community 'has been using data for longer, there is greater understanding of their value and of the need to invest in pooled data facilities' (Atkinson et al., 2010, 37). In short, data size matters less than what researchers need to do collaboratively with it.

Collaborative research data infrastructure

'Research data infrastructures and services' should have a major part in addressing the issues covered so far, by connecting the raw material (data) with human and machine capabilities for innovation. But how may 'data infrastructure' relate to other forms of e-infrastructure? One definition is as follows:

> The term e-infrastructure refers to this new research environment in which all researchers – whether working in the context of their home institutions or in national or multinational scientific initiatives – have shared access to unique or distributed scientific facilities (including data, instruments, computing and communications), regardless of their type and location in the world.
>
> e-IRG, n.d.

This suggests a view of e-infrastructures as conduits for data, rather than infrastructures of data. The overlap seems even greater in the RCUK e-Infrastructure Review Report, which defines e-infrastructure as the combination and interworking of:

- Digitally-based technology (hardware and software),
- Resources (data, services, digital libraries),
- Communications (protocols, access rights and networks), and
- People and organisational structures needed to support modern, internationally leading collaborative research be it in the arts and humanities or the sciences.

> RCUK, 2011b

To understand more clearly how any of the above can lead to 'data infrastructure' we may turn to basic questions about what makes anything 'infrastructural'. Star and Ruhleder (2001) set out some key dimensions of infrastructure that have influenced later work. Just as a 'tool' is meaningful only when it connects someone to useful activity (and the same might be said of a 'service') infrastructure is something that becomes sufficiently accepted and ingrained that it 'then sinks into an invisible background' (Star and Ruhleder, 2001, 111). According to their view it is more insightful to think of infrastructure as a relationship between practices than a thing in itself. What is 'infrastructure' to one person may be another's daily work. The infrastructural aspects of work can, from this perspective, be understood within eight dimensions:

1   embeddedness: structures, social arrangements and technologies are sunk into each other
2   transparency: there is invisible task support that does not have to be reinvented each time
3   reach or scope: these extend either spatially beyond a single site, and temporally beyond a single event or site
4   learned as part of membership: they comprise a set of artefacts and organizational arrangements that strangers and outsiders need to learn about
5   links with conventions of practice: creating infrastructure shapes and is shaped by the conventions of a community of practice
6   embodiment of standards: plugs into other infrastructures and tools in a standardized fashion
7   being built on an installed base: inherits strengths and limitations from backwards compatibility with previous infrastructure
8   becoming visible on breakdown: normally invisible operations become apparent when they fail.

Subsequent studies of e-infrastructure for scientific research and development (e.g. Edwards et al., 2009; Karasti, Baker and Halkola, 2006) have used these dimensions to highlight the processes of organizational change involved in development, as well as to prompt critical questions to help in understanding where particular infrastructure projects fit. Similarly they may help get the measure of the challenges in building data management and curation services so they may become 'part of the furniture' of research.

The role for curation in research infrastructure is expressed in *Riding the Wave*, which recommends the development of an 'international framework' for a collaborative data infrastructure. The authors see the outcomes depicted in the following way:

> Data generators and users gather, capture, transfer and process data – often, across the globe, in virtual research environments. They draw upon support services in their specific scientific communities - tools to help them find remote data, work with it, annotate it or interpret it. The support services, specific to each scientific domain and provided by institutes or companies, draw on a broad set of common data services that cut across the global system; these include systems to store and identify data, authenticate it, execute tasks, and mine it for unexpected insights. *At every layer in the system, there are appropriate provisions to curate data – and to ensure its trustworthiness.*
>
> Wood et al., 2010, 31

A collaborative research data infrastructure could be defined further as: 'a layered set of services to support the creation, discovery, use, reuse, and transformation of digital research objects; each layer comprising interoperable services that interface to lower layers, and supported by a common set of curation services, and measures to ensure trustworthiness'.

The DCC Curation Lifecycle (see Chapter 2) provides a high-level set of activities based on relevant standards, which help to expand on this definition. Table 10.1 offers a view of the various data management and curation services that would support a collaborative data infrastructure. Human actors and their support services (virtual research communities) perform curation across physical and online environments, enabled by governance frameworks and infrastructures. Planning and carrying out data management and the administration of research information are a level above the data infrastructure that supports these activities. Of course the main purpose of such infrastructure is to support research lifecycle activities such as data modelling, visualization, analysis and the publication of articles. Our focus here is on curation, however, so Table 10.1 shows curation and related research-support activities.

The curation lifecycle is shown in Table 10.1 as a vertical stack, with 'Appraise and select' as the boundary between higher-level activities performed in the research environment, supported by data infrastructure, with lower-level activities performed using services from the repository environment and its infrastructure.

Research domains or disciplines are users of research data infrastructures, freed of some of the constraints of time and place by 'virtual research communities'. Ideally these may be conceived at a level above the data infrastructure level depicted in Table 10.1. 'Research infrastructures' are mostly discipline specific, addressing even the lower levels in ways that have evolved historically to meet the conceptual and pragmatic needs of a domain. The layered approach described in Table 10.1 draws on similar distinctions in the data preservation community between 'conceptual', 'logical' and 'physical' levels of preservation.

Table 10.1 *Curation lifecycle, services and infrastructure*

Community governance	Curation lifecycle actions	Services	Infrastructures	
Legal frameworks	Conceive	Data management planning, research administration	Group, institution, community	Virtual research communities
Community norms	Create and receive	Identify, describe, annotate,	Data infrastructure	
Research assessments	Access, use and reuse	Search, deliver, notify, cite		
Data policies	Transform	Mine, extract, migrate		
Preservation plans	Appraise and select	Inventory, assess, dispose, register		
Repository audits	Ingest	Identify, describe, validate, deposit	Repository infrastructure	
	Preserve	Clean, check, refresh		
Data standards	Store	Control, replicate, move		
		Authenticate, execute, connect	Computing and networking e-infrastructures	

Table 10.1 is similar in structure to the framework presented by the e-SciDr project 'European e-Infrastructure of and for European e-Science Digital Repositories', which conceived the infrastructure 'for' repositories as services for authentication, authorization and security served by a grid management layer, on top of a physical infrastructure layer of networked computing resources (e-SciDr, 2008).

The concept of layered services is also found in cloud-based service provision. According to one common definition, cloud computing is a model for enabling convenient, on-demand network access to a shared pool of configurable computing resources (e.g. networks, servers, storage, applications and services), which can be rapidly provisioned and released with minimal management effort or service provider interaction. This cloud model promotes availability and is composed of five essential characteristics, three service models and four deployment models (Mell and Grance, 2009). The characteristics refer to on-demand self-service, broad network access, resource pooling, rapid elasticity and measured service. The service models are designed as three layers: software as a service, platform as a service and infrastructure as a service.

Roughly corresponding to Table 10.1, 'as a service' layers for curation can be envisaged:

- data management planning as a service, providing web-based tools to support the creation and monitoring of plans that comply with funder and institutional requirements, interfacing to cross-institutional research information systems
- data appraisal as a service providing on-demand tools for data valuation that interface with cloud-based repositories
- data discovery as a service, web-based provisioning of access to data across registry and repository services.

We return to cloud services later in the chapter, and meanwhile look at more familiar 'levels' of infrastructure: institutional, national and European.

Three levels of infrastructure design
Pan-European initiatives
Policy actors and background
The European Union has pursued a European Research Area (ERA) for multinational co-operation on research since its inception. The ERA's succession of Framework Programmes (FPs), which had reached FP8 at the time of writing, has become increasingly organized to serve 'flagship' initiatives. These are expected to deliver economic and societal impacts identified in the Europe 2020 strategy, which has the broad aim of 'smart sustainable growth that includes all citizens'. Those concerning scientific data cut across two themes: the digital agenda for Europe and the innovation union (CEU, 2010).

The focus on e-infrastructures has grown since the European Commission's 2009 communication on ICT infrastructures for e-science (CEC, 2009). This stressed the Commission's strategic role in underpinning European research and innovation policies, and led to the formation of two of the key policy actors in establishing European data infrastructures:

- the High level Expert Group on Scientific Data (HLEG), whose report *Riding the Wave* is discussed above; the HLEG is mandated by the Commission to 'prepare a "vision 2030" for the area of scientific data e-infrastructures describing the long term vision regarding scientific data access, curation and preservation as well as the challenges, strategy and actions necessary to realise the vision'
- the e-Infrastructure Reflection Group (e-IRG), which has a mandate to define a common policy for e-infrastructure development.

The European Strategy Forum on Research Infrastructures (ESFRI) is also a key actor here. Established in 2002 as a strategic instrument under the aegis of the EU Council of Research Ministers, its role is to 'develop the scientific integration of Europe and to strengthen its international outreach' (ECRI, n.d.). Its focus on 'research infrastructure' is broader than e-infrastructure, since it includes large-scale physical resources in a single location (e.g. the Large Hadron Collider) plus geographically distributed facilities such as the European Bioinformatics Institute, as well as the e-infrastructures necessary for accessing them and virtual organizations to support their use or provide entirely online facilities (ECRI, n.d.).

Complementing the HLEG on Scientific Data and its strategic thinking towards 2030, and the e-IRG's envisioning of the policy frameworks for e-infrastructure, ESFRI has helped co-ordinate the Commission's investment in e-infrastructure projects, which we return to below. Additional co-ordination is provided through the European e-Infrastructure Forum. The European E-infrastructure Forum connects Pan-European e-infrastructure providers in high performance computing, networking, secure data storage and services, and the European Grid infrastructure. Its role is to enable members to share and align policies (EEF, n.d.).

Supporting the policy work of these bodies is the community-building project GRDI2020. This is an FP7 'coordination action', with a remit to produce a roadmap towards 'global research data infrastructures' and convene meetings with stakeholders. The aim is to identify priorities, 'influence the development of a competitive global ICT infrastructure' and 'build a qualified, trans-European Research Data Infrastructure community whose members will be inspired by common use cases and will share experiences, plan, innovate, and reach out together, with strong commitment to tackle the main relevant technical challenges' (www.grdi2020.eu/StaticPage/About.aspx).

Cross-national collaboration on data infrastructure also occurs through the Knowledge Exchange (www.knowledge-exchange.info). This is a partnership between national bodies responsible for higher education infrastructure: the Joint Information

Systems Committee (JISC) in the UK, Denmark's Electronic Research Library (DEFF), the German Research Foundation (DFG) and the SURFfoundation in the Netherlands. The Knowledge Exchange partners' common interest is in making 'a layer of scholarly and scientific content openly available on the Internet' (KE, n.d.).

Other important actors are the European Heads of Research Councils (www.eurohorcs.org), an informal forum for cross-council research policy dialogue; the European Science Foundation (www.esf.org), a membership-based association for scientific research organizations; and EIROforum (www.eiroforum.org/), a collaboration between eight European intergovernmental scientific research organizations that are responsible for large scale infrastructures and laboratories.

Data management planning and research administration

The European Commission will be requesting data management and open content for all research projects in FP8. Vice President Neelie Kroes announced at the launch of the report *Riding the Wave* that 'we need to ensure that every future project funded by the EU has a clear plan on how to manage the data it generates. Such plans should foster openness and economies of scale, so that data can be reused many times rather than duplicated' (Europa, 2010).

At the time of writing (summer 2011) the specific policy measures to support this were unannounced. They will no doubt build on requirements already in place for FP7 projects. According to the Commission's contractual rules, project consortia must formulate plans for using and disseminating the results generated by their project. These currently cover such areas as intellectual property rights and the deposit of publications in public repositories. Projects are also obliged to retain all documentation for at least five years post-project (European Commission, 2010).

It is likely that as processes to support data management become better established, better integration will follow with research administration systems (see Chapter 5). Take-up of common research information systems based on the Common European Research Information Format standard could result in the growth of a research information infrastructure, driven by necessities to cut administrative costs through resource sharing.

From domain-based infrastructures to ERICS

Research e-infrastructures have grown around specific domain needs. Consider for example the World Large Computing Grid (WLCG), which enables the global particle physics community to make use of data collected from the Large Hadron Collider. This community is organized around very large scale and long-running experiments, such as ATLAS and CMS. Between the physical detectors and virtual organizations that serve these experiments, the WLCG provides curation, storage and transfer functions covering many of the services in Table 10.1. The European Union funds some activities of the European Organization for Nuclear Research (CERN), where physical facilities and much of the data management are hosted. However much is also funded and organized nationally; in the UK through the GridPP (www.gridpp.ac.uk) consortium, funded by the Science and Technology Facilities Council (STFC).

Particle physics offers significant examples of infrastructure that has been rapidly taken up across domains, spreading 'horizontally', yet the domain has other infrastructures that continue to develop 'vertically' in ways that reflect disciplinary cultures. In the former case we have the world wide web, famously the offspring of CERN, and in the latter case the open access 'pre-print' repository ArXive, which has been adopted relatively slowly by some communities outside physics (e.g. mathematics) and found to be less compatible with how other communities do their scholarly communication (Kling, Spector and McKim, 2002). It is understandable therefore that the e-IRG advocates an evolutionary approach to support virtual research communities, led by user requirements: 'VRC developments should proceed gradually, starting with domain-specific shared access to distributed resources, expanding to integrate different research activities, and ultimately including wider support infrastructure' (e-IRG, 2010).

The European Commission funds domain-specific data infrastructure projects, initially through FP7 and the ESFRI Roadmap (ESFRI, 2008). The Roadmap includes 44 projects and, according to the 2010 update report, ten had progressed to implementation with a further 16 not far behind (ESFRI, 2010). The projects are in broad 'thematic areas': social science and humanities, biological and medical science, environmental sciences, physical sciences and engineering, and energy. The EEF surveyed ESFRI projects to identify their common requirements. These commonly included data management and persistent storage services. Curation was identified as a priority in the social science and humanities and physical sciences and engineering areas (EEF, n.d.).

ESFRI infrastructures are typically conceived as a federated network of centres established in European member states, using web service-oriented architectures. Each is organized in a distributed hub structure, with the hubs co-ordinating data collection, management, distribution and analysis. Users are typically research centres, plus a variety of associated public or private partners providing data, technologies or services across different fields of academia and industry. Examples orientated to data provision include the following three projects:

1   The Council of European Social Science Data Archives (CESSDA; www.cessda.org) organization promotes data services for the European social science and humanities research community. The project fosters the development of national data archiving initiatives in countries that are not currently part of CESSDA, and by extending the network of organizations that host important data collections. The aim is for a 'one-stop-shop' for data discovery, access, analysis and delivery across the social science and humanities community. This entails developing a new generation of tools and services for data discovery,

integration, visualization, analysis and preservation.

2   Common Language Resources and Technology Infrastructure (CLARIN; www.clarin.eu) is a large-scale collaborative effort to create and co-ordinate language resources and technology and to make them available and useful to scholars of all disciplines, in particular the humanities and social sciences. Language resources may be collections (corpora) of written, recorded and multimodal interaction typically organized by a theme or genre of human interaction, and often including annotations of these and tools to support their analysis. CLARIN envisages a comprehensive service with tools and resources interoperable across languages and domains, aiming to overcome the present fragmented situation by making them available via web services. CLARIN will rely on a network of powerful centres that can offer a wide range of stable and highly available services, ranging from archiving services to advanced ontology services offering widely accepted and well defined domain concepts.

3   The European Clinical Research Infrastructures Network project (ECRIN; www.ecrin.org) integrates research capacities and capabilities to support multinational clinical trials. Clinical trials require access to large populations to develop new approaches and therapies effectively. Recognition of this at national level has encouraged co-ordination across research centres and trial units. ECRIN has multiple objectives to support patient enrolment in trials, data management, quality assurance, monitoring, ethics and regulatory affairs, and transparent reporting. ECRIN also supports harmonization of national legislation to protect trial participants, and frameworks for participation, education and training. There is a focus on compatibility of data and procedures throughout the pipeline from basic research to patient therapy. ECRIN addresses challenges related to long-term curation of clinical data and confidentiality of patient data.

In its blue paper the e-IRG observed, 'The worst possible scenario is that all new RI [research infrastructures] build their own data infrastructure resulting in 250–300 data silos of limited compatibility and interoperability' (e-IRG, 2010, 25). The follow-up white paper points to 'a high need to integrate the data sources to build a sustainable way of providing a good level of information and knowledge. This feature is currently missing from the European e-Infrastructure' (e-IRG, 2011). Their recommendation is a strategic roadmap to construct a new paradigm for data management, exchange and protection, and a process for embedding data infrastructure into e-infrastructure. The precursors of a common infrastructure are in a range of recent and ongoing European projects. Brief summaries of these follow below, in three areas: federated access and deposit to repositories, persistent identification and preservation.

Common repository infrastructures

The European Commission has an open access policy for authors to deposit research article outputs from FP7 projects. While policy towards data deposit for FP8 is still being formulated, output repositories will be significant providers of data infrastructure services.

OpenAIRE (www.openaire.eu), a three-year project from 2010, provides guidelines for repositories to comply with open access. This aims to offer a European help desk, national open access liaison offices, and a portal for scientific publication discovery services. OpenAIRE further seeks to 'explore the requirements, practices, incentives, workflows, data models, and technologies to deposit, access, and otherwise manipulate research datasets of various forms in combination with research publications' (OpenAIRE, 2010).

The OpenAIRE repository guidelines were based on work by the Digital Repository Infrastructure Vision for European Research (DRIVER) II Project. This built a pan-European federation of repositories, exchanging metadata using the Dublin Core standards, and the OAI-PMH transfer protocol. The project's validation tools, guidelines and registry enabled the DRIVER portal service (www.driver-repository.eu) to provide searching across the contents of 185 repositories in 21 countries. In 2009, a non-profit association Confederation of Open Access Repositories (COAR; http://coar-repositories.org) was established to sustain and promote the DRIVER federation by providing advocacy, guidance and training in open access models of information dissemination and data reuse.

Persistent identifier services

Several services are currently vying for primacy as a mechanism for their users to avoid 'link rot' by registering with the third-party service any online objects they wish to publish. The service then provides sustainable access to metadata associated with the object, a permanent identifier, and a means of 'resolving' that identifier so that requests for the object get redirected to the current location identified by its publisher. There are a variety of standards and international services. One of the largest is DataCite, a not-for-profit organization formed in London in 2009, which aims to establish easier access to scientific research data, promote its acceptance as a legitimate, citable contribution to the scientific record, and support data archiving. DataCite currently uses the Digital Object Identifier (DOI) standard, and 'mints' DOIs on behalf of partner organizations including the British Library. It also considers 'other identifier systems and services that help forward our objectives' (DataCite Metadata Working Group, 2011). PersID, an initiative launched by SURFfoundation in 2011, uses the URN-NBN standards on the grounds that these are based on open internet standards and are not vendor-specific (Cordewener, 2011).

Preservation services

The EU initiative Partnership for Accessing Data in Europe (PARADE; www.csc.fi/english/pages/parade) identified core requirements across the ESFRI infrastructure projects, including regular quality assessment, a high degree of interoperability at format and semantic level, and bit-stream preservation, guaranteeing data authenticity for a specified number of years.

The Alliance for Permanent Access (APA; www.alliancepermanentaccess.org) is an association of preservation projects including:

- Alliance for Permanent Access to the Records of Science in Europe Network (APARSEN), which aims to build a 'Virtual Centre of Digital Preservation Excellence' through the co-ordinated dissemination and exchange activities of its partners
- Science Data Infrastructure for Preservation – with focus on Earth Science (SCIDIP-ES), which aims to provide a scalable, robust e-infrastructure for preservation using components from its forerunner, the FP6 project CASPAR. The project has an initial focus on earth sciences
- Opportunities for Data Exchange (ODE), which intends to document best practices in the design of e-Infrastructures, plus 'success stories in data sharing . . . visionary policies' to enable data reuse, and the needs and opportunities for interoperability of data layers to fully enable e-Science' (APA, n.d.).

The Open Planets Foundation (OPF) similarly operates as a forum for exchanging solutions and expertise in digital preservation, building on research and development outputs of the FP6 PLANETS project (www.planets-project.eu). These include tools for preservation planning and for characterizing digital objects.

National approaches

The GRDI2020 project (www.grdi2020.eu) offers a comprehensive collection of EU member states' research infrastructure strategy documents, which gives a cross-national review of curation and preservation initiatives. Brief snapshots follow of programmes in Germany and the Netherlands.

Data publishing platforms in the Netherlands

National initiatives in the research infrastructure area have been co-ordinated through a national roadmap. The main actors in digital preservation and data infrastructure in the Netherlands include SURF, the 3TU Datacentrum and DANS:

- SURF has a similar role to the JISC in providing infrastructure to higher education. Its support for innovation in e-research, e-learning and e-administration is delivered by SURFfoundation (www.surffoundation.nl), whose SURFshare programme funds a range of initiatives including 'enhanced publications' projects in humanities, social science and geoscience disciplines.

- 3TU Datacentrum (www.datacentrum.3tu.nl) is a collaboration between three technical universities to provide a scientific research data archive, and includes within its remit long-term preservation, access, data citation and linking to publications.

- The Data Archiving and Networked Services (DANS) initiative has developed and promoted the Data Seal of Approval (www.datasealofapproval.org), internationally recognized as a self-assessment standard for digital data repositories in the social sciences and humanities.

German data infrastructure initiatives

German research organizations have been active for many years in promoting open access, particularly the Max-Planck Society (www.mpg.de). This is also a key player in research infrastructures, for example the CLARIN network described above. The German Federal Ministry for Education and Research (Bundesministerium für Bildung und Forschung; BMBF; www.bmbf.de) funds the Network of Expertise in Long-Term Storage of Digital Resources (nestor; www.langzeitarchivierung.de), a 'competence network' in preservation, which has been widely influential in setting standards for digital repositories.

Digital curation and preservation initiatives have been funded at national and federal state level, and in 2010 a joint Science Conference was held by the Federal and Länder Governments Commission on the Future of Information Infrastructure.

The German Research Foundation (Deutsche Forschungsgemeinschaft; DFG) issued a call for information infrastructures for research data, resulting in 27 projects starting in 2011 on:

- Data centres for entire disciplines, incl. high volume data.
- Systems for linking publications with research data.
- Systems offering a persistent identifier service.
- Workflow and software development for enhanced data handling.
- Long-term storage and archiving systems.

Winkler-Nees, 2011

UK data policies and infrastructure
Funding body data policies

The scene for UK data infrastructure development was set by several reports in 2007. One of these, the final report from the OST Preservation and Curation Working Group to the Office of Science and Technology, recommended that there should be:

- policy development in the long-term protection of 'valuable information from science data through to administrative data, and electronic publications'
- persistent national information infrastructure development: a national programme to 'enable the transformation and to pump-prime the development of the information infrastructure'
- research and development in digital curation and preservation 'to address long-term digital preservation and curation challenges' (Beagrie, 2007, 4).

These areas have each seen significant change. In policy development, the consultancy report to JISC *Dealing with Data* (Lyon, 2007) also identified a need for vigorous policy development by funders and research organizations to clarify roles and responsibilities. In 2007 the OECD released *Principles and Guidelines for Access to Research Data from Public Funding* (OECD, 2007), giving momentum to the research councils' data policy formation (covered in Chapter 3). Following the earlier example of the Research Information Network's *Principles and Guidelines for Stewardship of Digital Research Data* (RIN, 2007), in 2011 the UK Research Councils issued a statement of common principles on data policy. This 'overarching framework' for individual research council policies lists seven principles, which are on:

1 The 'public good' nature of publicly funded research data
2 The need for data management planning and preservation
3 Provision of metadata to aid discoverability
4 Constraints to ensure research is not damaged by inappropriate release
5 First use rights to recognise researchers' effort in collecting and analysing data
6 Recognition, by attributing data sources and abiding by terms and conditions
7 Cost-effective and efficient use of funds for data management and sharing

RCUK (n.d.)

Several research councils fund national data centres and attach importance to data infrastructure in the 'delivery plans' that identify funding strategies for 2011–2015. These place a lot of emphasis on funding larger, more collaborative, research projects and suggest that resource sharing and the 'seventh principle' (cost) will be key. The Economic and Social Research Council (ESRC) for example promises to: 'Sustain a basic national "core" infrastructure by investment in key data facilities, longitudinal datasets and methods; Protect all essential core elements of our data resources . . . scaling them back to the minimum level compatible with maintaining and developing a high quality national data infrastructure' (ESRC, 2010).

Developing tools and services at the institutional level

With the culmination of the UK e-Science Programme of Research and Development, which contributed to the 2004 founding of the Digital Curation Centre (DCC) (Atkins et al., 2010), the JISC has provided a crucial role in pump-priming infrastructure development in e-research tools and data management infrastructure, especially given a shift in cross-council funding from these to wider programmes intending to stimulate a digital economy.

Preservation initiatives undertaken at an institutional level have included Oxford University's project Embedding Institutional Data Curation Services in Research (http://eidcsr.oucs.ox.ac.uk). This launched the development of policy for the institution, seeking to join up existing institutional and departmental services to address the preservation challenges facing two 'data rich' research groups. Research workflows were examined and tools developed to aid integration with long-term file storage and the library digital asset management.

The first phase of the JISC's Managing Research Data Programme covered five areas from 2009 to 2011:

- research data management infrastructures
- citing, linking, integrating and publishing research data
- research data management planning support
- support tools for institutions to assess the costs and benefits of changes in practice
- discipline-specific training materials in data management (JISC, n.d.).

Institutional services and infrastructure have emerged from the first of these strands, involving the universities of Bath, Cambridge, Glasgow, Leicester, London (King's College) and Manchester, plus the two examples from Oxford and Southampton, which are described below.

The Supporting Data Management Infrastructure for the Humanities project (SUDAMIH), at the University of Oxford, continued the EIDCSR strategy. This involved the central Library and IT services engaging with the needs of specific research groups for data management and curation tools. In parallel, they carried out broader surveys of faculty requirements and developed services, guidelines and training. These sought to extrapolate across groups and disciplines from specific needs and solutions. Support for database management was found to be a common requirement of humanities scholars and, leveraging the central computing service's storage facilities, the project piloted an application called Database as a Service to address this: 'a web-based interface for creating and editing relational databases, querying them, and displaying results in various formats' (Wilson et al., 2010). The overview of the data management workflow shown in Figure 10.1 illustrates where this service fits, and which institutional actors are involved.

A broadly similar 'top-down and bottom-up' approach was adopted by the University

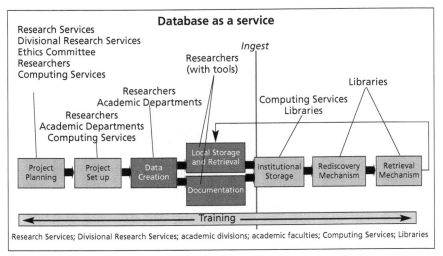

Figure 10.1 *The Sudamih project Database as a Service (Wilson, 2011)*

of Southampton's Institutional Data Management Blueprint project (IDMB). This envisaged infrastructure development as a long-term endeavour, requiring strategies for the short, medium and long-term. Short-term measures involved a cross-faculty review of data management practices and needs and the development of a 'one-stop shop' for advice and guidance. In IDMB the focus on particular research group requirements centred on an Archaeology project, Portus (funded separately by the Arts and Humanities Research Council). IDMB's medium-term plan features an institutional data repository, managed to support the research data lifecycle, with mandates for researchers to share data openly. The longer-term ambition inherent in the IDMB business plan is to provide coherent support across all disciplines, embed 'exemplary data management practice' across the institution and instil 'agile business planning for continual improvement' (Takeda, 2010).

Towards a UK research data service

In 2010, the creation of a UK research data service emerged as the core proposal from a joint project between Research Libraries UK (RLUK, a consortium of research libraries in the UK and Ireland) and the Russell Group of IT Directors (RUGIT). Funded by the Higher Education Funding Council for England (HEFCE), with support from the JISC, the objective of the UK Research Data Service (UKRDS) Project was to assess the feasibility and costs of developing and maintaining a national shared digital research data service for the UK higher education sector (UKRDS, 2010). One year later this concept of a UK-wide service received support with the announcement of activities to be pursued under the University Modernisation Fund (UMF), a £152 million initiative designed to support a 'sustained increase in student places at universities and colleges in a period of economic recovery by adopting greater savings and efficiencies' (HEFCE, n.d.). One element of this initiative is the development of shared services. In addition to the data service segment, there are two other related threads of activity:

- establishment of a 'service brokerage' for cloud or virtual services with the aim of persuading institutions effectively to rent servers and storage from trusted suppliers rather than build capital intensive data centres
- development and deployment within a software-as-a-service model of data management applications useful to researchers.

The UKRDS segment builds on the JISC's projects and programmes and is delivered principally by the DCC, with the aim of cultivating good practice in research data management, curation and preservation. The main strands of this work will:

- *Embed skills and capabilities within institutions* – There is a need to assist institutions in assessing and costing the changes needed to their organization and skills-base in order to exercise capability in research data management. This process will use appropriate methods and tools to assess data management requirements, activity and capacity at a department and research group level, such as the Collaborative Assessment of Research Data Infrastructure and Objectives (CARDIO) tool developed by the JISC-funded Integrated Data Management Planning (IDMP) Project. This may, for example, identify and address gaps in an institution's training provision or policy development.
- *Further develop an online tool for data management planning* (DMP Online) – This includes the provision of templates that allow researchers and their support services to prepare plans that meet the specific requirements of individual funding bodies. As described in Chapter 5, the provision of guidance tailored to individual institutions and disciplines is a further extension, with the option of enabling links to research administration systems.
- *Provide co-ordinating services* – Registries of metadata are envisaged, to enable inter-institution services for registering and discovering research datasets. The aim here is to alleviate the need for individual institutions to track where datasets are physically stored and curated. Co-ordination will include supporting the efficient flow of archived data to recommended places of deposit, for example in national data centres.

Clouds and horizons: issues to navigate

Star-gazing to predict the future trajectory of research data infrastructures is beyond the scope of this chapter. On the other hand, studies of previous e-infrastructure development highlight the issues likely to challenge, if not cloud, the vision for research data services and infrastructure. Barriers to collaboration have been studied extensively in e-infrastructure studies and Bos et al.'s (2007) study of scientific 'collaboratories' identified three main barriers to scientific research, moving from 'informal, one-to-one collaborations, which have long been common between scientists' to 'more tightly co-ordinated, large-scale organizational structures, which are a less natural fit'. The barriers are:

- the difficulty of transferring knowledge that requires specialist expertise and may be tacit: scientists 'can often negotiate common understandings with similar experts in extended one-to-one interactions but may have great difficulty communicating what they know to larger distributed groups'
- a culture of independence that affords freedom to pursue high risk ideas and resists 'controls that many corporate employees accept as normal'; scientific collaborations 'must work harder than other organizations to maintain open communication channels, adopt common toolsets, and keep groups focused on common goals'
- the plethora of difficulties encountered by cross-institutional research when traversing formal institutional boundaries, including the contentious matter of intellectual property rights issues, since 'universities often guard their intellectual property and funding in ways that hinder multi-site collaboration' (Bos et al., 2007).

These issues are likely to continue to affect data infrastructure development, as we discuss further below.

Representing disciplinary and local knowledge

As the e-IRG has pointed out, 'The data stored and shared in the pan-European infrastructure needs to be interoperable, easily discoverable, and its provenance must be known and trusted. Only after that, can the data be effectively used and re used' (e-IRG, 2010). Bioinformatics has been at the forefront of much of what we recognize today as 'data infrastructure' and key to its development has been the development of standards tools and services for 'packaging' – the metadata and documentation standards (Leonelli, 2009).

The 'tacit knowledge' in research limits the value of this packaging, and has long been recognized as a barrier to scientific communication (Mukherjee and Stern, 2009). Tacit knowledge is a core element of expertise but is by definition undocumented. It is acquired through bodily experience (e.g. learning to riding a bike) and collective social experience (e.g. learning to negotiate traffic) (Collins, 2007). While it is in principle feasible to make this kind of knowledge explicit and document it, the point is that it is normally taken for granted, or learned as part of becoming a member of a community of practice. The packaging needed to codify this knowledge is much broader than that referred to by 'packaging metadata'. It also includes what the Open Archival Information System standard for data preservation (CCSDS, 2002) defines as 'representation information' – all that is needed by a given community to understand a 'content data object'. Representation information entails understanding a string of dependencies: for example, the table headers defined in a code book, which refers to a glossary, which in turn invokes a broader standard, which in turn depends on understanding disciplinary conventions, and so on (Caplan, 2006). The amount that can feasibly be codified and the amount that will remain tacit of this and the 'preservation description information', which may record (for example) an object's context and provenance, will vary widely between disciplines, domains and even research group (Lyon et al., 2010).

Representation information that is tacit, widely distributed and very expensive will limit the practical and economic case for sharing and reusing research data, and more especially of reproducing its analysis. This affects even 'data intensive' fields. Some, such as neuroimaging (Whyte et al., 2008) and particle physics (Gray, Carozzi and Woan, 2011), are especially challenging, as they involve the rapid development of the instruments and models used. Data may be captured in a computational environment whose software components comprise an interdependent network whose nodes are quickly outdated. Coupled with that, understanding the raw data and analysing it requires the close collaboration of many specialists, and the data is a record of events that are unique or can only be reproduced at great cost.

Complex cases like this may well become more common. Strategies for making it possible to reanalyse their datasets and make them manageable will involve breaking down the problem, perhaps by establishing the scientific and economic 'reuse case' at different stages in the data lifecycle. For example, the Data Preservation in High Energy Physics Working Group has used a four-level model for analysing reuse cases, from raw data at the lowest level to analysis results at the highest level (South, 2011).

Depending on the domain and research context it may be pragmatic and cost-effective to approach curation from the top level first, dealing with datasets that relate to published articles, such as the spreadsheets and figures comprising 'supplementary material' for publication. Emerging repository services specializing in this area include Dryad (www.datadryad.org) and Figshare (http://figshare.com). Longer-term solutions will involve automatically capturing more of the semantic relations between research datasets and the software components used in their analysis, implementing generic models of 'research objects' and their workflows (Bechhofer et al., 2010). Capturing day-to-day notes and exchanges in electronic lab notebooks may also be a very useful aid to preserving the research record, especially when employed alongside semantic representations of the research objects concerned (Frey, 2009).

Standardization and interoperability

Research, especially basic 'curiosity-driven' research, inevitably encounters 'unknown unknowns'. These may require innovation in methods, software, data or file structures and, as innovation is competitive, standardization can only progress where collaboration brings reciprocal gains through interoperability. The review of the UK e-science programme by Atkins et al. (2010) recommends 'openness as a general policy' and allies this with the use of international standards. Nevertheless, lack of agreement on data and metadata standards is one of the biggest barriers to infrastructure take-up according to Voss et al., 2009).

Astronomy, for example, has benefited from sustained efforts of the International Virtual Observatory Alliance international collaboration on 'virtual observatory' standards. These enable data captured at real observatory facilities to be curated and very quickly shared among collaborators. Yet the standards have taken decades to become accepted, and have had to accommodate fundamental differences in methods of measurement between sub-domains – for example between high-energy and ground-based astronomy. Realizing the benefits of open standards may involve many cost-benefit tradeoffs before they become accepted as the only option and acquire the invisibility that goes with the status of infrastructure (RIN, 2010). This may involve research groups in making 'political' decisions on their prospective collaborators, and bring in issues around intellectual property rights and cross-jurisdiction questions about legal rights and responsibilities.

Collaboration in a competitive environment
Legal frameworks and intellectual property rights governance
Legal issues represent the most significant barrier to sharing data (Kuipers and van der Hoeven, 2009) and they are the target of slow but significant developments coalescing around the topics of legal instruments, intellectual property rights policy, secure data services and guidelines. At the European level, the legal framework for European Research Infrastructure Consortia, established in 2009, has enabled these projects to acquire the status of legal entities, simplifying the creation of contracts and agreements. However, the e-Infrastructure Reflection Group states, 'Legal structures, like ERIC, should become easier to implement, should enable international co-operation on a non-governmental level, and should be adapted to also support distributed immaterial infrastructures like data' and calls for the overhaul of copyright and IPR frameworks: 'IPR arrangements have to facilitate interoperability of infrastructure and services instead of hindering them' (e-IRG, 2011).

Public domain licensing models for data from the Creative Commons project and Open Knowledge Foundation offer options to tackle the rights clearance issues that data reuse presents for researchers and institutions. The competing demands to protect and commercialize research results may complicate the decisions. Guidance is available from the DCC (Ball, 2011) and a risk management approach to rights clearance is recommended (Strategic Content Alliance, 2009).

Assessing research and infrastructure

A string of high-level reports have called for new ways to measure the value of data and reward those who use it (e.g. Wood et al., 2010; Lyon, 2007). If funders and institutions were to give more credit to dataset creation and curation, reward should flow to those datasets that are found to be more useful and reusable for research purposes and to the services that provide them. This requires the introduction of mechanisms for funders and institutions to identify well used (or reused) datasets, most probably on the basis of their citation rates, and their provision by useful and usable services.

Progress has been slow; despite 'infrastructure' being a recognized category for research assessment exercises in the UK, submissions are few. From some perspectives the missing element is an established set of metrics that may be used to assess 'non-traditional outputs' transparently, as bibliometrics are used to measure publication impacts (e.g. Priem and Hemminger, 2010). The standards being developed in this area may be crucial. Standards-based services for identifying and tracking datasets (Datacite, Persid), researchers and contributors (ORCID; www.orcid.org) and outcomes (RCUK Research Outcomes Project; www.rcuk.ac.uk/research/ResearchOutcomes) may become key elements in more efficient research administration, using current research information systems that comply with the Common European Research Information Format standard.

Underlying the lack of measures to assess and reward effort on datasets is a similar lack in measuring the effectiveness of tools or services used to generate, share and preserve datasets. Standards and software developments are rewarded by the citation of articles that are written about their novel aspects. More appropriate rewards could be based on take-up, usability or reliability (Atkins et al., 2010, RIN, 2010).

Addressing resource issues through broader participation

The ESFRI has described research infrastructures as '"grinders" to wear down old, inefficient and isolated form of managing research' (Rizzuto and Hudson, 2010). We might want to insert the word 'data' in that statement, but who pays for the investment in curation and with what consequences? A survey in *Science* (Science, 2011) found that only 8.9% of respondents said their research group or lab had sufficient funds to curate their research data. And the investment needed at this level may be substantial; one study for the project Keeping Research Data Safe found there were significant set-up costs for a university in establishing requirements, developing policies and applying standards for a data curation service (Wilson et al., 2010).

Greater industry involvement in data infrastructures at the cross-institutional level may be the consequence of this resource gap. When the Council of the EU recently deliberated on the overlaps between the Innovation Union and Digital Agenda for Europe flagships it urged the European Commission (EC) to 'leverage more private investment in ICTs through the strategic use of pre-commercial procurement and, where appropriate, effective industry-driven research partnerships', recommended 'greater focus on demand- and user-driven partnerships' and advised that the EC should 'support joint ICT research infrastructures and innovation clusters, cultural and creative industries, develop further world-class e-infrastructures and establish an EU strategy for cloud computing notably for government and science but also for SME's' (CEU, 2010).

Resonating with these concerns, the e-IRG white paper points to 'unnecessary distinctions between national and international e-Infrastructure services'. These should be abolished, and 'national and community regulations or practices that inhibit open and equal public and private co-operation in the use of e-Infrastructures should be reviewed, allowing equal treatment of users in public and private research'. The draft continues 'best practices and lessons learned from Research Infrastructures show that opening access to RIs for the full European user base, catalyses the development of an EU knowledge market' (e-IRG, 2010).

Conclusion

Services comprising a collaborative research data infrastructure will involve many actors and it is not yet clear how these will be shaped around domains and institutions. Will the role of institutions be to provide generic data repositories that fill the gaps between directly funded disciplinary services, sometimes as a temporary 'staging post' until these evolve to meet niche requirements? Will institutions seek to specialize in areas of local research strength, in effect becoming nodes in international domain-based collaborations? What about the roles of nationally funded data centres? Some have traditionally catered for single disciplines, and may try to establish more diverse roles, as funders jointly fund large inter-disciplinary collaborations around major scientific and societal problems.

It seems likely that whoever provides data management, curation and preservation services will be expected to cater for cross-disciplinary virtual communities, while drawing their capabilities from regional innovation networks based around clusters of institutions and the physical facilities and tacit expertise in their vicinity. This will make regional collaboration between library, IT and research support services attractive. Whether the services operate at institutional, national or international level will depend on the level of scale at which the governance frameworks can fund their operation and resolve breakdowns in trust. More and earlier collaboration with non-academic users will be likely as funders seek to stimulate innovation. Since this will add to the range of stakeholders whose data management requirements must be identified and planned for, it will increase the complexity of data management provision, adding to the pressure on services to scale up.

Building infrastructure calls for both short-term and long-term strategies (Ribes and Finholt, 2009), as exemplified by the University of Southampton's Institutional Data Management Blueprint. The need for an incremental approach coupled with long-term vision has interesting parallels in the history of other infrastructures, such as enterprise resource planning. Long-term studies of the 'biography' of packaged software shows how vendors of packaged enterprise resource planning tools and services have progressed step-by-step, successfully enrolling new 'domains' of the enterprise. This has meant reconciling current and emergent requirements, including gateways to accommodate competing standards, anticipating and managing drift in requirements arising from pressure to increase the number and diversity of users (Pollock and Williams, 2010).

Whatever the extent of top-down mandates, the take-up by researchers of standards-based services will be critical. Services for research data management provided through institutions and nationally funded services such as DCC in the UK, SURF in the Netherlands and DFG in Germany should build a more effective bridge between researchers and 'demand led' services for research information and impact recording.

References

APA (n.d.) *Projects*, Alliance for Permanent Access,
   www.alliancepermanentaccess.org/index.php/current-projects.

Atkins, D. , Borgman, C., Bindoff, N., Ellisman, M., Feldman, S., Foster, I. et al. (2010) Building a UK Foundation for the Transformative Enhancement of Research and Innovation: report of the international panel for the 2009 review of the UK research councils e-science programme. Retrieved from:
   www.epsrc.ac.uk/SiteCollectionDocuments/Publications/reports/RCUKe-ScienceReviewReport.pdf.

Atkinson, M., De Roure, D., van Hemert, J., Jha, S., Mann, B., Viglas, S. and Williams, C. (2010) *Data-Intensive Research Workshop Report*, e-Science Institute.

Ball, A. (2011) *How to License Research Data*, Digital Curation Centre,
   www.dcc.ac.uk/resources/how-guides/license-research-data.

Beagrie, N. (2007) *E-infrastructure Strategy for Research: final report from the OSI preservation and curation working group*, Office of Science and Innovation.

Bechhofer, S., De Roure, D., Gamble, M., Goble, C. and Buchan, I. (2010) Research Objects: Towards Exchange and Reuse of Digital Knowledge. In *The Future of the Web for Collaborative Science (FWCS 2010)*, April 2010, Raleigh, NC,
   http://eprints.ecs.soton.ac.uk/18555.

Bos, N., Zimmerman, A., Olson, J., Yew, J., Yerkie, J., Dahl, E. and Olson, G. (2007) From Shared Databases to Communities of Practice: a taxonomy of collaboratories, *Journal of Computer-Mediated Communication*, **12** (2).

Caplan, P. (2006) Instalment on 'Preservation Metadata', *DCC Curation Manual*, July.

CCSDS (2002) *Reference Model for an Open Archival Information System (OAIS)*, Consultative Committee for Space Data Systems, 650.0-B-1, Blue Book.

CEC (2009) COM(2009) *108 ICT Infrastructures for e-Science, Commission of the European Communities*, 3 May, eur-lex.europa.eu/LexUriServ/LexUriServ.do?uri=COM:2009:0108.

CERN (2011) *Worldwide LHC Computing Grid*. Retrieved from:
http://press.web.cern.ch/public/en/LHC/Computing-en.html.

CEU (2010) *Council Conclusions on 'Cross fertilization between Europe 2020 Flagship Initiatives Digital Agenda for Europe and Innovation Union'*, Council of the European Union, 3 December, http://ec.europa.eu/information_society/newsroom/cf/news-dae.cfm?pillar_id=50&section=Documents.

Collins, H. (2007) Bicycling on the Moon: collective tacit knowledge and somatic-limit tacit knowledge, *Organization Studies*, **28** (2), 257.

Cordewener, B. (2011) *PersID – I: Project report*, SURFfoundation, http://persistent-identifier.nl/?identifier=urn:nbn:nl:ui:13-oss-dl6.

DataCite Metadata Working Group (2011) *DataCite Metadata Scheme for the Publication and Citation of Research Data* (Version 2.1), http://dx.doi.org/10.5438/0003.

Digital Data Archiving for Palaeontological Research (n.d.) *An Open Letter in Support of Palaeontological Digital Data Archiving*, http://supportpalaeodataarchiving.co.uk.

Donnelly, M. and North, R. (2011) The Milieu and the Message: talking to researchers about data curation issues in a large and diverse e-science project, *International Journal of Digital Curation*, **6** (1), www.ijdc.net/index.php/ijdc/article/view/161.

ECRI (n.d.) *Highlights*, European Commission Research & Innovation – Infrastructure, http://ec.europa.eu/research/infrastructures.

Edwards, P. N., Bowker, G. C., Jackson, S. J. and Williams, R. (2009) Introduction: an agenda for infrastructure studies, *Journal of the Association for Information Systems*, **10** (5), 364–74.

EEF (n.d.) *Mission*, European E-infrastructure Forum, www.einfrastructure-forum.eu.

e-IRG (n.d.) *Welcome to the Website of the e-Infrastructure Reflection Group*, www.e-irg.eu.

e-IRG (2010) *Blue Paper*, e-Infrastructure Reflection Group, www.e-irg.eu/images/stories/eirg_bluepaper2010_final.pdf.

e-IRG (2011) *White Paper*, e-Infrastructure Reflection Group, www.e-irg.eu/publications/white-papers.html.

e-SciDR (2008) *Towards a European e-Infrastructure for e-Science a report for the European Commission*, Digital Archiving Consultancy Limited, http://e-scidr.eu/report.

ESFRI (2008) *Roadmap 2008*, European Strategy Forum on Research Infrastructures, ec.europa.eu/research/infrastructures/pdf/esfri_report_20090123.pdf.

ESFRI (2010) *Strategy Report and Roadmap Update 2010*, European Strategy Forum on Research Infrastructures, http://ec.europa.eu/research/infrastructures/pdf/esfri-strategy_report_and_roadmap.pdf.

ESRC (2010) *ESRC Delivery Plan 2011–2015*, Economic and Social Research Council, www.esrc.ac.uk/news-and-events/news/13751/esrc-delivery-plan-2011-2015.aspx.

Europa (2010) press release, Neelie Kroes, Vice-President of the European Commission, Unlocking the Full Value of Scientific Data: formal presentation of the report *Riding the Wave: how Europe can gain from the raising tide of scientific data*, 6 October, http://europa.eu/rapid/pressReleasesAction.do?reference=SPEECH/10/518.

European Commission (2010) *Guidance Notes on Project Reporting*, www.admin.ox.ac.uk/rdm/managedata/funderpolicy/ec.

Frey, J. G. (2009) The Value of the Semantic Web in the Laboratory, *Drug Discovery Today*, **14** (11–12), 552–61.

Gray, N., Carozzi, T. and Woan, G. (2011) *Managing Research Data – Gravitational Waves Final Report*. Retrieved from: http://purl.org/nxg/projects/mrd-gw/report.

HEFCE (n.d.) *Student places, efficiency, and strategic subjects*, Higher Education Funding Council for England, www.hefce.ac.uk/finance/fundinghe/places.

Hey, A. J. G., Tansley, S. and Tolle, K. M. (2009) *The Fourth Paradigm: data-intensive scientific discovery*, Microsoft Research.

Hey, T. and Trefethen, A. (2003) *The Data Deluge: an e-science perspective*, http://eprints.ecs.soton.ac.uk/7648/1/The_Data_Deluge.pdf.

Irshad, T. and Ure, J. (2009) *Clinical Data from Home to Health Centre: the Curation Lifecycle in Telehealth Research*, SCARP Case Study No. 3, Digital Curation Centre. Retrieved from www.dcc.ac.uk/scarp.

JISC (n.d.) *Managing Research Data (JISCMRD)*, Joint Information Systems Committee, www.jisc.ac.uk/whatwedo/programmes/mrd.aspx.

Karasti, H., Baker, K. S. and Halkola, E. (2006) Enriching the Notion of Data Curation in E-science: data managing and information infrastructuring in the long term ecological research (LTER) network, *Computer Supported Cooperative Work*, **15** (4), 321–58.

KE (n.d.) *Welcome to Knowledge Exchange*, Knowledge Exchange, www.knowledge-exchange.info.

Kling, R., Spector, L. and McKim, G. (2002) Locally Controlled Scholarly Publishing via the Internet: The Guild Model, *Proceedings of the American Society for Information Science and Technology*, **39** (1), 228-38.

Kuipers, T. and van der Hoeven, J. (2009) *PARSE Insight Survey Report*, www.parse-insight.eu/publications.php#d3-4.

Leonelli, S. (2009) On the Locality of Data and Claims about Phenomena, *Philosophy of Science*, **76**, 737–49.

Lyon, L. (2007) *Dealing with Data: roles, rights, responsibilities and relationships*, Consultancy Report to JISC, UKOLN, www.ukoln.ac.uk/ukoln/staff/e.j.lyon/reports/dealing_with_data_report-final.pdf.

Lyon, L. (2009) *Open Science at Web-scale: optimising participation and predictive potential*, Joint Information Systems Committee, www.jisc.ac.uk/publications/reports/2009/opensciencerpt.aspx.

Lyon, L., Rusbridge, C., Neilson, C. and Whyte, A. (2010) *Disciplinary Approaches to Sharing, Curation, Reuse and Preservation: DCC SCARP final report*, Digital Curation Centre, www.dcc.ac.uk/sites/default/files/documents/scarp/SCARP-FinalReport-Final-SENT.pdf.

Mell, P. and Grance, T. (2009) *The NIST Definition of Cloud Computing*, National Institute of Standards and Technology.

Mukherjee, A. and Stern, S. (2009) Disclosure or Secrecy? The dynamics of open science, *International Journal of Industrial Organization*, **27** (3), 449–62.

OECD (2007) *OECD Principles and Guidelines for Access to Research Data from Public Funding*, Organisation for Economic Co-operation and Development.

OpenAIRE (2010) *Objectives*, www.openaire.eu/en/about-openaire/general-information/objectives.

Pollock, N. and Williams, R. (2010) E-infrastructures: how do we know and understand them? Strategic ethnography and the biography of artefacts, *Computer Supported Cooperative Work*, 1–36.

Priem, J. and Hemminger, B. H. (2010) Scientometrics 2.0: new metrics of scholarly impact on the social web, *First Monday*, **15** (7).

RCUK (n.d.) *RCUK Common Principles on Data Policy*, Research Councils UK, www.rcuk.ac.uk/research/Pages/DataPolicy.aspx.

RCUK (2011a) *Common Principles on Data Policy*, www.rcuk.ac.uk/research/Pages/DataPolicy.aspx.

RCUK (2011b) *e-Infrastructure*. Retrieved from: www.rcuk.ac.uk/research/xrcprogrammes/eInfrastructure/Pages/home.aspx.

Ribes, D. and Finholt, T. A. (2009) The Long Now of Technology Infrastructure: articulating tensions in development, *Journal of the Association for Information Systems*, **10** (5), 375–98.

RIN (2007) *Principles and Guidelines for Stewardship of Digital Research Data*. Retrieved from: www.rin.ac.uk/our-work/data-management-and -curation/stewardship-digital-research-data-principles-and-guidelines.

RIN (2010) *Open to All? Case studies of openness in research*, Research Information Network, www.rin.ac.uk/our-work/data-management-and-curation/open-science-case-studies.

Rizutto, C. and Hudson, R. (2010) *Inspiring Excellence: research infrastructures and the Europe 2020 strategy*, European Strategy Forum on Research Infrastructures, http://ec.europa.eu/research/infrastructures/index_en.cfm?pg=esfri-publications.

Science (2011) Challenges and Opportunities: introduction to special issue on dealing with data, **331** (6018), 692–93.

South, D. M. (2011) *Data Preservation in High Energy Physics*, Cornell University Library, http://arxiv.org/abs/1101.3186.

Star, S. L. and Ruhleder, K. (2001) Steps toward an Ecology of Infrastructure: design and access for large information spaces. In Yates, J. and Van Maanen, J. (eds), *Information Technology and Organizational Transformation: history, rhetoric, and practice*, Sage.

Strategic Content Alliance (2009) *IPR Risk Assessments*, www.jisc.ac.uk/publications/programmerelated/2009/scaiprtoolkit/2riskassessments.aspx.

Takeda, K. (2010) *IDMB Initial Findings Report*, University of Southampton, www.southamptondata.org.

UKRDS (2010) *Proposal and Business Plan for the Initial Pathfinder Development Phase*, UK Research Data Service, www.ukrds.ac.uk.

Voss, A., Asgari-Targhi, M., Procter, R., Halfpenny, P., Fragkouli, E., Anderson, S., Hughes, L. et al. (2009) Adoption of e-Infrastructure Services: inhibitors, enablers and opportunities, www.escholar.manchester.ac.uk/api/datastream?publicationPid=uk-ac-man-scw:117650&datastreamId=FULL-TEXT.PDF.

Whyte, A. and Pryor, G. (2011) Open Science in Practice: researcher perspectives and participation, *International Journal of Digital Curation*, **6** (1), www.ijdc.net/index.php/ijdc/article/view/173.

Whyte, A., Job, D., Giles, S. and Lawrie, S. (2008) Meeting Curation Challenges in a Neuroimaging Group, *International Journal of Digital Curation*, **3** (1), http://ijdc.net/index.php/ijdc/article/view/74.

Wilson, J. (2011) The Sudamih Project: findings and conclusions. Presented at the *JISC Managing Research Data International Workshop*, Birmingham, 8 March, http://sudamih.oucs.ox.ac.uk/documents.xml.

Wilson, J. A. J., Fraser, M. A., Martinez-Uribe, L., Jeffreys, P., Patrick, M., Akram, A. and Mansoori, T. (2010) Developing Infrastructure for Research Data Management at the University of Oxford, *Ariadne*, **65**.

Winkler-Nees, S. (2011) New DFG Information Infrastructure Projects, Presented at the *JISC Managing Research Data International Workshop*, Birmingham, 28 March, www.jisc.ac.uk/whatwedo/programmes/mrd/rdmevents/mrdinternationalworkshop.aspx.

Wood, J., Andersson, T., Bachem, A., Best, C., Genova, F., Lopez, D. R. and Los, W. et al. (2010) *Riding the Wave: how Europe can gain from the rising tide of scientific data*, High Level Expert Group on Scientific Data, European Commission, http://cordis.europa.eu/fp7/ict/e-infrastructure/docs/hlg-sdi-report.pdf.

Wuchty, S., Jones, B. F. and Uzzi, B. (2007) The Increasing Dominance of Teams in Production of Knowledge, *Science*, **316** (5827), 1036–39.

Index